MACAULAY

Zareer Masani has an Oxford doctorate and is the author of four previous historical books, including a widely acclaimed biography of the former Indian Prime Minister Indira Gandhi. He spent two decades as a current affairs producer for the BBC and is now a freelance broadcaster on BBC Radio. A Macaulay child himself, he is the son of the late Indian politician Minoo Masani and grandson of the eminent historian Sir Rustom Masani.

ZAREER MASANI

Macaulay

Britain's Liberal Imperialist

VINTAGE BOOKS
London

Published by Vintage 2014

2 4 6 8 10 9 7 5 3 1

First published in Great Britain in 2013 by
The Bodley Head

Vintage
Random House, 20 Vauxhall Bridge Road,
London SW1V 2SA

A Penguin Random House Company

www.vintage-books.co.uk

www.penguinrandomhouse.com

A CIP catalogue record for this book
is available from the British Library

ISBN 9780099587026

Penguin Random House is committed to a sustainable future
for our business, our readers and our planet. This book is
made from Forest Stewardship Council® certified paper.

Printed and bound by Clays Ltd, St Ives plc

To my History teachers in Bombay,
who were proud to be Macaulay's children

Contents

Acknowledgements

My thanks are due to several friends and colleagues who encouraged me to write the book and offered valuable suggestions: in particular Mark Tully, Gillian Wright, Margaret Macmillan, Farrokh Suntook, John Saddler, Mayerlene Engineer and David Ward. I owe a particular debt to my editor, Meru Gokhale of Random House India, and Katherine Ailes at The Bodley Head, whose very thoughtful and perceptive comments helped me flesh out the historical context and make it more accessible.

Introduction

Thomas Babington Macaulay, historian and statesman, classical scholar, poet and essayist, was one of the towering intellects of the nineteenth century. As a prominent British parliamentarian, he played a key role in the passing of the Great Reform Act of 1832, which opened up British democracy to the booming new industrial cities and their dynamic middle classes. But his greatest achievements were global. He was the first Western thinker to predict that the future of global modernity, science and capitalism lay with an Anglo-Saxon model of development, based on the English language, liberal political and economic ideas and representative government.

As a politician, Macaulay was the first to formulate a coherent doctrine of 'just wars' and of British-led, liberal interventionism across the globe. That makes him—for better or worse—the ideological precursor of Margaret Thatcher, Tony Blair and Western military interventions in Kosovo, Iraq, Afghanistan and Libya. He was an ardent supporter of the controversial First Opium War against China (see Chapter Ten); and the high point of his long and varied career was as a colonial administrator in India, where he had the chance to put his ideas into practice, sowing the seeds of modernization and globalisation in the British Empire, and by extension across the world.

It's astonishing that there has been no comprehensive biography of Macaulay since the excessively reverential late nineteenth-century volume by his nephew, the historian Sir George Otto Trevelyan. A couple of more recent studies from the perspective of post-colonial and Marxist theory have tended to trivialise his achievements by quoting him out of historical context and judging him by anachronistic 21st century standards of political correctness.

Though largely forgotten in the land of his birth, Macaulay and his legacies are still alive and hotly contested in the Indian sub-continent, where he had the chance to put his ideas into practice. The term 'Macaulay's Children' used to be a pejorative label for anglicized Indians, and he is still the *bête noire* of many Indian nationalists, especially the Hindu chauvenists of the newly elected BJP government. But for all their rhetoric, India still relies on Macaulay's legacies in its bid to become an economic superpower, and the time is ripe for a more balanced reappraisal of his contribution to Indian nation-building. It's no accident that he is still celebrated as a saviour by many Dalits, * who believe that his progressive educational ideas freed them from caste tyranny.

As a bookish intellectual, Macaulay was an unlikely model of an imperial nation-builder; and his four-year stay in India was prompted by no more than a need to boost his sagging private income. He went out in 1834 as adviser to the enlightened Governor-General, Lord William Bentinck, who collaborated with Indian reformers like Raja Ram Mohan Roy to implement dramatic social reforms such as the abolition of sati. ** It was a crucial watershed

---

* The lower castes, regarded as 'untouchables' by traditional Hindu society.
** The enforced immolation of Hindu widows on the funeral pyres of their husbands.

in the evolution of the Raj from a trading company into an inter-ventionist colonial power with a civilizing mission.

The earlier generation of British adventurers, who had established the East India Company as the dominant power in the subcontinent, had been far more concerned with trade and plunder than with governance. Many of them had also been more eager to explore exotic Indian cultures than to impose their own. But by the time of Macaulay's arrival, British attitudes had become sharply polarised between the so-called Orientalists, who wanted to study and preserve Indian traditions and institutions, and the liberal reformers who wanted to modernise and transform them on Western lines.

Macaulay enthusiastically took up cudgels against the Orientalist faction in British India, which had so far supported the funding of classical languages like Sanskrit, Persian and Arabic, which had been the preserve of Mughal India's ruling elite. Macaulay, taking his stand on modernising and utilitarian grounds, led a heated debate about the merits of traditional Indian education and its Western alternatives. And he won the argument with his famous Education Minute, making English language education the basis of 'a class who may be interpreters between us and the millions whom we govern; a class of persons, Indian in blood and colour, but English in taste, in opinions, in morals and in intellect'.

This new imperial vision of assimilation via language was played out in the classrooms of the schools and colleges which now sprang up across British India, most of which are still thriving centres of learning for India's westernized elite. My own former school, the Cathedral in Bombay, is one of them, its ethos summed up by the school anthem, sung to the tune of the Harrow Boating Song, with the opening lines: 'Prima in Indis, gateway of India, door of the East with its face to the West'.

Macaulay was notoriously dismissive, if not downright hostile and contemptuous, towards native Indian, and particularly Hindu, customs and religious superstitions. Despite being a formidable linguist, he made no attempt to master any Indian languages, and his knowledge of Sanskrit and Arabic texts was confined to a few European translations and summaries. Though confident of the superiority of Western scientific knowledge, he believed passionately that, once Indians acquired it, they could and should become the political equals of their colonial masters, a doctrine that was well in advance of most of his British contemporaries.

Macaulay also argued, and history has proved him right, that English as the language of modernity would complement and revitalize native languages, rather than replace them. In the immediate post-Independence period, there were strenuous efforts by Central and State governments to replace English with Hindi, the official national language, and also the various regional vernaculars. Linguistic nationalism became a major political force; there were language riots, and state boundaries were redrawn on linguistic lines. And yet, sixty years on, the pendulum has swung decisively back in favour of English as the language of global success, with even the most chauvinistic Indian politicians from parties like the ruling BJP sending their own children to English-medium schools.

Macaulay spent the last two decades of his life back in Britain as its leading historian, a talented poet (every schoolboy learnt his *Lays of Ancient Rome*), and a distinguished parliamentarian who became Secretary for War, enunciated a new concept of 'just wars' and waged three successful military campaigns against China, Egypt and Afghanistan. Macaulay continued to write and speak on India till his death in 1859, and his thoughts on the Mutiny of 1857* and on the founders of British rule, Robert Clive and Warren Hastings,** were particularly interesting. He played a key role in the creation of the 'heaven-born' Indian Civil Service, or ICS, when he chaired a government committee which opened it up to recruitment by competitive examination. It was a momentous decision that gave India the benefit of an able, incorruptible, highly educated and professional civil service, well in advance of Britain itself.

Without English as its official language, it's unlikely that the Raj could have introduced the comprehensive new Indian Penal Code which Macaulay also drafted, or that the ICS could have brought the rule of law to the most remote villages in the subcontinent. And it's no coincidence that Macaulay's Children also included the Western-educated lawyers who eventually led India to independence. A distinguished succession of nationalist leaders, including Motilal and Jawaharlal Nehru, Muhammed Ali Jinnah and Mahatma Gandhi himself, studied British law in London and practised it in the courts of the Raj before they learned how to turn its liberal and egalitarian principles against the colonial power.

Whatever one thinks of Macaulay's personal prejudices, and he had many, his institutional legacies, I would argue, are the glue that still holds independent India together as a multi-lingual,

---

* Hailed by nationalists as India's First War of Independance, this began as a mutiny of Indian sepoys in the East India Company's army, but escalated into a series of localised uprisings against British rule.
** The first British Govenor of Bengal, Lord Clive of India, as he came to be known, was a dynamic young adventurer who defeated the tottering Mughal empire in the 1750s and established the East India Company as the major power in the subcontinent. His highly talented successor, Warren Hastings, had the grander title of Governer-General of all British India, and further consolidated the Company's territorial power with a controversial expansionist policy.

democratic, federal state with English as its lingua franca. Without Macaulay, India, like China and Japan, would no doubt eventually have industrialized and modernized, but it would most likely not have been a unified country, rather an arena for several competing and possibly hostile regional states each with its own language, and it's unlikely that most of them would have been democracies.

Macaulay was undoubtedly a cultural racist by today's standards; but then so were the overwhelming majority of his nineteenth-century contemporaries, whether European, Indian or Chinese, who believed their own culture, religion and values to be intrinsically superior to those of others. What made Macaulay unique among nineteenth-century intellectuals and policy-makers was his universalist, assimilationist vision of a global political and economic space in which different races and nations might share a common citizenship based on liberal political values, free markets and free trade—a world not unlike what many of us aspire to in the twenty-first century.

A century and a half after his time, the Macaulay model remains the template for Western influence and intervention in the wider developing world. Empires in the formal sense may have disappeared, but Macaulay's ideas about an imperial mission to inform and educate still underpin the way the West exports its values to the rest of the world, especially through 'soft' power and the subtle transfer of cultural and economic norms.

1

Clever Tom

It is the 25th of October 2006, and an unusual birthday party is being held in a small apartment perched high up in one of the many ugly tower blocks that have sprung up in the sprawling suburbs of Delhi. The host is Chandra Bhan Prasad, a stout, very jovial middle-aged social activist of the Dalit community, and his guests are a motley collection of Dalit intellectuals, Delhi academics and foreign journalists. They are celebrating the 206th birthday of Thomas Babington, Lord Macaulay, the man who brought the English language and British education to India, and thence arguably to the rest of the world.

Macaulay's Delhi birthday party owes far more to local Indian rituals than to the classical Western values and ideals he espoused. Indian pakoras and kebabs circulate along with liberal supplies of Scotch whisky; and the climax of the event is the unveiling of a portrait of the newly invented goddess of English. In the best traditions of the colourful bazaar posters of Hindu deities, this hybrid reincarnation of the American Statue of Liberty is pictured against a blazing map of India, standing on a giant computer, wearing a sari and a wide-brimmed straw hat and holding aloft a massive pink pen.

A Dalit poet sings a hymn of praise to the new deity, with the refrain:

Oh Devi Ma, please let us learn English!
Even the dogs understand English.

Then Chandra Bhan Prasad addresses his guests and announces: 'Empowered by Goddess English, Dalits can take their place in the new globalized world . . . Imagine, if we had followed only indigenous study, we would be like Afghanistan or Nepal today.' And he adds, with a humorous twinkle in his eye: 'Hereafter, the first sounds all newborn Dalit babies will hear from their parents is—abcd. Immediately after birth, parents will walk up to the child and whisper in the ear—abcd.'[1]

~

The man who inspired this post-colonial celebration in Delhi was born in a location which could not have been further removed in geography and culture. Rothley Temple in rural Leicestershire was the country seat of Thomas Babington, uncle to the new arrival, who was named after him. His mother, Selena Macaulay, had been invited to spend her confinement there by her sister-in-law, 'who belonged to the school of matrons who hold that the advantage of country air outweighs that of London doctors'.[2]

It was here, on St Crispin's Day, the anniversary of English victory at Agincourt, as he liked to say, that Macaulay first opened his eyes 'in a room panelled from ceiling to floor, like every corner of the ancient mansion, with oak almost black from age, looking eastward across the park, and southward through an ivy-shaded window into a little garden'.[3] His mother, Selena, was the pretty young daughter of a Quaker bookseller in Bristol. She had married for love an earnest and high-minded social reformer called Zachary Macaulay. He was a lean, rather severe-looking man, descended from a pious family of Scottish Presbyterian preachers and ministers and was actively involved in the campaign to abolish the slave trade.

Zachary had experienced slavery at first-hand for five years on a West Indian sugar estate. It had been a huge change from his early life in Scotland. Writing home to a friend, he described himself 'in a field of canes, amidst perhaps a hundred of the sable [black] race, cursing and bawling, while the noise of the whip resounding on their shoulders, and the cries of the poor wretches, would make you imagine that some unhappy accident had carried you to the doleful shades'.[4] Zachary arrived there as a bookkeeper at the age of sixteen, soon rose to become manager, but returned to England aged twenty-one, convinced of the iniquity of slavery and 'tired of trying to find a compromise between right and wrong'.[5] His views on slavery were closely linked to his conversion to Evangelical Christianity under the influence of his brother-in-law, Thomas Babington, who was active in both the Evangelical and Abolitionist movements. It was through Babington that young Zachary obtained his new posting as an administrator and eventually Governor of the West African colony of Sierra Leone, established as a haven for newly liberated slaves from the West Indies.

From 1794 to 1799, Zachary had ruled the new colony with a stern hand, trying to reform the black settlers, many of whom, according to his journals, were openly rebellious, constantly drunk, riddled with venereal disease and unwilling to work. He also had to endure the bombardment and looting of the settlement by troops of the new French Republic.

According to his grandson, 'his very deficiencies stood him in good stead' in his 'arduous and uninviting task' as Governor: '. . . It was well for him that nature had denied him any sense of the ridiculous. Unconscious of what was absurd around him, and incapable of being flurried, frightened, or fatigued, he stood as a centre of order and authority amidst the seething chaos of inexperience and insubordination.'[6]

In 1795, his health broken by fever and anxiety, Zachary had returned to England on home leave; and it was then that he met and fell in love with the pretty and intelligent Selena Mills. They were secretly engaged, but he returned to Sierra Leone soon after, and they waited to be married till his final return to England three years later, when he was appointed to the London-based job of Secretary to the Sierra Leone Company, which owned the colony. Their marriage produced nine children, and the eldest, called 'Clever Tom' by his parents' intellectual circle, was born just a year after their wedding.

~

The new century into which Tom Macaulay was born in 1800 saw the world on the cusp of major transformations, in which Britain was playing a dominant role. The French Revolution had shaken the traditional European order to its very foundations, but the revolutionary tide had been stemmed due largely to British resistance. The Napoleonic Wars, which raged throughout Tom's childhood till 1815, were essentially a struggle between France and Britain for mastery of Europe and, by extension, for global empire too. Britain's victory made it the unrivalled global super-power for a century to come, based on its naval supremacy. And this coincided with a dramatic economic boom at home, stimulated by hugely expanded trade, scientific and technological innovation and rapid industrialization.

Tom's childhood was dominated by the needs and demands of an overbearing and humourless father, of whom his grandson later wrote: '. . . fate seemed determined that Zachary Macaulay should not be indulged in any great share of happiness.' The pattern was set early on, the day after Tom's birth, when Zachary was thrown from his horse and broke both arms, 'and he spent in a sick-room the remainder of the only holiday worth the name which . . . he ever took during his married life'.[7] As a result of this accident, the young couple stayed on in their stately surroundings at Rothley Temple, and their baby was baptised in its private chapel, with his uncle Thomas Babington as godfather.

When they returned to London, Zachary and Selena took up residence in a dismal backstreet in the heart of the city of London, in a house where the Sierra Leone Company had its office. There were no local parks where the baby could be taken and no greenery for him to look out on. One of his earliest memories was of standing at the nursery window by his father's side, looking at a cloud of black smoke pouring out of a tall chimney. He asked if that was hell, 'an inquiry that was received with a grave displeasure which at the time he could not understand'.[8] Although it offended Zachary's stern religiosity, it was an extraordinarily precocious and perceptive comment from an infant less than two years old. It won him the title of 'Baby Genius' from one of his parents' friends, who predicted that 'he says such extraordinary things that he will be ruined by praise'.[9]

Zachary soon decided to supplement his salary as Company Secretary by setting up his own business to trade with Africa and the East Indies. The success of this venture enabled the rapidly growing family to move to the far more salubrious, leafy suburb of Clapham, to a large and comfortable house a stone's throw from the unspoilt wilderness of Clapham Common, with its gorse bushes, poplar groves and ponds. Here, Tom spent most of his childhood, surrounded by a brood of eight younger brothers and sisters.

Clapham, in those years and well into the twentieth century, was not just a rustic retreat from central London, but the hub of one of the most influential intellectual groups in British cultural history, the famous Clapham Sect. They were a combination of political and social reformers and Evangelical Christians, brought together by the parliamentary campaign for the abolition of slavery. Tom was seven when the Abolitionists succeeded in getting an Act through Parliament to outlaw the slave trade, and their efforts and debates were part of his early childhood. The Baby Genius must have been a child after their own hearts. We are told that by the age of three 'he read incessantly, for the most part lying on the rug before the fire, with his book on the ground, and a piece of bread and butter in his hand'. A parlour-maid recalled how this extraordinary infant in his frilly frock used to perch on the table near her while she polished the silver, 'expounding to her out of a volume as big as himself'.[10]

Like most of his Clapham circle, Zachary was fiercely religious, and on Sundays the family were subjected to three sermons a day, two in church and one at home delivered by the stern *pater familias*. So it is surprising to learn that the Baby Genius found time to indulge in pastimes as frivolous as baking plum and apple pies.[11] Although the theatre was out of bounds for the children of the Clapham Evangelicals, they were allowed games of blind man's buff and fancy dress parties, at one of which little Tom dressed up as Napoleon Bonaparte.

The Napoleon complex, so often associated with short

people, stayed with Macaulay in later life. Even as a child of four, he was unusually conscious of his own dignity. About this time, he accompanied his father on a visit to the society hostess Lady Waldegrave at her stately mansion at Strawberry Hill. A pretty, slight child with an abundance of fair hair, Tom was dressed in a green coat with a red collar and cuffs, a frill at the throat and white trousers. Unfortunately, a clumsy servant who was waiting on them spilt hot coffee over his legs. Shortly after, when his solicitous hostess asked how he was, the solemn little boy replied stoically: 'Thank you, madam, the agony is abated.'[12]

His nephew and first biographer later wrote that 'these were probably the years of his greatest literary activity'. At the age of seven, he began 'a compendium of Universal History . . . and . . . contrived to give a tolerably connected view of the leading events from the Creation to the present time.' True to his Evangelical roots, he began work on a paper aimed at persuading the people of the south Indian kingdom of Travancore to embrace Christianity. 'On reading it,' his proud mother wrote approvingly, 'I found it to contain a very clear idea of the leading facts and doctrines of that religion.' He began work on an epic poem in six cantos, but after writing three embarked instead on another ode celebrating the achievements of the Macaulay clan. He was particularly inspired by the exploits of his uncle, General Colin Macaulay, who had fallen prisoner to Tipu Sultan, but later marched in the force that defeated and killed 'the tyrant of Mysore'. General Macaulay ended his career as the autocratic British Resident at the princely court of Travancore.[13] His adventures and exploits would have given little Tom an early and exciting introduction to Britain's rapidly expanding Indian empire. When the General finally retired to Britain in 1810, after suppressing a local uprising in Travancore, his eight-year-old nephew greeted him with a long paean of praise which he had composed himself and which began:

'Now safe returned from Asia's parching strand,
Welcome, thrice welcome to thy native land.'[14]

Macaulay's biographer nephew notes approvingly that 'the voluminous writings of his childhood . . . are not only perfectly correct in spelling and grammar, but display the same lucidity of meaning, and scrupulous accuracy in punctuation and the other minor details of the literary art, which characterize his mature works'. By the age of six, he had already begun collecting the enormous and encyclopedic library that was his most prized possession in later life. It was a period when books were still a hand-made and expensive luxury; and half a century would pass before mass production brought them within reach of middle-class households.

Tom's childhood library was liberally endowed with gifts from his parents' bluestocking friend, Hannah More, an influential member of the Clapham Sect. Complimenting him on 'two letters, so neat and free from blots', she announced: 'By this obvious improvement you have entitled yourself to another book. You must go to Hatchard's and choose. I think we have nearly exhausted the Epics. What say you to a little good prose? Johnson's Hebrides, or Walton's Lives, unless you would like a neat edition of . . . Paradise Lost for your own eating? In any case choose something which you do not possess. I want you to become a complete Frenchman, that I may give you Racine, the only dramatic poet I know in any modern language that is perfectly pure and good.'[15]

With mentors like these, he hardly needed any formal schooling. But his parents, though aware they had produced a prodigy, prudently 'abstained from any word or act which might foster in him a perception of his own genius with as much care as a wise millionaire expends on keeping his son ignorant of the fact that he is destined to be richer than his comrades'. Aged only a few years, he was sent very reluctantly to a small day-school in Clapham, which had originally been set up by the local Abolitionists to educate African youths 'sent over to imbibe Western civilization at the fountain-head'. 'The poor fellows,' we are told, 'had found as much difficulty keeping alive at Clapham as Englishmen experience at Sierra Leone.' So by the time young Tom arrived, the school, bereft of Africans, had the less exotic task of educating the young white children of its founders. When Tom's mother warned him that he would have to learn to study there 'without the solace of bread and butter', he is reported to have replied: 'Yes, Mama, industry shall be my bread and attention my butter.'[16]

~

Based on his early precocity and phenomenal memory, Macaulay was proclaimed a genius and awarded an IQ of 180 to 190 by twentieth-century American social scientists.[17] Like many child prodigies, he had an unhappy and lonely time at school. When he outgrew the Clapham school, his parents had initially thought of sending him as a day scholar to Westminster, the leading London-based public school. But for better or worse, they eventually decided to send him to a small, private boarding school near Cambridge, run by a stern Evangelical clergyman.

Tom was twelve when he was sent away to boarding school, and his letters home, especially to his mother, are a poignant record of an intense homesickness which would today be diagnosed as clinical depression. His emotional symptoms got no better with time. Returning to school after his summer holidays in his second year, he poured out his soul to his mother: 'There is nobody here to pity me or to comfort me, and if I were to say I was sorry at being from home, I should be called a baby . . . So I have nothing to do but to sit and cry in my room, and think of home and wish for the holidays. I am ten times more uneasy than I was last half year.' A month later he writes reproaching her for not writing to him more often: 'You must consider that you have seven little creatures at home, besides Papa, to make you happy, and that I have nobody to supply the place of a mother or of a father here.'[18]

Tom must undoubtedly have been singled out for ragging and bullying at school by 'his utter inability to play any sort of game'.[19] But he found refuge and solace in his copious reading and also took an unusually active interest in the politics and current affairs of the day. Amidst his laments about missing home day and night, he also found time to write to his mother supporting a new parliamentary bill to repeal the disabilities imposed on Catholics, condemning the Prince Regent's 'barbarous manner of treating his wife' and 'hoping that Parliament will never be so base as to consent to a divorce between them'.[20] The prince, later George IV, had separated from his wife, Caroline of Brunswick, because he found her ugly and repulsive. Tom's championship of the unfortunate princess, who refused to be dumped, was perhaps an early example of his instinctive sympathy for the underdog.

Although he held passionate opinions, he was open to persuasion by contrary evidence. In a school debate, he was chosen to speak against the proposition that the Crusades were beneficial to Europe. 'I shall speak against my conscience in opposing the Crusades,' he wrote home, 'but there are such a number of specious arguments against them that I shall be in no want of matter.'[21] Even so, a week later he wrote to his father that he had had second thoughts, because 'when I came to consider it carefully, the Crusaders put to death 70,000 Mahometans in the streets of Jerusalem though they implored mercy on their knees'.[22]

Significantly for his later role in imperial policy, Tom, though only thirteen, took a keen interest in the parliamentary and wider public debate about the Charter Bill redefining the rule of the East India Company in India. His father, along with other Evangelicals, was campaigning to add a controversial new clause to the Bill which would permit Christian proselytizing in India. The Company had so far maintained a strict embargo on Christian missionaries for fear of alienating the Indian princes and notables on whom its presence depended; and the Evangelicals' demands met with strong opposition across the country, not least at the University of Cambridge, where Tom Macaulay aspired to study after he left school. Since he later grew up to become an avowed agnostic, it is ironical that, as a thirteen-year-old schoolboy, he saw Christianity as a necessary precondition for modern, scientific learning.

'It is rather strange,' he wrote to his mother, 'that Cambridge, the abode of learning and religion for so many years, should hesitate an instant to do her utmost in order to promote science and Christianity through such a vast tract of country.'[23] The University had just deferred consideration of a petition to the Parliament, drafted by Tom's father, to allow missionaries into British India. But his indignation turned to delight when residents of a Scottish country parish signed the petition in large numbers. 'I am very much pleased,' he congratulated his father, 'that the nation seems to take such interest in the introduction of Christianity in India. My Scotch blood begins to boil at the mention of the 1750 names that went up . . . Ask Mamma and Selena [one of his younger sisters] if they do not now admit my argument with regard to the superior advantages of the Scotch over the English peasantry.'[24]

Father and son were united in their passionate belief in Britain's imperial mission and their indignation against those who challenged it. 'Vipers are said to devour their parents,' Tom wrote to Zachary in 1816. 'The Americans have attempted to do this. But if I were John Bull . . . I would drub our graceless offspring into reverence, if not into love.'[25] A year later he had composed a long, celebratory ode to Britannia:

Let golden plenty nod on all our plains,
While at thy feet benignant Commerce pours
From her full lap the spoils of distant shores,
The spicy sweets of India's dusky breast . . .

The poem goes on to eulogize the British Empire for bringing the world 'Mild Peace', 'Awful Law', 'solemn Justice' and 'Bright Virtue', with 'Art, genius, science' in its train.[26]

Despite their shared views on empire and Tom's ardent support for his father's Evangelism, relations between the two became increasingly strained as Tom grew to adolescence and young adulthood. By the age of sixteen, he is described by one of his favourite sisters as having grown fat and ungainly, careless in dress and deportment and lacking good manners.[27] Much of this was probably in reaction to the constant teasing and bullying he had to endure at school. But his father kept berating him for his weaknesses and setting him tasks which he hoped would help to reform him. 'Loud-speaking, affected pronunciation in reading, late lying in bed, neglect of cleanliness', so ran a catalogue of his faults in one of Zachary's letters of admonishment to fifteen-year-old Tom.[28]

~

Despite his father's criticisms, Tom's academic brilliance meant that he had no difficulty in achieving his goal of going up to Cambridge, where he arrived in October 1818 at Trinity, one of its most august colleges. Here he emerged from his emotional chrysalis, acquired a large circle of friends and admirers and developed intellectual tastes and opinions very different from those of his overbearing father. Till the end of his life, Tom would consider Trinity his intellectual home, regarding it 'as an ancient Greek, or a mediaeval Italian, felt towards his native city'.[29]

He was soon at the centre of a scintillating intellectual circle of undergraduates who eschewed the hedonistic pleasures of the fashionable set. While the latter spent their time going to the races and to balls or playing billiards, cricket and tennis, Tom and his friends spent their days and nights reading, sharing and debating poetry, philosophy and politics. 'So long as a door was open, or a light burning,' his nephew later wrote, 'Macaulay was always in the mood for conversation and companionship.' In later life, he often recalled the student days 'when he supped at midnight on milk-punch and roast turkey, drank tea in floods' and sat up till the bell rang for morning chapel. Sometimes, on a warm, summer night, 'the whole party would pour out into the moonlight, and ramble for mile after mile through the country, till the noise of their wide-flowing talk mingled with the twittering of the birds in the hedges'.[30]

It was on nights like these that Tom encountered the Utilitarian ideas that soon radicalized him and led him to discard the far more traditionalist and conservative opinions he had inherited from his father. 'The report of this conversion,' we are told, 'of which the most was made by ill-natured tale-bearers . . ., created some consternation in the family circle.'[31] These were the years when the political philosopher Jeremy Bentham, the founding father of Utilitarianism, was developing and publicizing the rational, empirical ideology that was to become so characteristic of modern British thinking. Its key principle was that all actions, laws and institutions must be judged by their utility in maximizing the greatest happiness of the greatest number; an idea that was deeply subversive of traditionalist values.

Utilitarianism both fuelled and responded to a new appetite for radical political and economic reform, now that the external threat from France had receded. The so-called 'Peterloo Massacre' of 1819, in which eleven people were killed and many more injured by troops firing on a peaceful public meeting in Manchester, was a major catalyst in Tom's conversion to the cause of radical parliamentary reform and democratic constitutional change. But his father continued to support the Tory government of the day and even accused it of being supine in not acting more vigorously to suppress sedition.[32]

When his parents wrote warning Tom against associating with democratic societies at Cambridge, he replied defiantly that he was not 'one of "the sons of Anarchy and confusion"' and that he owed his opinions to great minds like Cicero, Tacitus and Milton, who had saved the world from superstition and slavery. 'I can never repent speaking of them with indignation,' he insisted, referring to events at Peterloo. 'When I cease to feel the injuries of others, warmly detest wanton cruelty, and to feel my soul [rise] against oppression, I shall think myself unworthy to be your son . . .'[33]

Father and son also clashed on the less serious issue of Tom's hunger for the latest novels. Zachary had a puritanical distrust of what we today would call creative fiction, and he was alarmed by a report that Tom had become known in Cambridge as 'the novel-reader'. His son replied with an unrepentant letter attributing such criticism to men who were 'mere mathematical blocks . . . without one liberal idea or elegant image, beings so stupid in conversation, so uninformed on every subject of history, of letters and of taste'. 'It is in such circles,' Tom declared, 'which, I am happy to say, I hardly know but by report, that knowledge of modern literature is called novel-reading—a commodious name, invented by ignorance and applied by envy . . . To me the attacks of such men are valuable as compliments.'[34]

His father's disapproval was reinforced when Tom failed to get Honours in his Cambridge degree exams because of his failure in Mathematics, his academic Achilles' heel.[35] Zachary sarcastically attributed this to his son's preference for what he called 'more tasteful pursuits'.[36] These included a passion for public debate, which made him one of the Cambridge Union's legendary orators.

His physical appearance was a disadvantage in such public performances: a Cambridge contemporary described him as 'little graced with aught of manly beauty—short, obese, rough-featured, coarse-complexioned, with lank hair and small grey eyes . . .his voice abrupt, unmusical'. But the same account went on to say that, once he spoke, his audience was overwhelmed by his 'rich mind', 'swift flow', 'deep impassioned thought' and 'exhaustless store of multifarious learning'.[37] These combined to give him a reputation for invincibility: the side he led won fourteen out of seventeen debates according to Union records from 1822 to 1824.

Under the influence of his new Utilitarian ideas, Tom had by this time broken decisively with his father's Evangelical Christianity. He later joked to one of his sisters that Zachary condemned 'smoking, eating underdone meat, liking high game, —lying late in a morning, and all things which give pleasure to others and none to himself to be absolute sins'.[38] Matters came to a head over a brilliant and extraordinarily versatile series of essays Tom had written for a new literary magazine called *Knight's Quarterly*, on subjects ranging from Dante, Petrarch and Milton to the French Revolution, Napoleon and even Zachary's *cause célebre*, the abolition of slavery. His contributions included two love poems which contained erotic passages that would have outraged Zachary and his Clapham circle:

How fondly could I play for hours
with thy long curling tresses,
And press thy hand and clasp thy neck
with fanciful caresses.[39]

Unfortunately, journalistic and poetic forays of this sort came to an abrupt halt when Zachary objected to their frivolity. Tom wrote to his editor making it clear that he did not 'in the slightest degree partake his [Zachary's] scruples', cited 'the complete discrepancy which exists between his opinions and mine', but concluded that he felt compelled 'to respect prejudices which I do not in the slightest degree share' and stop contributing to the magazine, a sacrifice which gave him 'considerable pain'.[40]

By this time, the only points on which father and son were united were the abolition of slavery and championship of George IV's rejected queen. Accused of adultery and sued for divorce by her husband, Caroline was barred from his coronation, even though she tried to force her way into Westminster Abbey. For a time, she had the support of many in the Whig Party and the wider public, because George IV—obese, arrogant and pleasure-loving—was deeply unpopular and seen to be politically aligned with the Tories. Among Queen Caroline's most ardent knights errant was the young Trinity undergraduate who composed this ode of welcome for her:

Though tyrant hatred still denies
Each right that fits thy station,
To thee a people's love supplies
A nobler coronation:[41]

In 1824, Tom made up for his mathematical disaster in the Cambridge Tripos* two years earlier by winning a much-coveted fellowship at Trinity in an arduous and hotly contested round of exams. It was a seven-year fellowship which did not require residence at Cambridge and brought with it an income that made him for the first time financially independent. Tom had been anxious for some time to relieve Zachary of financial burdens, especially as the family business had declined and disappeared while he devoted himself to the anti-slavery campaign. In his final year at Cambridge, Tom had taken on the private tutoring of two pupils for a fee of 100 guineas (approximately £5,200 in today's money) to relieve his father of the burden of supporting him.[42] He was also remarkably conscious of his duty as the eldest son to help support his younger siblings.

Six years at Cambridge, for all their intellectual delights, had been enough to quench his love of academia, and it was the

---

* A three-part exam called the Mathematics Tripos was at that time the only road to a Cambridge honours degree.

world of action that beckoned now. He began reading for the Bar* and happily abandoned Trinity for the new family home in Bloomsbury, in the heart of central London. His love of city life, and of London in particular, appears to have been rooted early on. As a schoolboy of fourteen, he had already composed a paean to urban living:

> Poets may talk of the beauties of nature, the enjoyments of a country life, and rural innocence: but there is another kind of life which, though unsung by bards, is yet to me infinitely superior to the dull uniformity of country life. London is the place for me. Its smoky atmosphere, and its muddy river, charm me more than the pure air of Hertfordshire, and the crystal currents of the river Rib. Nothing is equal to the splendid varieties of London life, the fine flow of London talk, and the dazzling brilliancy of London spectacles.[43]

For the next decade, this heaving and thriving metropolis would be the stage for Macaulay's own dazzling rise to fame and fortune as a journalist, politician and man of letters.

---

* To qualify as an advocate in the British courts, one had not only to take the law exams but also to serve an apprenticeship in a Barrister's chambers and take a prescribed number of dinners at the Inns of Court.

2

The Making of a Whig

While at Cambridge, Macaulay is reported to have announced to a contemporary: 'I have been a Tory; I am a Radical; *but I never will be a Whig.*'[1] And yet, a decade later, he was one of the leading young parliamentarians of the Whig Party and a favoured recruit to its aristocratic social circle in London. The distinction between English Radicalism and Whiggism at this time was the former's rejection of all established traditions and institutions that failed to meet strictly Utilitarian criteria. The Whig tradition, on the other hand, believed in gradual parliamentary reform led, as during the Glorious Revolution of 1689,* by powerful and wealthy liberal aristocrats and balanced by a continuing respect for the hereditary privileges of the Crown and the peers of the realm.

During his radical phase, Macaulay was credited by his sister with a 'great admiration for American institutions, . . . and a disposition to question everything hitherto considered

---

* When William of Orange overthrew James II, and Parliament passed a new Bill of Rights, subordinating the powers of the Crown to those of Parliament.

settled', which caused 'great grief' to his family.[2] Yet an essay he wrote at the time about ancient Greece showed the limits of his belief in full democracy as the solution to everything. 'A good government, like a good coat,' he wrote, 'is that which fits the body for which it is designed.' He went on to argue that, while pure democracy might be the ideal form of government, it was crucial that power be exercised by educated people, and that might well require a small elite to act in the interests of the wider, uneducated masses. The example he cited was that of free trade which, though in the interests of all, would never find majority support under universal suffrage.[3]

Macaulay was called to the Bar* in 1826, but made no serious attempt to practise law as a profession. 'After the first year or two of the period during which he called himself a barrister,' writes his nephew, 'he gave up even the pretence of reading law, and spent many more hours under the gallery of the House of Commons, than in all the Courts together.'[4] It was the making of laws, or the unmaking of unjust ones, that now became his main preoccupation.

In June 1824, at a public meeting in London organized by his father's Anti-Slavery Society, Macaulay made his first ever public speech to wide acclaim and much publicity. The meeting was chaired by no less than the King's brother, with other luminaries like William Wilberforce on the platform. Young Macaulay's passionate attack on slavery in Britain's West Indian colonies was hailed in the *Edinburgh Review*, a leading Whig periodical, as 'a display of eloquence so signal . . . that the most practised orator may well admire how it should have come from one who then for the first time addressed a public assembly'. Wilberforce himself

---

* Macaulay was allowed to argue cases at the Bar of the Court after completing his law exams and apprenticeship in chambers.

spoke congratulating Zachary, the proud father, on 'the gratification he has this day enjoyed in hearing one so dear to him plead such a cause in such a manner'. But stern Zachary, we are told, 'took it in his own sad way', sitting expressionless and doodling on a piece of paper while his son spoke and was applauded and cheered. At home, later that evening, his only grudging comment was 'to remark that it was ungraceful in so young a man to speak with folded arms in the presence of royalty'.[5]

This maiden speech, delivered by a young, 24-year-old barrister, was significant not merely for its assault on slavery, but because it enunciated for the first time a coherent ideological justification for liberal imperialism. Britain's 'peculiar distinction', Macaulay had proclaimed, was 'not that she has conquered so splendidly—but that she has ruled only to bless, and conquered only to spare. Her mightiest empire is that of her manners, her language and her laws; her proudest victories, those which she has achieved over ignorance and ferocity; her most durable trophies, those which she has erected in the hearts of civilized and liberated nations. The strong moral feeling of the English people, their hatred of injustice, their disposition to make every sacrifice, rather than participate in crime—these have long been their glory, their strength, their safety.'[6] It was a concept of Anglo-Saxon benevolence which has underpinned two centuries of British military intervention around the world, echoed in our own times by the rhetoric of Tony Blair and David Cameron.

During the six years that followed, young Macaulay, though nominally a barrister, focused most of his energies on political and historical journalism, establishing himself as a highly successful and widely read reviewer and essayist for the prestigious *Edinburgh Review*. His reputation was made early on with a 42-page article on the Republican poet, John Milton. 'Like Lord Byron,' we are told, 'he awoke one morning and found himself famous.'[7] The essay demonstrated Macaulay's mastery of rhetoric and literary style and set out his own political creed in a way that helped launch him as a rising star in the ranks of the Whig Party, now preparing to take power on a platform of radical parliamentary reform.

'There is only one cure for the evils which newly acquired freedom produces,' he wrote, 'and that cure is freedom . . . Many politicians of our time are in the habit of laying it down as a self-evident proposition, that no people ought to be free till they are fit to use their freedom. The maxim is worthy of the fool in the old story, who resolved not to go into the water till he had learnt to swim. If men are to wait for liberty till they become wise and good in slavery, they may indeed wait for ever.'[8]

Such radical rhetoric, along with his celebration of the so-called English Revolution of 1649 and the execution of King Charles I, was at odds with his own more Whiggish insistence elsewhere that democracy and the vote should be confined to the educated and propertied middle classes. 'Our fervent wish,' he wrote in another essay, ' . . . is that we may see such a reform in the House of Commons as may render its votes the express image of the middle orders of Britain.'[9] In yet another essay, he praised the middle class as 'too numerous to be corrupted by government', 'too intelligent to be duped by demagogues' and unlikely 'to carry its zeal for reform to lengths inconsistent with the security of property and the maintenance of social order'.[10]

For Macaulay, such contradictions were part of the complexity of human nature and therefore of politics too. Though heavily influenced by Utilitarian philosophers like Jeremy Bentham and his ideological heir, James Mill, he disliked what he considered their over-rationality; and he wrote a series of essays criticizing their failure to address the irrational in human behaviour or to explain the conflict between morality and pleasure in human choices. 'Innumerable martyrs,' he wrote, 'have exulted in torments which made the spectators shudder; and to use a more homely illustration, there are few wives who do not long to be mothers.'[11]

Though staunchly opposed to populist attempts to stir up revolution, Macaulay had an instinctive sympathy for the underdog which made him champion a series of minority causes during these early years in his political career. The first was the long overdue repeal of laws barring Catholics from Parliament and public office, especially unjust in Ireland, where they were the overwhelming majority of the population. In 1826, Macaulay mobilized a party of young Whig MAs from the Inns of Court to travel post-haste by stagecoach to Cambridge, arriving just in time to reverse a University Senate petition opposing Catholic emancipation. The Tory press, we are told, were outraged 'at the deliberate opinion of the University having been overridden by a coachful of "godless and briefless barristers"'.[12]

Writing about England's conversion from Catholicism to Protestantism, Macaulay made it clear that his own preference would have been for a secular state which allowed 'perfect freedom of conscience'; and he did not shrink from attacking a Whig icon like Elizabeth I for subjecting Catholics 'to a persecution even more odious than the persecution with which her sister [the Catholic 'Bloody Mary' of Protestant mythology] had harassed the Protestants'.[13]

He had by this time rejected his father's fierce Evangelical Christianity for an agnosticism that he retained for the rest of his life. This was, no doubt, partly a reaction to the severity of his childhood upbringing, subjected to Zachary's constant sermonizing, and partly the result of his own far more scientific and sceptical mind. Yet, despite such disagreements with his father, Tom wholeheartedly shared Zachary's opposition to slavery; and he wrote articles remarkably modern in their tone and methodology demolishing myths about the racial inferiority of black Africans and analysing racist hostility and exploitation in economic and social terms.[14]

He was equally vociferous in his attacks on anti-Semitism at a time when Jews, like Catholics, were still banned from Parliament. In a style which became his hallmark, he used satire and ridicule to demolish the idea that someone should be denied civil rights 'because he wears a beard, does not eat ham, goes to the synagogue on Saturdays, instead of going to the church on Sundays'.[15]

His speeches and essays revealed a fiercely original and questioning mind, an encyclopedic range of knowledge and opinions that were never predictable. One moment he was full of admiration for Oliver Cromwell, another ridiculing Samuel Johnson and another defending the poet Byron from prudish attacks on his sexuality.[16] Despite his support for the rights of Catholics, he was firmly against any concessions to Irish nationalism. And he saw no contradiction between demanding greater democracy for England while imposing imprisonment without trial in Ireland.[17]

Macaulay's journalism brought him an impressive annual income of almost £200 which, together with nearly £300 (£10,000 and £15,000 respectively in today's money) from his Trinity fellowship, was enough for him to live comfortably enough at home in Bloomsbury with his parents. In 1828, his income was supplemented by the grand sum of £900 (£45,000 today) a year from a government sinecure as a Commissioner for Bankruptcy, a largely honorific post which involved little practical work. Ironically, he saw no contradiction in accepting such financial patronage, while campaigning to rid Parliament of the notorious 'pocket' and 'rotten' boroughs through the control of which corrupt oligarchs could run the government of the country. Two years later, he showed even fewer scruples about himself entering Parliament as the nominee for just such a pocket borough in Wiltshire. The Whig grandee who controlled it had generously declared 'that he had been much struck by the articles on Mill, and that he wished to be the means of first introducing their author to public life'.[18]

London in the 1830s was already the world's largest city and expanding rapidly, with contrasts of affluence and poverty every bit as dramatic as we see in contemporary Indian metropolises like Mumbai and Kolkata. In the West End were the fashionable, clean and quiet, tree-lined streets of Mayfair and Belgravia, with their expensive stone-and-white stucco houses and ornamental garden squares. Further east was the city's grimy underbelly, with its slums and open sewers, pavements crowded with hawkers and muddy, congested roads, full of carts, cattle and rubbish. Further north stretched the recently created, palatial, neo-classical avenues and parks of the Regency period, and to the west the semi-rural peace and quiet of Kensington. It was there at Holland House (now Holland Park), the stately Kensington home of Lord and Lady Holland, that Whig society had its cultural and political centre; and Tom Macaulay would soon create a favoured place for himself in this charmed circle.

Macaulay's arrival on the back benches of the House of Commons marked the culmination of a decade of political ambition, and it coincided with a historic shift in British politics. Almost half a century of conservative Tory rule was about to give way to a return of the Whigs to power with a programme of sweeping constitutional change. As an essayist and polemicist,

Macaulay had played an important part in creating educated public support for such change, and now he had the opportunity to participate directly in implementing it.

Consistent with his sympathy for minority rights, his maiden speech in the House was in support of allowing Jews to enter Parliament. Citing the economic and political power Jews could and did exercise by virtue of their wealth, he argued that it was ludicrous to deny them formal political rights. To this pragmatic, Utilitarian argument he added the plea that 'on every principle of moral obligation the Jew has a right to political power'.[19]

The speech went down so well that London's Jewish community, led by a prominent banker, held a grand party at Westminster to felicitate its author. Macaulay wrote to his sister the next day describing the event in improvized doggerel of the sort he was fond of composing in his letters to the family:

I dined with a Jew,
Such Christians are few,
He gave me no ham,
But plenty of lamb.
And three sorts of fishes,
And thirty made dishes.
I drank his champagne
Again and again.
I drank up his hock
Until ten o' clock.
O Christians whose feasts
Are scarce fit for beasts,
Example take you
By this worthy old Jew.[20]

Despite his sympathy for persecuted minorities, his sense of humour encompassed jokes that we today might consider anti-Semitic. After attending a lavish costume ball hosted by the same Jewish banker, he told his sister that it was 'not such as we *exclusives* think quite the thing . . . Jewesses by dozens and Jews by scores'. Nonetheless, he added in a limerick about the occasion:

The dull crowd that flocks
To an opera box
Had much better come to the Jewesses' ball.
For it costs a good guinea
To hear Paganini
And here are twelve fiddlers for nothing at all.[21]

Macaulay's sharp wit and rhetorical skills came into their own during the parliamentary debates about the Great Reform Act of 1832, which disenfranchised sixty pocket and rotten boroughs, halved the representation of another forty-eight, redistributed forty-two new seats to industrial cities and gave the vote to the middle classes. It was the most dramatic constitutional change in British history since the Glorious Revolution of 1689; and describing the crucial second reading of the Bill to a friend, Macaulay was conscious that: 'It was like seeing Caesar stabbed in the Senate House, or seeing Oliver [Cromwell] taking the mace from the table, a sight to be seen only once and never to be forgotten.'[22]

During the fifteen-month parliamentary battle that followed between Whigs and Tories, Lords and Commons, Macaulay emerged as one of the most articulate and persuasive speakers in favour of the Reform Bill. His style of speaking was eccentric to say the least, his 'inconceivable velocity', as one listener put it, like that of an express train which refused to stop at any station. His voice was described as 'pitched in alto, monotonous and rather shrill'. Another description called him 'a little man of small voice, and affected utterance, clipping his words, and hissing like a serpent'.[23] A popular Tory periodical cruelly described him as 'an ugly, . . . splay-footed, shapeless little dumpling of a fellow, with a featureless face . . . large glimmering eyes and a mouth from ear to ear', but went on to admit that, once he got going, his speech was 'so well worded, and so volubly and forcibly delivered . . . there is such an endless string of epigram and antithesis . . . such a flashing of epithets – such an accumulation of images . . . and the voice is so trumpetlike and the action so grotesquely emphatic, that you might hear a pin drop in the House'.[24]

What he lacked in physical charms or elegance of presentation, he more than made up for in razor-sharp argument, inexhaustible historical learning and a superbly rich and colourful prose, not unlike that of Winston Churchill. And although he never read out written speeches, his apparently extempore orations were carefully prepared, memorized and practised at home on his ever-eager sisters.[25]

His first speech on the Reform Bill was made the day after its introduction, and it was a parliamentary sell out. The Speaker of the Commons himself later told Macaulay 'that in all his prolonged experience he had never seen the House in such a state of excitement' and even the Tory leader, Sir Robert Peel, conceded: 'Portions of the speech were as beautiful as anything I have ever heard or read. It reminded one of the old times.'[26] For Macaulay himself, the proudest compliment came from Lady Holland, the wealthy and aristocratic doyenne of Whig society in London, who 'gave me a most gracious reception . . . shook my hand very warmly, and told me in her imperial decisive manner that she had talked with all the principal men on our side about my speech . . . that they all agreed that it was the best that had been made since the death of Fox,* and that it was more like Fox's speaking than anybody's else'.[27]

The speech itself was a shrewd, strategic appeal to the forces of conservatism to embrace or at least accept reform, rather than face the certain alternative of violent revolution as demonstrated in neighbouring France, which had just thrown out its ancient Bourbon monarchy for the second time in 40 years. 'Reform, that you may preserve,' Macaulay exhorted the House, warning that 'everything at home and abroad forebodes ruin to those who persist in a hopeless struggle against the spirit of the age'. And he concluded with a terrifying forecast of political Armageddon as the cost of failure: 'Save the greatest, the fairest, and the most highly civilized community that ever existed, from calamities which may in a few days sweep away all the rich heritage of so many ages of wisdom and glory. The danger is terrible. The time is short.'[28]

In the stormy debates that followed, as the Bill was twice passed by the Commons, defeated in the Lords and then re-launched in the Commons, Macaulay made it clear that he was no advocate of universal suffrage as a basic human right. For him, the right to vote was inseparable from a level of education and property that would ensure it was exercised responsibly. He made no apology for the fact that the extension of the franchise by the new Bill would restrict it to householders whose homes had an annual rentable value of £10, thus excluding the vast majority of the working class.

Macaulay's prolific speeches and writings during these turbulent times laid the foundations of what was to become

---

* Charles James Fox (1749–1806), the hero of Whig radicalism, renowned for his parliamentary oratory.

the dominant Whig interpretation of English history as an ancient and continuous march towards democracy dating back to *Magna Carta*. With his encyclopedic knowledge of classical and world history, Macaulay was fond of citing precedents in the conflicts between patricians and plebeians in ancient Rome, in the American and French Revolutions and even in the slave revolts of the Caribbean.

He was also, in a way that makes him very modern for our times, convinced of the bonds between political and economic freedom. Unlike his contemporaries in the Romantic movement, he warmly welcomed the Industrial Revolution and celebrated its material benefits with the same fervour that the Romantics worshipped nature. When his own rural constituency, one of the pocket boroughs abolished by the new reforms, was swept away, Macaulay was delighted to seek re-election for the newly enfranchised, industrial city of Leeds. One of his election speeches savagely contrasted 'the squalid misery, the dependence, and . . . the comparative stupidity, which . . . characterizes the agricultural population' with the superior intelligence and dynamism of the people of Leeds.[29]

Macaulay's main backers in Leeds were its business community, no doubt because he was by now an ardent champion of laissez-faire capitalism, minimal state intervention and free trade. In response to campaigns to abolish child labour and regulate factory working hours, he maintained that such measures would only address the symptoms rather than the causes of poverty and make matters worse by driving business out of the country. During his election campaign, he had proudly insisted that, if returned to Parliament, he would be as independent of his new electors as he had been of his former aristocratic patrons. 'Under the old system I have never been the flatterer of the great,' he wrote in an open letter. 'Under the new system I will not be the flatterer of the people.'[30]

~

Though no flatterer of the great, Macaulay had become adept at making his way by sheer intelligence and charm into the highest echelons of the Whig aristocracy, centred on Holland House. The first impressions he made, however, were not always favourable. 'Not a ray of intellect beams from his countenance,' wrote one bemused peer of the realm. 'A lump of more ordinary clay never enclosed a powerful mind and a lively imagination.'[31] The historian Thomas Carlyle was more scathing when he described him as 'a short squat thickset man of vulgar but resolute energetic appearance', inclined to corpulence and 'intrinsically common', while grudgingly conceding that he was 'the young man of most force at present before the world'.[32]

Macaulay himself had no illusions about his own looks and often said his portraits flattered him. His intellectual self-confidence more than made up for any diffidence about his appearance. The vast erudition, learning and wit which made him such a formidable parliamentarian were employed with equal success at the tables of the rich and famous. But his brilliance also made him enemies among those he put down or overshadowed. One perceptive biographer attributed to him 'a sort of conversational killer instinct, delight in the demonstration of knowledge for the sake of victory rather than for its own sake'.[33] His sister Margaret, to whom he was closest at this time, attributed such excesses to an underlying shyness and dislike of the company of those outside his intimate circle. She compared his lack of good manners and dislike of hypocrisy with that of Dr Johnson, as also his habit of contradicting

31

others and taking the opposite side in any argument.[34]

Macaulay, even at the peak of his London success in the early 1830s, had a healthy cynicism about the glittering round of parties he dutifully attended. 'I would much rather be quietly walking with you, my darling,' he wrote to his sister Hannah after a grand breakfast at Holland House. 'And the great use of going to these fine places is to learn how happy it is possible to be without them. Indeed I care so little for them that I certainly should not have gone today, but that I thought that I should be able to find materials for a letter which you might like'.[35]

Two years later, he was even more scathing about the Whig elite, telling Hannah he was 'sick of Lords with no brains in their heads, and Ladies with paint and plaister on their cheeks, and politics and politicians, and that reeking furnace of a House'.[36] 'I am the only *parvenu* I ever heard of,' he declared, 'who, after being courted into splendid circles, and after having succeeded beyond expectation in political life, acquired in a few months a profound contempt for rank, fashion, power, popularity and money, . . . for all pleasures but those which derive from the exercise of the intellect and the affections.'[37]

Perhaps young Macaulay was protesting too much, given his own undoubted love of fame and success. But there is little doubt that he was happiest at home within the family circle, and most of all with Margaret and Hannah, the two sisters whom he loved most dearly and whose loss was to cause him the greatest sorrow in his life.

3

Brotherly Love

Two eminent twentieth-century authors, Lytton Strachey and J.H. Plumb, both attributed Macaulay's faults to his lack of 'the embracing fluidity of love', of 'the roots of life, sexual passion, and the sense of tragedy that it arouses—the biting, painful sense of the transience of living and loving men'.[1] These were harsh judgements based on his apparent lack of sexual interest in either gender and his status as a lifelong bachelor. But they ignore his intense, passionate and deep attachments to his inner circle of family and friends.

His closest and only intimate friend was a fellow barrister whom he met in 1827, Thomas Flower Ellis. The latter first described his new friend as 'an amusing person; somewhat boyish in his manner, but very original'.[2] They shared, we are told, 'an insatiable love of the classics', 'similarity of character, not very perceptible on the surface' and 'an intimacy . . . as important to the happiness of both concerned as ever united two men'. There is no evidence that their friendship was sexual, but Macaulay poured out his heart and mind to Ellis in the hundreds of long letters he wrote to him in the course of his life. Unlike him, Ellis married, but his wife died young, and Macaulay was his greatest comfort and support through those difficult times.

Why did Macaulay himself show no inclination for marriage or even courtship with any of the eligible young women he met during his busy social life in London? It was certainly not because he disliked the company of women; quite the contrary. He had grown up with five younger sisters of assorted age and temperament; and he had been close to his mother, whose gentle but intelligent presence had sheltered him from his father's disciplinarian excesses. When she died of a sudden illness in May 1831, he was away from London and first heard of it in the newspapers. He rushed home 'in an agony of distress', his sister Margaret noted in her journal, 'and gave way at first to violent bursts of feeling'. But he then decided to pull himself together, comfort the rest of the family and divert them from their grief. 'I never saw him appear to greater advantage,' said his grateful sister, 'never loved him more dearly.'[3]

Surprisingly, Macaulay also confided to Margaret how much more he would have suffered had it been her or their sister Hannah who had died.[4] It is not clear how or why the internal chemistry of their large family had brought these three siblings so close together, but by this time they were locked in a love triangle that was no less passionate for not being sexual, at least in any conscious sense. The evidence was there in their daily intimacies and in the long letters they wrote each other whenever they were separated.

Margaret, the youngest of the three, recorded in her journal that this special relationship with her brother had begun when she was twelve and he twice her age: 'I shall never forget my delight and enchantment when I first found that he seemed to like talking to me. His manner was very flattering to such a child, for he always took as much pains to amuse me, and to inform me on anything I wished to know, as he could have done to the greatest person in the land.'

His sisters were the audience to whom he first read the drafts of his speeches and essays. 'When we find fault,' said Margaret, 'as I very often do with his being too severe upon people, he takes it with the greatest kindness, and often alters what we do not like.' She went on to say that he could be over-hasty but was quick to accept correction and never lost his temper. His only fault, apparently, was a passion for puns. When his sisters laid a bet that he could not make 200 puns in one evening, he won it in two hours with a flood of puns, 'most of them miserably bad'.[5] Another entry in Margaret's journal noted approvingly:

> Tom is very much improved in his appearance during the last two or three years. His figure is not so bad for a man of thirty . . . He dresses better, and his manners, from seeing a great deal of society, are very much improved. When silent and occupied in thought, walking up and down the room as he always does, his hands clenched and muscles working with the intense exertion of his mind, strangers would think his countenance stern; but I remember a writing-master of ours . . . saying, 'Ladies, your brother looks like a lump of good humour.'[6]

These were idyllic years spent in the cosy informality of the family's comfortable Bloomsbury home. As Margaret later recalled in a letter to Hannah, Tom 'used to lie in bed with his unshorn face, you opposite the window with your feet up on the bed, reading the *Spectator* resting on your knee, I opposite you, or at the foot of the bed, working'.[7] Most afternoons the three spent walking together around the streets and squares of central

London, 'deep in the mazes of the most subtle metaphysics . . ., engaged over Dryden's poetry and the great men of that time; . . . making jokes all the way along Bond Street, and talking politics everywhere'.

Macaulay himself seems to have assumed that this state of happy domesticity would continue indefinitely. 'How sweet and perfect a love is that of brothers and sisters when happy circumstances have brought it to its full maturity,' he wrote to Hannah and Margaret, adding for good measure one of his doggerels:

> My mistress is a jilt—
> My wife—ah! bad's the best,
> So give me my little sisters
> And plague take all the rest.[8]

During another brief separation, he addressed to Hannah what can only be described as a passionate love letter:

> My dear, dear girl, my sister—my darling—my own sweet friend—you cannot tell how . . . I pine for your society, for your voice, for your caresses. I write this with all the weakness of a woman in my heart and in my eyes . . . Farewell my dearest, and believe that there is nothing on Earth that I love as I love you.[9]

'I do not know how love in a cottage may do with a wife,' Macaulay told his two favourite sisters. 'But I am sure that it would suit me with a sister.'[10] His sisters, though equally devoted, were more realistic and seem to have foreseen that this happy idyll would eventually have to make way for matrimony and the role that their strongly Christian family circle expected of them. 'I felt that there was one I idolized,' Hannah confessed about her brother, 'one I loved more than God, one on whom I depended alone for happiness, and in one moment we might be separated for ever. And yet I cannot endure the thought of ever loving him less than I do at this moment, though I feel how criminal it is . . .'[11]

A few months later the happy threesome was shattered when Margaret became engaged and then married to a Quaker family friend. She was motivated by a sense of feminine duty, rather than any romantic attachment, and never fully recovered from the emotional wrench of separation from her beloved brother. 'You will not know till you are parted from him as I am,' she warned Hannah, 'how much you love him.'[12] Macaulay, too, was devastated. Margaret's wedding day coincided with his election victory at Leeds against a strong Tory candidate. 'It is all I can do to hide my tears, and to command my voice . . .' he wrote to Hannah while his supporters celebrated. 'Dearest, dearest girl, you alone are now left to me. Whom have I on Earth but thee . . . and what is there in heaven that I desire in comparison of thee?'[13]

Macaulay's biographer nephew, and Hannah's future son, was clearly embarrassed by his uncle's maudlin outpourings and conceded that 'his affections were only too tender, and his sensibilities only too acute . . . It must be acknowledged that, where he loved, he loved more entirely, and more exclusively, than was well for himself. It was improvident in him to concentrate such intensity of feeling upon relations who, however deeply they were attached to him, could not . . . requite him with the whole of their time, and the whole of their heart. He suffered much for that improvidence'.[14]

His uncle, he tells us, 'never again recovered that tone of thorough boyishness' after Margaret's marriage. But Macaulay, to his credit, made no attempt to discourage her from marrying or to play on her guilt and heartache about leaving him, although he told her it was 'a parting scarcely less solemn than that of a deathbed'. He also began to prepare himself for the double blow that might follow when Hannah followed her sister's example. 'The attachment between brothers and sisters,' he philosophized, 'blameless, amiable, and delightful as it is, is so liable to be superseded by other attachments that no wise man ought to suffer it to become indispensable to his happiness . . . But to me it has been in the place of a first love.' He admitted that he had only his 'own want of foresight' to blame for his grief. As for the prospect of Hannah too flying the nest, he predicted: 'From that moment, with a heart formed, if ever any man's heart was formed for domestic happiness, I shall have nothing left in this world but ambition. There is no wound, however, which time and necessity do not render endurable.'[15]

~

Fortunately for Macaulay, the loss of his sister Margaret coincided with the opening of a new chapter in his public life, which demanded most of his energies for the next six years and produced arguably his most enduring achievements. This was his involvement with the governance of India, until recently just a lucrative trading base for a private British company, but now, since the loss of the American colonies, the main arena for Britain's imperial ambitions.

In June 1832, just days after the passing of the Great Reform Act, Britain's most important constitutional change since the Revolution of 1689, Macaulay was rewarded for his parliamentary eloquence with his first government post. He was appointed one of the Commissioners of the Board of Control, the quango through which the British Crown managed the affairs of the East India Company. For all the scorn he was fond of pouring on ministerial patronage, he could not conceal his pleasure in this first taste of the perks of office. 'I am sitting in a very handsome well furnished room, with a large window looking out on the Thames,' he proudly informed Hannah and Margaret, who were spending the summer away from London, 'and writing to you with government ink and a government pen on government paper and under a government seal.'[16] A few months later, he had been promoted to the post of Secretary to the Board with a generous salary of £1,500 a year (£75,000 in today's money), no doubt very welcome because his previous sinecure as Commissioner of Bankrupts had just been abolished.

Stirred perhaps by childhood memories of his uncle's adventures in the wars against Tipu Sultan, Macaulay took to his new Indian brief like a duck to water. Within days of his appointment, he was writing to his sisters:

> I am already deep in Zemindars, Ryots, Polygars, Courts of Phoujdary, and Courts of Nizamut Adawlut. I can tell you which of the native Powers are subsidiary, and which independent, and read you lectures of an hour on our diplomatic transactions at the courts of Lucknow, Nagpore, Hydrabad and Poonah . . . Am I not in fair training to be as great a bore as if I had myself been in India? . . . that is to say, as great a bore as the greatest.[17]

Macaulay had little time or sympathy for 'such pests as those curry-coloured old watering-place Nabobs', the Anglo-Indians*—retired or on home leave—who were wont

---

* In the nineteenth century, 'Anglo-indian' referred to British settlers, not Indians of mixed descent.

to try and lobby the Commissioners.[18] But he was equally vitriolic about the iniquities of the Indian caste system and the complex intrigues and corruption of Indian princes. Plagued with issues as perplexing as the debts of the Nawab of Oudh and legal appeals by some Indians to the Privy Council against the abolition of sati, Macaulay let off steam in one of his characteristic doggerels:

Oh the charming month of May
When I was in Opposition,
I walked ten miles a day,
And lounged at the Exhibition.
Oh the hateful month of May
Now that I am in power.
No longer can I ramble
In the streets to the East of the Tower.
The Niggers in one hemisphere
The Brahmins in the other
Disturb my dinner and my sleep
With 'An't I a man and a brother?'*[19]

The reference to 'niggers' (a term more common but less pejorative in the nineteenth century) was inspired by his successful efforts to amend a new government Bill to phase out slavery over a twelve-year period. Macaulay, egged on by his Abolitionist father, had argued that this was too generous to the slave-owning planters of the West Indies; and he had succeeded in getting the term reduced to six years.

Meanwhile, his diligent research into Indian administration and customs produced its own new crop of bad puns, to which his sisters were subjected. 'A pun! A pun! . . . well suited to a

---

* This was a reference to the motto of his father's Anti-Slavery Society.

Commissioner for the Affairs of India,' he quipped to Hannah and Margaret. 'What city in Hindostan [sic] tells the whole history of Desdemona?* . . . Moor-she'd-a-bad. Huzza! How witty!'[20]

An important voice at this time in favour of the abolition of sati, the promotion of women's rights and other radical reforms in India was that of the greatest of all Hindu social reformers, Raja Ram Mohan Roy, who had arrived in London in 1830 as the ambassador of the now defunct Mughal Emperor Akbar II. Roy had been closely allied with the reform-minded British Governor-General in India, Lord William Bentinck, and was a leading supporter of the latter's policy of liberal interventionism in the three British-ruled provinces of Bengal, Madras and Bombay. Roy believed passionately that the British administration had a duty to help modernize Muslim and Hindu society in India, as opposed to the Orientalist policy of non-interference in local customs, which had prevailed so far. He stayed on in England till his death in September 1833, and Macaulay must almost certainly have met him during this three-year period, though it is unclear when and where.

Writing to his sister Hannah in June 1831, Macaulay said he had hoped to meet Roy at the home of the Whig historian Sir James Mackintosh, but left 'in despair' after waiting till midnight. He was already familiar, he wrote, with Roy's 'peculiar' religious thinking and his belief that Hinduism and Christianity had common roots in a 'pure Theism', which Hindu idolatry and superstition had perverted into 'the source of all sorts of absurdities and crimes'. Roy acknowledged that Christian morality was 'superior to any . . . in the most ancient and purest records of the Hindu theology', and he was 'firmly convinced that in twenty-five years the *caste* will be

---

* A reference to Shakespeare's *Othello, the Moor of Venice*.

no more—that there will not be a Brahmin in Hindustan who will not eat beef'. Macaulay added that Roy, himself a Brahmin, did not eat beef 'solely from a disgust like that which we feel to a food to which we are not used—snails or frogs for example'.[21]

Whether or not Roy and Macaulay actually met in London, there was an undoubted meeting of minds in their shared iconoclasm, rejection of conventional morality and faith in the then nebulous concept of universal human rights. Macaulay had grown up in a family staunchly committed to the abolition of slavery, and he had written articles declaring that there could be no rational objection to mixed marriages between black and white, except for an educational and economic gap which must disappear in time.[22] He was proud of what he considered his own racially mixed origins as the child of a Scottish Celtic father and an Anglo-Saxon mother. Despite his insistence that the political franchise must be restricted to the educated, he was even open to the prospect of educated women getting the vote, an extremely remote and revolutionary concept in the first half of the nineteenth century.[23]

Macaulay's arrival at the heart of Britain's imperial government coincided with a major legislative overhaul of the East India Company's rule in India; and he soon became the most articulate protagonist of what was still only a budding sense of imperial mission. Underlying his view of empire was the assumption, rooted in his own Scottish family's assimilation into Britishness, that British subjects anywhere in the world could share common values, language and political rights.

The Charter Act of 1813 had opened the door to a policy of Western penetration of the subcontinent by abolishing the East India Company's trading monopoly in India, allowing Christian missionaries to proselytize there and setting aside public revenues for 'native education' (long before any State grants for education were available in Britain itself). The latter two objectives had been closely linked in the minds of Evangelicals like Charles Grant,* who were convinced that the English language, rather than the vernaculars, would be the most successful means of replacing Hindu superstition with a modern, rational approach that would be both scientific and Christian. The Charter Act of 1833, in the drafting of which Macaulay was closely involved, took these early modernizing aims to their logical conclusion.

Macaulay, as we know, had little sympathy for Evangelical Christianity, and the imperial proselytizing he had in mind was essentially secular, cultural and political, inspired by the classical, pagan civilisations of ancient Greece and Rome, to whose literature he was so addicted. It was his job to present the new Bill for its crucial Second Reading in the House of Commons, and it passed by a huge majority. 'I made the best speech, by general agreement, and in my own opinion, that I ever made in my life,' he boasted to Hannah. 'I was an hour and three-quarters up. And such compliments as I had . . . you never heard . . . An old member said to me, "Sir, having heard that speech may console the young people for never having heard Mr Burke."'[24]

The comparison with Edmund Burke's legendary oratory may have flattered him, but the imperial mission his speech outlined had little in common with Burke's overriding emphasis on protecting India's traditional culture and institutions from Western incursions. Instead, Macaulay started with the premise

---

* Adviser to the Governor-General, Lord Cornwallis, later Chairman of the East India Company, and closely associated with Zachary Macaulay and the Clapham Sect. His son, also called Charles Grant, was Chairman of the Board of Control when Macaulay joined it.

that the British had found India in a state as chaotic as that of Europe during the Dark Ages, with the Mughal Empire, like that of Rome, having crumbled 'under the vices of a bad internal administration, and under the assaults of barbarous invaders'. As for the common people of India, they 'were ground down to the dust by the oppressor without and the oppressor within', subject at once to 'all the evils of despotism, and all the evils of anarchy', with desolation in their cities and famine stalking the land.[25]

It was true, Macaulay conceded, that the early history of British conquest had been 'chequered with guilt and shame', due to 'rapacious, imperious and corrupt' White Nabobs, who had been carried away by the wealth and power suddenly at their disposal. But half a century later, he could 'see scarcely a trace of the vices which blemished . . . the first conquerors of Bengal'. They had been replaced by a new generation of colonial administrators who were committed to the task of maintaining peace, order and good government for very modest remuneration. The creation of a professional civil service offering India 'the best talents which England can spare' would, Macaulay argued, be greatly furthered by the proposed new system of recruitment by open and competitive examination, replacing the old network of patronage and nepotism the Company's Directors had operated so far.

The new Raj, he proclaimed, would be 'an enlightened and paternal despotism', based, like the ancient empires of Greece and Rome, on the rule of law, and it would build institutions in which Indians might eventually rise to the highest offices. He was proud of having helped to draft the 'noble clause, which enacts that no native of our Indian empire shall by reason of his colour, his descent, or his religion, be incapable of holding office'. Even if that ultimately meant Indian Independence, it would be far preferable for Britain itself than a policy of narrow imperial domination. Macaulay waxed lyrical in Parliament:

> The public mind of India may expand under our system till it has outgrown that system; that by good government we may educate our subjects into a capacity for better government; that, having been instructed in European knowledge, they may, in some future age, demand European institutions . . . Whenever it comes, it will be the proudest day in English history. To have found a great people sunk in the lowest depths of slavery and superstition, to have so ruled them as to have made them desirous and capable of all the privileges of citizens, would indeed be a title to glory all our own.

Looking ahead to an age of globalization through free trade, Macaulay declared that Britain as a great trading and manufacturing nation could only benefit from India's wealth and prosperity. He predicted:

> It is scarcely possible to calculate the benefits which we might derive from the diffusion of European civilization among the vast population of the East. It would be, on the most selfish view of the case, far better for us that the people of India were well governed and independent of us, than ill governed and subject to us; that they were ruled by their own kings, but wearing our broadcloth, and working with our cutlery, than that they were performing their salams to English . . . magistrates, but were too ignorant to value, or too poor to buy, English manufactures. To trade with civilized men is infinitely more profitable than to govern savages.

It was a remarkably prophetic, if patronizing, vision of future globalization, and it was based on an overriding confidence that the new world order would be led by the Anglo-Saxon language and values of the British Whig tradition. Macaulay asked rhetorically:

> What is power worth if it is founded on vice, on ignorance and on misery; if we can hold it only by violating the most sacred duties which as governors we owe to the governed, and which, as a people blessed with far more than an ordinary measure of political liberty and of intellectual light, we owe to a race debased by three thousand years of despotism and priestcraft? We are free, we are civilized, to little purpose, if we grudge to any portion of the human race an equal measure of freedom and civilization.

This ideological commitment to a doctrine of universal human rights sounds remarkably modern in its anticipation of the language and rhetoric of twentieth- and twenty-first-century Western interventions everywhere from Sierra Leone to Iraq and Afghanistan, whatever one might think of their underlying motivation or practical outcomes. Macaulay ended his remarkable speech with what must be the first clear articulation of the current concept of soft power. Britain might suffer military defeats in the future, 'but there are triumphs which are followed by no reverse. There is an empire exempt from all natural causes of decay. Those triumphs are the pacific triumphs of reason over barbarism; that empire is the imperishable empire of our arts and our morals, our literature and our laws.'

But such a grand imperial vision had yet to grasp the public imagination of pre-Victorian Britain. Macaulay himself lamented the very thin attendance in Parliament during the debates and 'the strange indifference of all classes of people, members of Parliament, reporters and the public to Indian politics'. But he congratulated himself: 'The very cause of the negligence of the reporters and of the thinness of the House is that we have framed our measure so carefully as to give little occasion for debate . . . Many other members assure me that they never remember to have seen a Bill better drawn or better conducted . . .'[26]

The Act which he so nimbly piloted through the Commons in July 1833 opened a momentous new chapter in Britain's imperial role and arguably enunciated for the first time the goal of a unified Indian state. It effectively nationalized the East India Company and created a centralized government of British India accountable to the British Crown, namely the Governor-General-in-Council based in Calcutta. That supreme government in India was given law-making powers, with a Law Commission to advise on a uniform legal code that would apply equally to British and Indian subjects of the Crown. A month later, Macaulay himself had the doubtful distinction of being offered the newly created post of Law Member of the Governor-General's Council, with the task of advising on its new legislative role.

~

For the intellectual darling of the fashionable Whig society and a rising star of the party's parliamentary benches to abandon London and seek his fortune on the remote frontiers of empire might seem like an astonishing career move. The post would mean an unbroken absence of several years from England, since the sea passage in those pre-Suez times took several months. And for all his grand imperial designs and his dutiful background research at the Board of Control, Macaulay had shown little real interest in India or its culture. His main motive in accepting the post, as he admitted freely to his family, was pecuniary.

The post of Law Member, joining the three other members who made up the Governor-General's Council, was 'one of the highest dignity and consideration', Macaulay assured his sister Hannah, even though his voting rights would be restricted to legislative, rather than executive, decisions. It carried a princely salary of £10,000 a year, and he had been assured that he could live 'in splendour' in Calcutta for half that sum, enabling him to return to England six years later with a fortune of £30,000 (£500,000 and £1.5 million respectively in todays money). 'I am not fond of money, or anxious about it,' he declared, but his recent experiences as a junior member of government had convinced him of the need to be independent of official patronage. At present, he was trapped in a circle of economic dependence, because his only means of earning a living was by writing, but he had little time to write because of the demands of active politics. He also foresaw a political split in the government, which would compel him to resign his office or 'lose my political character'. 'In England,' he concluded, 'I see nothing before me, for some time to come, but poverty, unpopularity and the breaking up of old connections.'[27]

'I feel that the sacrifice which I am about to make is great,' Macaulay wrote to a Whig grandee who had been his patron, but went on to explain that 'every day makes me more sensible of the importance of a competence. Without a competence it is not very easy for a public man to be honest: it is almost impossible for him to be thought so.' India was to provide this competence, enabling him to return to British politics a wealthy man, free of anyone's grace and favour. It was also to provide for his large family, for which he was now the sole breadwinner, with his father ailing and indigent and three unmarried sisters.

'A family which I love most fondly is dependent on me,' Macaulay wrote emotionally to his patron. 'Unless I would see my father left in his old age to the charity of less near relations; my youngest brother unable to obtain a good professional education; my sisters, who are more to me than sisters ever were to a brother, forced to turn governesses . . ., I must do something . . . An opportunity has offered itself.'[28]

Although he never said so, his decision to make such a radical break with his old life cannot have been unconnected with the depression into which Margaret's marriage had plunged him less than a year ago. She was settled far away in a small country estate near Liverpool, already busy raising a family of her own. Macaulay's life in London must have been a constant reminder to him of her absence and of all the happy times they had shared on its bustling streets. As though writing about a lover who had jilted him, he assured Hannah that his relationship with Margaret was over. 'She is dead to me . . .,' he declared melodramatically. 'Instead of wishing to be near her, I shrink from it.'[29] He was certainly exaggerating, because he continued to write long and intimate letters to Margaret. But his emotions now focused more intensely on the sister who remained with him—his beloved 'Nancy', as he called Hannah. His main pre-condition for taking the job in India was that she must accompany him as his official hostess and housekeeper.

Macaulay's choice of a lucrative Indian exile may well have been motivated in part by a desire to provide for his family. But it did him no credit that he constantly reminded them of this and even used it as a weapon to force Hannah into going with him, much against her own wishes. 'Whether the period of my exile shall be one of misery, or of comfort . . . depends on you . . .,' he begged her in the same letter that announced the new job offer. 'I can scarcely see the words which I am writing through the tears that force themselves into my eyes. Will you, my own darling . . . will you go with me? . . . I can bribe you only by telling you that, if you will go with me, I will love you better than I love you now, if I can.'[30]

Having delivered this unashamed piece of emotional blackmail, he hastened to assure her 'that the climate would be quite as likely to do you good as harm'.[31] This could hardly have been much comfort at a time when mortality rates among the British community in India were more than double those back home. And Hannah, who had so far shown no interest in anything remotely exotic or adventurous, was being asked to abandon all the physical and emotional comforts of her happy family circle for several years of exile in the distant tropics. Her response, not surprisingly, was one of horror. She replied instantly to her brother's request, saying she 'abhorred the idea' and saw India only as a 'region of disease and death', and she made 'an agonized appeal to him entreating him to give it up'.[32] Macaulay promptly offered to give up the idea if she insisted, while reminding her that his main motive in considering the job was to provide for her future.[33]

In the weeks that followed, Hannah gave way to this combination of pressure and pleading, drawing from her brother an effusion of gratitude inspired by the erotic poetry of 'The Song of Solomon': '. . . there is love, I believe, which, as the Bible says, many waters cannot quench nor the floods drown . . . And such love is mine for my Nancy, and, I think, hers for me.'[34]

～

Despite Hannah's acquiescence, there were still practical hurdles to be overcome before the pair could set sail on their new venture. Although his appointment had the support of the Prime Minister,

Earl Grey, and of Charles Grant (the younger), the powerful
Chairman of the Board of Control, it initially provoked a 'furious'
response from the Chair and Vice-Chair of the Board of Directors,
because they held Macaulay personally responsible for abolishing
their powers in the new Charter Act. 'They put their opposition on
the ground of my youth,' he informed Hannah, 'a very flattering
objection to a man who this week completes his thirty-third year...'
And he added with exasperation: '... they seemed quite obstinate;
– as indeed they are on all occasions the most stupid pair of mules
that I ever saw.'[35]

Just as he was thinking of bowing out of the contest to make
way for someone less controversial, a sudden *coup d'état* at
India House replaced the hostile pair of mules with new Chairs
of Directors friendly to the government and 'very strongly'
in Macaulay's favour.[36] The appointment was clinched when
the political philosopher and historian James Mill,* 'my old
enemy'[37] as Macaulay described him, decided to support his
candidature. Mill at this time was Chief Examiner for the East
India Company's training college and its senior-most figure
after the Chairs of Directors. 'Mill said, very handsomely, that
he would advise the Company to take me,' Macaulay wrote to
Hannah, 'for, as public men went, I was much above the average,
and, if they rejected me, he thought it very unlikely that they
would get anybody so fit.'

With the job now in the bag, he began to plan well in advance
and in meticulous detail how he and Hannah would travel and

---

* Father of the political philosopher John Stuart Mill, James Mill had
published in 1817 a definitive, eight-volume history of British India,
which had hugely influenced a whole generation of East India Company
administrators with its paternalistic view of British rule lifting India out
of Oriental despotism and superstition. Though sympathetic to Mill's
historical interpretation, Macaulay had been sharply critical of his
Utilitarian political theorizing.

what they would need to take with them. Even before the formal announcement, he was 'beset by advertising dealers begging leave to make up a hundred cotton shirts for me, and fifty muslin gowns for you, and by clerks out of place begging to be my secretaries'.[38] But he decided prudently that they should take only what they needed for the journey and buy the rest—'plate, wine, coaches, furniture, glass, china'—more economically in Calcutta. With careful accounting, they would keep their entire expenses for the passage within the limit of £1,200 allowed by the Company, including a clothing allowance of £300 (£60,000 and £15,000 respectively in today's money) for Hannah 'to lay out as you like'.[39]

They would take one servant each with them; and Macaulay was most insistent that Hannah must choose hers 'with great caution'. In the past, the Company's rule had been that all maidservants shipped out from Britain to India must be returned within two years because of their tendency to 'treat the natives with gross insolence; an insolence natural enough to people accustomed to stand in a subordinate relation to others when, for the first time, they find a great population placed in a servile relation towards them'. It was also feared that these unattached young women might 'become mistresses of the wealthy Europeans, and . . . flaunt about in magnificent palanquins, bringing discredit on their country by the immorality of their lives and the vulgarity of their manners'.

Macaulay himself seems to have been unduly concerned about the havoc that might be caused to their future Calcutta home by an unsuitable English maidservant 'if she should be ill-tempered and arrogant'. He also felt responsible for her moral well-being having brought her 'into the midst of temptations of which she cannot be aware'. 'If she should be weak and vain,' he lectured Hannah, 'she will probably form connections that will ruin her morals and her reputation.' And if she were 'young and attractive', he had no doubt that she would soon marry and have to be replaced by a native ayah from one of the Christian mission schools.

His attention to such domestic arrangements was motivated less by any puritanical morality than by the magisterial role he now envisaged for himself in the newly created post of Law Member in Calcutta. At a celebratory dinner for him at India House, one distinguished guest noted that Macaulay 'rather gave himself the airs of a Lycurgus, and spoke as if he were about to bestow on the swarming millions of India the blessings of rudimentary legislation'.[40] While warning Hannah against choosing an English maid who might oppress their Indian servants, he grandly declared that his new post 'is to be, in a peculiar manner, the guardian of the people of India against the European settlers' and that he must not allow the abuse of power 'to bring scandal on my own house'.[41]

He was equally concerned that Hannah, whose social life so far had been restricted to the family circle, must be groomed for her new role as his hostess in the social world of colonial Calcutta. He arranged for friends of his to invite her to a London season of parties where she would meet 'the best set in town'. 'Even to have mixed a little in a circle so brilliant will be of advantage to you in India,' he lectured her. 'You have neglected . . . frivolous accomplishments. You have not been at places of fashionable diversion: and it is, therefore, the more desirable that you should appear among the dancing, pianoforte-playing, opera-going damsels at Calcutta as one who has seen society better than any that they ever approached.'[42]

Lest Hannah waver in her resolve to accompany him, he sent her descriptions of the suburban splendour of Chowringhee with its fine houses and verandahs, one of which would soon be theirs.[43] And after dining with the former Advocate-General of Bengal, he reassured her that nothing could be pleasanter than the Calcutta climate 'except in August and September'. 'His looks do credit to Bengal,' Macaulay ran on, 'for a healthier man of his age I never saw.' As for insects and snakes, the secret of survival, according to this cheerful, old gentleman, was simple: 'Always, sir, manage to have at your table some fleshy, blooming, young . . . cadet, just come out that the mosquitoes may stick to him and leave the rest of the company alone.'[44]

Macaulay lost no opportunity to remind poor Hannah that it was really for her own sake and the family's finances that they would be embarking on this hazardous, tropical adventure. His social patroness, Lady Holland, he told her was 'quite hysterical about my going; paid me such compliments as I cannot repeat, cried, raved . . . "You are sacrificed to your family . . . You are too good to them. They are always making a tool of you . . . now sending you to India to make money for them. . ."' Lady Holland, he told Hannah, had brushed aside his concerns about the great sacrifice Hannah was making. 'Oh what dupes you men are,' the grande dame had exclaimed. 'How women turn you round their fingers. Make me believe that any girl who has no fortune would not jump at the chance of visiting Calcutta as the sister of such a man and in such a situation.'[45]

Meanwhile, there was the question of which ship to take, a major decision since it would be their home for several months. Offers were pouring in from various captains eager to land a passenger as illustrious as a Member of the Governor-General's Council. 'I really am mobbed with gentlemen begging to have the honour of taking me to India . . .,' Macaulay told Hannah. 'The fact is that a Member of Council is a great catch . . . because other people are attracted by him. Every father of a young writer* . . . likes to have his son on board the same vessel with

---

* A writer was a Company civil servant.

the great man, to dine at the same table, and to have a chance of attracting his notice.'[46]

They eventually fixed on a ship called *The Asia* whose very likable captain was 'an agreeable, intelligent, polished man of forty . . . and very good-looking, considering what storms and changes of climate he has gone through'.[47] Macaulay instructed him to make Hannah's cabin 'as neat as possible, without regard to expense' and to furnish it 'simply . . . but prettily'. 'When you see it,' he assured Hannah, 'if any addition occurs to you, it shall be made. He assured me that he can make it all that a lady's cabin can be for a small sum.'

Among the possessions they would take with them would be 'a very large and very fine dinner set and tea set', plated rather than solid silver cutlery,[48] and of course a large library of the books from which Macaulay could never be parted. 'I have my eye on all the bookstalls,' he announced gleefully to Hannah, 'and I shall no longer suffer you, when we walk together in London, to drag me past them as you used to do.'[49] His special interest at this time was in Voltaire, whose biography he was proposing to write, but his other proposed choices for the voyage demonstrated both his eclectic tastes and his multilingual skills. They ranged from Jane Austen's novels to Gibbon on the Roman Empire, Don Quixote in Spanish, Homer in Greek, Horace in Latin and Italian poetry. He had already arranged with the *Edinburgh Review* that he would continue writing for it from India, in return for payment in kind with a regular supply of books he would order.[50]

There had been much discussion between brother and sister about which would be the best month to sail, so that they could time their arrival four months later at an opportune time in the Bengal climate. They had decided that departure in early February would be best because June and July were 'agreeable months' in Calcutta, based presumably on the assumption that the monsoon would by then have broken.

On the eve of their departure, Macaulay wrote to his father to assure him that he and Hannah were 'both of us looking forward firmly and cheerfully to our voyage and to our sojourn in India'.[51] Nothing could have been further from the truth, though brother and sister put a brave face on it and tried to conceal their feelings from each other. On the day they sailed, Hannah wrote to Margaret, the beloved sister they were leaving behind, confiding how desperately unhappy she was: 'It is impossible that I could be called upon to such a sacrifice as I have really made . . . Tom has no conception what I am feeling.'[52]

Tom's own feelings were scarcely more cheerful, as he had confided to Margaret a month earlier. 'Why is it,' he wrote, 'that I cannot trust myself to finish this letter without locking my door lest I should be found crying like a child?' And he added, in a reference to her recent marriage: 'It is not the separation which is to take place six weeks hence that makes me weep, but the separation which took place last year.'[53]

A month later his spirits were buoyed up by a generous farewell gift from the Jewish banker, Isaac Goldsmid. 'The Jew of Jews,' he joked to Margaret, 'has sent me a most superb gold tabatière with an inscription on the lid setting forth my services to the cause of civil and religious liberty. It will do excellently to hand round our table after great dinners at Calcutta.'[54] It must also have been a reminder to him of the challenge awaiting him to perform far greater services in distant India.

4

Mangoes and Maharajas

Macaulay was famously dubbed 'the least Indian of Indian civil servants' by the future Liberal prime minister, William Ewart Gladstone.[1] As he sailed towards India, his voracious appetite for foreign languages and books made no concessions to his destination. The handful of Hindustani and Persian grammars he had packed lay neglected. And despite his pride in mastering any language in a fortnight, no Indian tongue ever joined the list. Instead, he spent the four-month voyage mostly closeted in his cabin, devouring 'Greek, Latin, Spanish, Italian, French and English; folios, quartos, octavos and duodecimos'.[2] As he later proudly announced in a letter to his old friend Thomas Ellis, he managed to consume 'the Iliad and the Odyssey, Virgil, Horace, Caesar's commentaries, Bacon's *De Augmentis*, Dante, Petrarch, Ariosto, Tasso, Don Quixote, Gibbon's *Rome*, Mill's *India*, all the seventy volumes of Voltaire, Sismondi's *History of France*, and the seven thick folios of the Biographia Britannica'.[3]

His bibliomania was aided by extraordinary powers of speed-reading, a photographic memory and an ability to carry on reading a book while walking, eating and performing most of his other daily business. It was also helped by the fact that he studiously avoided his fellow-passengers. 'Except at meals,' he informed his sister Margaret, 'I hardly exchanged a word with any human being.' Hannah, on the other hand, was showing new signs of independence and had clearly decided to make the best of the journey she had dreaded: 'she was extremely social; danced with the gentlemen in the evenings, and read novels and sermons with the ladies in the mornings.'

Macaulay had no time for the other young British women on board, 'all rather plain and all very vulgar'. 'One Miss Haldane in particular,' he grumbled, 'was a perfect nuisance, and was always romping and joking with a coarse, raw-boned Scotchman, the very abstract and essence of every thing that is most unpleasant in the Scotch character.'[4] His own Scottish ancestry probably made him doubly intolerant of such antics.

After a largely uneventful voyage that was 'monotony itself', *The Asia* reached its destination at Madras on June 10, 1834. The first Indian they set eyes on was a boatman who rowed up to the ship on a raft. 'He came on board with nothing on him but a pointed yellow cap,' Macaulay wrote home to Margaret, 'and walked among us with a self-possession and civility which, coupled with his colour and his nakedness, nearly made me die of laughing.' He did not record the reaction of his vulgar, young female compatriots.

The naked boatman was followed by 'more responsible messengers' from the Governor-General, Lord Bentinck, who was awaiting the Law Member of his Council in the newly established hill-station of Ootacamund (Ooty) in the Nilgiri Hills. Greeted by a ceremonial salute of fifteen guns as they came on shore, Macaulay was overwhelmed by the excitement and exoticism of his new surroundings: 'nothing but dark faces and bodies with white turbans and flaming robes, – the trees not our trees, . . . the very smell of the atmosphere like that of a hothouse, . . . the architecture as strange as the vegetation, I was quite stunned.'[5]

Brother and sister drove in state to Government House, and at each door of their carriage 'trotted a boy in an oriental costume of scarlet and gold'. Such boys, Macaulay was assured, could 'run by the side of a carriage without being distressed for fourteen or fifteen miles at a time'. The new arrivals were handsomely lodged in the Madras Governor's stately residence, each with their own suite of rooms. The rooms looked enormous, compared with those of Georgian London. Macaulay's dressing-room had a ceiling 'as high as a church' and four huge doors, 'each as large as the door of a house in Grosvenor Square'. The doors were slatted like Venetian blinds to let cooling breezes blow though the rooms. The floors were covered with rush matting, the white ceilings were of painted wood and the walls covered with a very fine *chunam* plaster, which looked 'exactly like the whitest and purest marble'.

The next morning, he woke to the delights of being shaved by the Governor's barber, who 'shaves me so much better than I can shave myself that I mean, . . . while I remain in India, to leave the superintendence of my chin to others'. There followed a lavish breakfast, waited upon by five servants, with the coffee 'excellent, . . . the butter good and cool, . . . the bread, the eggs, the milk, all quite equal to those of an English country house'. But never one to offer uncritical praise, Macaulay complained that 'all the tropical fruits together are not worth any of our commonest English productions—cherry, strawberry, currant, apple, pear, peach'. 'The mango,' he grumbled, clearly not having experienced the far more refined Alphonso variety, 'eats like honey and turpentine—the plantain like a rotten pear.' Even the

Indian pineapple, which he deemed 'the best fruit that I have found here', was far inferior to its English cousin.

Fond of judging by comparison, he had plenty of opportunity in the months that followed to discover major contrasts, but also occasional similarities, between the tidy and ordered English world he had left behind and the vast and chaotic subcontinent opening up before him. Though he never wavered in his preference for all things English and European, even Macaulay was not immune to India's exotic allure and excitement:

> The burning sun, the strange vegetation of the palm and the cocoa-tree, the rice-field, the tank, the huge trees, older than the Mogul empire, under which the village crowds assemble, the thatched roof of the peasant's hut, the rich tracery of the mosque where the imaum prays with his face to Mecca, the drums, and banners, and gaudy idols, the devotee swinging in the air, the graceful maiden, with the pitcher on her head, descending the steps to the riverside, the black faces, the long beards, the yellow streaks of sect, the turbans and the flowing robes, the spears and the silver maces, the elephants with their canopies of state, the gorgeous palanquin of the prince, and the close litter of the noble lady . . .[6]

~

On his drives into the countryside around Madras, Macaulay found the local villages 'much on an equality with the villages of Wales and Scotland' (though presumably not of more prosperous England). They consisted of low, whitewashed huts, with projecting roofs to offer shaded areas in front. And he saw signs that their inhabitants had 'more than the mere necessaries of life'. 'The timber over the door is generally carved,' he noted approvingly, 'and sometimes with a taste and skill that reminded me of the wood-work of some of our fine Gothic chapels and cathedrals.'[7]

He was less positive about the native population, based on the advice he received from 'a native of some fortune in Madras'. This gentleman had warned him that 'the great evil is that men swear falsely in this country' and that 'no judge knows what to believe'. The answer, according to this Anglophile Indian, was drastic but simple: 'Let your honour cut off the great toe of the right foot of every man who swears falsely, whereby your honour's fame will be extended.' 'An exquisite specimen of legislative wisdom', Macaulay joked, but not one he intended to apply in his future role as a lawmaker.[8]

He would later dismissively refer to Indians as 'a people who have much in common with children'.[9] His first impressions of India's ruling classes were undoubtedly coloured by two early visits he made to the courts of princes who had become British pensioners, deprived of any real power and confined to a largely ornamental role. The first was the Muslim Nawab of the Carnatic, a young boy of 10, whose forefathers had been the autonomous, hereditary, southern viceroys of the Mughal Emperor in Delhi. The British province of Madras had been carved out of their territories and the titular Nawabs retired on a lavish income of £100,000 (£5 million in today's money), ten times Macaulay's own generous salary. Even so, he found the Nawab's palace gardens thronged by Muslim beggars and the palace guard of honour that welcomed him dressed in the ragged, cast-off clothes of British sepoys.* 'They looked like scarecrows,' he exclaimed, 'and had less precision and order in

---

* Indian troops employed by the East India Company.

their movements than any awkward squad that I ever saw in St James's Park.'[10]

The court interpreter, however, turned out to be 'a handsome, intelligent-looking man, whose mind has evidently been enlarged by much intercourse with Englishmen'; and the Regent, the Nawab's uncle, 'talked with as much profundity and wit as most princes in Europe'. He eagerly questioned Macaulay about how old the King of England was and how many sons he had to succeed him. He was 'greatly concerned' to discover that poor William IV was 68 and childless.*

The next day, as protocol demanded, the Nawab returned the visit and arrived at Government House with a cavalry escort 'more miserable, if possible, than his infantry'. He was accompanied by the same intelligent interpreter, 'who was evidently scarcely able to suppress his laughter at the nonsense which he was employed to translate'. Macaulay drew some serious inferences from the amusing contrast between this untutored prince and his articulate courtier, and he 'could not but feel for the poor little fellow who is brought up in such a way that he is quite sure to indulge in every excess and to acquire no useful knowledge'.

He was informed that the boy, though both intelligent and affectionate, was surrounded by flatterers, cosseted by a mother and grandmother 'who will not let him swallow English physic for fear of poison and are always covering him with amulets for fear of enchantment', and that his education was limited to reading the Koran for a few hours every day. Here, Macaulay was quick to notice, was a major lost opportunity for what we today would call Western nation-building:

---

* William IV succeeded his brother, George IV, who had also died childless in 1830. In the absence of a male heir, the crown passed to their niece Victoria on William's death in 1837.

I really think that our government should have insisted
. . . that his education be superintended by some
Englishman. If the Nabob had been so brought up as
to turn out an accomplished gentleman, and a good
scholar, with his influence over the Mahometans, with his
immense wealth, and with his high birth, he would have
been the most useful agent that our government could
have had in the great work of civilizing the Carnatic. It
is now, I am afraid, too late. He will kill himself, in all
probability, before he is thirty, by indulgence in every
species of sensuality.

A couple of weeks later, on his way from Madras to Ooty
in the Nilgiris, Macaulay had the opportunity to compare this
example of Muslim feudal decadence with the Hindu Raja of
Mysore. The British had recently restored the Wadiyar dynasty
to their throne, which had previously been usurped by the
formidable Muslim warlord Hyder Ali and his son Tipu Sultan.
But the young Raja had proved so incompetent that his British
protectors had been forced to depose him all over again and
take direct control of his state.

The deposed Raja, eager to impress his influential visitor, sent
a grand escort to bring Macaulay to his palace. It was 'better
managed' than the retinue of the Nawab of the Carnatic, the
soldiers better dressed and drilled and their oriental costumes
very striking. The procession was led by a richly caparisoned
elephant, followed by a long stream of silver spears and floating
banners. For the rest, Macaulay found little to praise. 'Music,'
he lamented, 'detestable like all the music that I have heard in
India, preceded the carriage and the whole rabble of Mysore
followed in my train.' Nor was he impressed when they arrived
at the Raja's grand durbar hall. 'The pillars,' he observed, 'were

gaudily painted and carved, and the whole look of the thing was like that of a booth for strolling players on a large scale . . . Everywhere I saw that mixture of splendour and shabbiness which characterizes the native courts.'[11]

'His Highness' turned out to be 'a tolerably good-looking man, if he had not a trick which is very common here of always chewing betel nut. He keeps such a quantity of it in his cheek that his face looks quite distorted, and the juice of it makes his mouth a very unpleasing object.' If that were not enough, the hall of private audience in which the Raja received him had a positively nightmarish quality: 'The whole room had the look of a toyshop. Everything was like Tunbridge ware. The roof, the walls, the pillars, the railing, were of wood cut into little knobs, cups and points, coloured and varnished . . . Whatever was not painted and carved wood was pier glass, and the glasses reflected the room backward and forward in such a way as to make it seem a perfect universe of knick-knackeries.'

The Raja then took his guest into his private closet, 'a little room which had more of an English look than any that I had seen in India. It was crowded with English furniture, carpets, sofas, chairs, glasses, tables and a dozen clocks of ivory and gilt metal. It was not much unlike the drawing room of a rich, vulgar, Cockney cheesemonger who has taken a villa at Clapton or Walworth, and has shown his own taste in the furnishing of the apartments.' The Raja's picture gallery consisted of six or seven coloured English prints, 'not much inferior to those which I have seen in the . . . parlour of a country inn'.[12]

Just in case their visitor was still unimpressed, the courtiers then insisted on showing him the Raja's wardrobe, jewels and regalia, and his fine white Arab horse, caparisoned in gold and jewels. Finally, he was introduced to the household gods and had his first encounter with what was for him the bizarre figure of Ganesh, 'a fat man with a paunch like Daniel Lambert's [the fattest man in England], an elephant's head and trunk, a dozen hands, and a serpent's tail.'[13]

Based on encounters such as these, Macaulay formed an enduring if stereotypical image of 'the Hindoo talents, quick observation, tact, dexterity, perseverance, and the Hindoo vices, servility, greediness and treachery'.[14] Having likened the Mysore Raja's crude attempts at Westernization to the tasteless ostentation of a *nouveau riche* Cockney tradesman, Macaulay laid the blame for his poor education squarely at the door of the former Governor-General, Lord Wellesley, who had placed him on his throne after defeating Tipu Sultan.

> If he had been put . . . under good tuition, if he had been made an accomplished English gentleman, what a different aspect his court would have exhibited . . . To give a person immense power, to place him in the midst of the strongest temptations, to neglect his education, and then to degrade him from his high station because he has not been found equal to the duties of it, seems to me to be a most absurd and cruel policy . . . Whatever power I have shall be exerted to prevent the repetition of such fatal errors in future.[15]

~

Macaulay would never for a moment have considered the possibility that decadent Indian princes might be reinvigorated by a revival of their nobler past traditions. In an essay he later wrote on Lord Clive, the founder of British power in the sub-continent, he conceded that the Mughal Empire had been 'one of the most extensive and splendid in the world', with buildings whose 'beauty and magnificence . . . amazed even travellers who had seen St Peter's'.[16] But 'this great empire, powerful and prosperous as it appears on a superficial view, was yet, even in its best days, far worse governed than the worst governed parts of Europe now are. The administration was tainted with all the vices of Oriental despotism, and with all the vices inseparable from the domination of race over race.' As for the later Mughals after Aurangzeb, he wrote, 'a succession of nominal sovereigns, sunk in indolence and debauchery, sauntered away life in secluded palaces, chewing bang, fondling concubines, and listening to buffoons.'

Yet, he was not complacent about the permanence of the British power that had filled India's political vacuum. Within weeks of his arrival, and twenty-three years before the 1857 Mutiny, Macaulay had sized up the weak foundations of the East India Company's rule and predicted how easily it might crumble. 'Every enemy is formidable in India,' he warned. 'We are strangers there. We are as one in two or three thousand to the natives. The higher classes whom we have deprived of their power would do anything to throw off our yoke. A serious check in any part of India would raise half the country against us.'[17]

His reflections on the ephemeral nature of military power on its own were reinforced by a visit to Seringapatam, the ruined stronghold where Tipu Sultan, the most formidable opponent of the British, had made his last stand. It had always been a place of romantic interest to him. His uncle, the General, had been imprisoned there for four years and was later among the British forces that successfully besieged and captured the fortress. 'From a child, I used to hear it talked of every day,' Macaulay recalled, as 'the scene of the greatest events of Indian history' and 'the residence of the greatest of Indian princes'.[18] His childhood imagination had been captured by a painting of the fall of Seringapatam displayed in a Clapham shop-window, which he used to stare at when he passed by.

His visit to the site itself, 'everything silent and desolate', produced mixed emotions. Although the fortress was intact, Tipu's palace was in ruins. 'I am surprised,' Macaulay lamented, 'that more care was not taken by the English to preserve so splendid a memorial of the greatness of him whom they had conquered.' The palace courtyards, which he likened to the quadrangles of Oxford colleges, were completely overrun by weeds and flowers; but the Durbar Hall, 'once considered as the finest in India', still retained faint traces of its old magnificence in the faded gilding of its high wooden pillars, resting on pedestals of black granite.

Macaulay was delighted to find that the nearby mosque and family mausoleum which Tipu had built were being very well maintained at British government expense. A narrow path, bordered by flower-beds and cypress trees, led up from the fort to the front of the mausoleum. Unlike the other, more garish, princely buildings he visited, Macaulay thought it 'very beautiful' with a façade which 'closely resembles the prettiest and most richly carved of our small Gothic chapels'. Inside, he admired the three tombs—of Tipu Sultan, his mother and his father, Hyder Ali—'all covered with magnificent palls embroidered in gold with verses from the Koran'.

Macaulay's admiration for Tipu, who had been demonized in so many British accounts of his wars against them, stands in stark contrast to his indictment of the weak and decadent princely pensioners whom the British had adopted in his place. Apart from Seringapatam, he found little to admire during his journey to Ooty, which took more than a week. He was 'grievously' disappointed by the arid countryside of the plains and amazed that two-thirds of the land appeared to be uncultivated.

Hannah had been left behind in Madras, because the journey was deemed too arduous for her. Since the country roads were not good enough for a carriage, Macaulay travelled mostly by palanquin carried by two alternating teams of six bearers. Unlike England, there were no country inns where they could break journey, so they travelled by day and night.[19] With a train of thirty-eight people, it must have been an impressive convoy, including a second palanquin for Macaulay's new valet, a 'half-caste' whose name—'which I never hear without laughing'—was Peter Prim. There is no record of what became of the servant who had shipped out with him from England, nor for that matter of Hannah's carefully chosen English maid. Prim was a devout Catholic, with a habit of 'crossing himself and turning up the whites of his eyes', and over-fond of giving his master unwanted advice.[20]

The party travelled slowly at a speed of about four miles an hour, changing bearers every fifteen miles. Macaulay was entertained by their rhythmic chanting. He had heard that 'they generally chant extemporaneous eulogies on the person whom they carry, interspersed at intervals with sounds between grunting and howling'. A British official who understood their language had made out the words of one such song, which went: 'There is a fat hog—a great fat hog—how heavy he is—hum—shake him—hum—shake him well—hum—shake the fat hog—hum'. 'Whether they paid a similar compliment to me I cannot say,' Macaulay joked. 'They might have done so, I fear, without any breach of veracity.'[21]

He was less tolerant of the music with which local villagers welcomed his passage, with sounds 'like a cat-call, and a drum which made a noise like a kettle beaten with a poker'. He complained of being woken at night at each village where they changed bearers, to be greeted and garlanded by local dignitaries, accompanied by village musicians 'whose noise was as odious to me as the squeaking of a slate-pencil or the scraping up of ashes under a grate'. While admitting his own lack of a musical ear, he concluded nevertheless that 'the national music of India is most deplorably bad . . . Whether the boatmen or the bearers make the more horrible noise, whether the vocal or instrumental music be the worse, I cannot decide'.

Such diatribes gave way to delight and wonder as they began the climb up the Nilgiris. 'The magnificence of the scenery . . . ,' he enthused, 'is really beyond description. Imagine the vegetation of Windsor Forest or Blenheim spread over the mountains of Cumberland.' His own descriptions relied as ever on homegrown comparisons. The plant life reminded him of 'the fern and heath of England'; the grass, which had been so brown and scarce in the plains below, was now 'as thick and as richly green as in the meadows of Leicestershire in a wet spring'. The greatest surprise was that 'the temperature was that of England, or rather cooler'.[22] Such evocations of 'the green and pleasant land' he had left behind were symptomatic of his homesickness, but also, like so much European travel writing of this period, based on an implicit assumption of cultural superiority.

After reaching a plateau on the summit, they travelled for another eighteen miles through thick forests, until a turn in the road brought them into an amphitheatre of green hills encircling a small lake. Its banks were dotted with neat, pretty cottages, many with thatched roofs, and there was a pretty, neo-Gothic church. They had reached Ooty, soon to become one of the favourite hill-stations of the Raj. The whole small colony had 'very much the look of a rising English watering place'. The largest of the houses, a handsome stone building, was the residence of the Governor-General; and Macaulay was taken straight there as soon as he arrived.

Lord William Bentinck, second son of the Earl of Portland,

had already had an illustrious career as a diplomat and military commander before he took over the stewardship of British India. Influenced by Utilitarian ideals and his friendship with Indian reformers like Raja Ram Mohan Roy, he had already embarked on an ambitious programme of liberal intervention in traditional Indian laws and customs. Macaulay found the great man—'rectitude, openness and good nature personified'— sitting by a fire in his carpeted library. But critical as ever, he judged that Bentinck's abilities were 'not quite on a level with his moral qualities'.[23] As for the Governor-General's entourage, he dismissed them as 'clever people, but not exactly on a par . . . with the society to which I belonged in London'.[24]

~

For the next two months, Macaulay experienced the joys and discomforts of an Indian hill-station. He had been allocated a pretty and very English cottage with a garden to match, full of laburnums and geraniums. But his stay coincided with the monsoon, which brought bad weather beyond any that he had experienced before. It rained for eighteen hours a day, severely restricting his outdoor exercise. 'My beds are heaped with blankets,' he complained soon after his arrival, 'and my black servants are coughing round me in all directions.'[25] He was distressed to see that 'they were exposed to the temperature of an English November in garments no warmer than an English shirt'.[26]

Six weeks later, the servants were looking 'rather less miserable', because he had bought them thick woollen clothes.[27] But poor Peter Prim, his valet, had fallen ill and died of a liver abscess. He had struggled against death for ten days, lying in a room adjoining his master's. Macaulay had done what he could to look after him; and, at the end, he had sent his palanquin to fetch a local Catholic priest to administer the last rites, 'a tall, venerable-looking man with a black beard' who knew neither English nor Latin. When the Indian Catholics of the neighbourhood assembled for Prim's funeral, Macaulay was struck by 'the contrast between their oriental dresses and complexions and the European character of their rites'. They thanked him so profusely for his kindness to Prim, that he thought it 'said little for the general conduct of masters in India', because he had done 'absolutely nothing more than common humanity required'.[28]

In this, his first Indian home, he found himself with a large retinue of servants, including half a dozen bearers, who were always in attendance in case he needed to be carried in his palanquin. His daily routine was simple and very regular. He rose at 6.30, walked for two hours before breakfast (weather permitting), worked on his official duties till 5 in the afternoon, then took another long walk, dressed for dinner at 7.30 (always with the Governor-General) and was in bed by 10. 'Nobody here eats tiffin*,' he wrote with relief, 'and I am glad to find that it is a decaying fashion.'[29] On his walks, he often encountered riding parties which had 'also much the look of flirting parties, consisting of smart English damsels escorted by young officers'. But he complained that his own social life was unbelievably dull and monotonous: 'It is so distant from the civilized world that we think ourselves happy if the post from Calcutta arrives on the sixteenth day.'[30]

Ootacamund had been born little more than a decade ago; and the surrounding forests were still full of wild animals. 'The tigers prefer the situation to the plains below,' Macaulay shrewdly

---

* Anglo-Indian slang for an afternoon meal.

conjectured, 'for the same reason which takes so many Europeans to India. They encounter an uncongenial climate for the sake of what they can get.'[31] He found relief from his boredom by starting work on what was to become one of his best-remembered books, *The Lays of Ancient Rome,* a collection of epic poems which he composed in the heroic style of the Roman poets. He also found solace in the arms of *Clarissa,* the picaresque novel, which, on his recommendation, became Ooty's favourite reading. Macaulay later told the novelist Thackeray that the heroine and her misfortunes put 'the whole station in a passion of excitement': 'The Governor's wife seized the book; the Secretary waited for it; the Chief Justice could not read it for tears.'[32]

Finally, at the end of August, the Governor-General gave his stimulating and entertaining new Councillor leave to depart for Calcutta, where his sister Hannah was already installed in style at Government House as the cosseted guest of Lady Bentinck. At the last minute, his departure was unexpectedly delayed by a domestic drama with echoes of Shakespeare's *Othello.* The cause of it all was Macaulay's new manservant, also a Christian like his deceased predecessor, but in this instance a native Indian convert from the recently established colonial township of Bangalore. His master bluntly described him as 'such a Christian as the missionaries make in this part of the world, . . . that is to say a man who superadds drunkenness to the other vices of the natives'.[33] This unlikely adulterer managed to attract the violent jealousy of one of the Governor-General's cooks, a man with a temper as bad as Othello's and a wife whom Macaulay described as 'an ugly, impudent Pariah girl'. 'The place of the handkerchief,' he wrote in his very colourful account, 'was supplied by a small piece of sugar-candy which Desdemona was detected in the act of sucking, and which had found its way from my canisters to her fingers.'

And so it was that, on the eve of his departure from Ooty, Macaulay found his peaceful cottage besieged by 'a mob of blackguards', accompanied by a native judge 'who spoke tolerable English' and had come to arrest his servant. For the government's new Law Member, it was to be an educative, if ludicrous, lesson in how *not* to administer British justice in a remote Indian village. Macaulay himself was uncertain of his servant's innocence, based on his own 'very poor opinion' of his morals. Perhaps he had in mind the warning he had received from the Indian gentleman in Madras that none of his compatriots could be trusted to tell the truth. But Macaulay also suspected that the servant's accusers were persecuting him for his Christian faith; so he came to his rescue and offered to pay off the jealous husband. But the mob insisted that the offender go to jail and await trial at some distant date.

Macaulay suspected that this was a ruse to ensure that the man lost his job because he would be unable to accompany his master. So he got the British Commandant to order an immediate trial. The Court sat all night 'in violent contention', at the end of which the exhausted Indian judge pronounced a verdict of Not Guilty. Macaulay later declared that, without his knowledge, 'this respectable magistrate' had been paid a bribe of 20 rupees for his cooperation. 'Even if I had known it,' he confessed, 'such is the state of Indian morality that there would have been nothing uncommon or disgraceful in the transaction.'

The matter, however, did not end there. The next morning, as Macaulay prepared to set out on his journey down to the plains, a crowd of angry locals, furious at being thwarted of their prey, mobbed his servant's palanquin as it pulled out from the gate. Hearing the fracas, Macaulay looked out of his window to see that the mob 'had torn off his turban, stripped him almost naked, and were . . . about to pull him to pieces'. In an unusual display of physical courage, he picked up a sword and ran out to defend the man whose innocence he had doubted, even though he feared the mob might turn on him as well. 'Even in their rage,' he later wrote with an air of gloating, 'they retained a great respect for my race and station. I supported the poor wretch in my arms. For, like most of his countrymen, he is a chicken-hearted fellow, and was almost fainting away.'

The crowd surrounded them, shaking their fists and refusing to allow Macaulay to put his servant back in the palanquin. Luckily for them, the sahib's barber, 'a fine fellow' and a retired Company sepoy, ran for help to Lord Bentinck's house next door and returned with a posse of policemen. Led by Macaulay, the whole crowd then made their way to the house of the local British Commandant. 'I was not long detained here,' Macaulay noted with satisfaction. 'Nothing can be . . . more expeditious than the administration of justice in this country, when the judge is a Colonel, and the plaintiff a Councillor. I told my story in three words. In three minutes the rioters were marched off to prison, and my servant, with a sepoy to guard him, was fairly on his road and out of danger.'

It was a dramatic end to his otherwise uneventful and very monotonous holiday in the hills. He would probably have been amused to learn that the incident became part of local folklore, with highly colourful versions being circulated, in which the servant was alleged to have seduced the cook's wife on behalf of his master, who was the real adulterer.[34]

~

Early the next morning after the *Othello*-like tragicomedy, the journey back to Madras got off to a miserably wet start. The rain poured down in torrents, the fog was thick around them, and they had to cross ten or twelve mountain streams which rose above the girdles of the palanquin bearers. Their first night was spent in a miserable barn with a stone floor and bare walls, and the sahib had to sleep with his twenty-four bearers and other servants all crowded in around him 'without any partition'.

The next morning they were rewarded with a 'gloriously beautiful' view of the jungles below the Nilgiris as they descended from the fog and rain into 'a vast ocean of foliage on which the sun was shining gloriously'. 'I am very little given to cant about the beauties of nature,' Macaulay wrote, 'but I was moved almost to tears.' As always, he found a home-grown comparison, likening 'this prodigious jungle, as old as the world and planted by nature' to 'the fine works of the great English landscape gardeners'. Their journey continued past hundreds of gigantic trees, 'the smallest of which would bear a comparison with any of those oaks which are shewn as prodigies in England', and through grasses and wild flowers as high as their heads. An euphoric Macaulay was moved to exclaim that these scenes 'might have been part of the garden of Eden'.[35]

On his way back to Madras, he was impressed by his visit to the new town of Bangalore, which he declared would have been his favourite place of residence in India because of its cool climate all the year round.[36] But he was now eager to reach Calcutta and be reunited with Hannah. He sailed from Madras on the 16th of September, three months after he had arrived there, and was seen off with all due ceremony and the fifteen-gun salute to which he was entitled. He was on a British ship with a fervently Evangelical captain, 'a good sort of person who understands his profession', Macaulay noted, 'but who is not overburdened with brains'.[37] He was so anxious to prevent any flirtation between his male and female passengers that he banned dancing and even psalm-singing on board. Macaulay entertained himself by learning Portuguese, and, a week later, when they landed at Calcutta, was 'almost as well acquainted with it as I care to be'.

As they sailed in to Calcutta, he found the banks of the Hooghly River 'far prettier than I expected . . . of the richest green, well wooded, and sprinkled with pretty villages'. 'They are far superior . . . ,' he conceded, 'to the banks of the Thames or the Humber.' Unlike the arid countryside around Madras, he was surprised to find Bengal 'more verdant than Leicestershire in a moist April', clearly his benchmark of pastoral bliss. At the end of the monsoon, 'the bright, cheerful, silky green of the rice-fields was in all its beauty'.

The coffee-coloured river, boiling with debris, was less picturesque, with several half-burnt, naked corpses from the funeral pyres on its banks sweeping alongside their ship. 'In India death and everything connected with it become familiar subjects of contemplation,' Macaulay noted. 'Six months ago I could not have believed that I should look on with composure while the crows were feasting on a dead man within twenty yards of me.'[38]

He was received at Fort William with the now familiar fifteen-gun salute and escorted to Government House, where he would spend the next six weeks as the honoured guest of Lady Bentinck. 'Calcutta is called, and not without some reason, the city of palaces,' he wrote to his editor at the *Edinburgh Review*.[39] The view from his windows was 'not unlike that from the houses in Park Lane', and the Calcutta Esplanade he thought similar to Hyde Park.[40] Extending for miles behind the Esplanade was the Black Town, 'about three times as large as Liverpool', with a native population of nearly half a million.

He was impressed by the imperial grandeur of the stone-and-plaster neo-Classical villas of the English Quarter: 'The size, the loftiness, the brilliant whiteness . . . of these large mansions, and the immense profusion of columns, though not always happily disposed, give a certain splendour to the general effect.' But he complained that the houses were 'vilely arranged inside'. The rooms had to be very large to cope with the heat and all opened into each other, with the result that 'there is seldom any way to your library but through your dining room or to your dining room but through your drawing room.' Much of the furniture was 'deplorably shabby' with 'chairs and tables of the meanest sort', below the standard of an English servants' hall. He had already noted in Madras the showy exteriors and shabby interiors of most European homes, an indication that their occupants regarded themselves as visitors in India rather than permanent settlers.[41]

After his trials at Ooty, life at the Governor-General's palatial home was a welcome taste of the pomp and circumstance that colonial Calcutta could offer in compensation for its hot and humid climate. Hannah had her own very airy sitting-room, which was twice as large and twice as high as their Bloomsbury drawing-room, with three large French windows. Whenever they drove out with Lady Bentinck, they were attended by two horsemen from the Governor-General's bodyguard 'in blazing uniforms and with drawn swords'. Dinner was always a formal affair, served at eight after an evening gun announced the hour. 'The dining room,' Macaulay enthused, 'is a very splendid hall of marble, opening into a semi-circular portico. It is delightfully cool. The meat and the cookery are much better than in Madras, and might indeed be considered as very good in London.'[42]

Never short of a criticism or two, he complained bitterly about the local fish and fruit. 'There is no fish in India,' he declared in one of his typically sweeping condemnations, 'which can be compared to the fourth-rate or fifth-rate fish of Europe.'

'The tropical fruits are wretched,' he continued in similar vein. 'The best of them is inferior to our apricot or gooseberry. I never touch them.' He had tasted the local palm-wine, but found it to be like insipid ginger-beer, so reverted to French claret. As a child he had envied his father the tropical delicacies he had supposedly enjoyed during his years in West Africa. 'I have now enjoyed them all,' he joked, 'and I have found . . . that all is vanity.'

He also disliked the lack of privacy involved in being constantly surrounded by servants, especially the pankhawalas who pulled the ceiling fans, or pankhas, that kept them cool. 'There is a dislike generally felt here towards native attendants who know our language,' he explained in a letter home. 'And certainly . . . it is pleasant to be able to say what you will at table without fearing the tongues of servants. The servants indeed are so constantly about us here—fanning us—pulling punkahs—and so forth—that, if they understood all that we might say, we should be under constant restraint.'[43] His own knowledge of Hindustani, he confessed, was confined to a few of the commonest phrases like 'coop tunda', by which he meant 'khoob thanda' or 'very cold'.

Since neither Macaulay nor his contemporaries felt any such compunctions about their dinner table conversation being overheard by servants back home in England, their distrust of English-speaking Indians, or babus as they were derisively called, can only be explained by a desire to maintain racial barriers in the colonies. It is ironical that the educational and legal reforms Macaulay himself was about to champion for the next four years were designed to break down precisely such barriers between the rulers and the ruled. As the Charter Act of 1833 (see page 43) had spelled out, his role in the newly created post of Law Member would be to establish the rule of law, and more specifically to protect Indians from predatory European settlers.

For all his past fears about this tropical exile, he was in remarkably good spirits now that he had arrived in Calcutta. He even professed to be enjoying its dreaded climate. While Hannah kept her pankha-pullers at work night and day and threatened to dock their wages unless they pulled harder, Macaulay hardly felt the heat, seldom had his pankha pulled, even during the hottest part of the day and felt generally very pleased with himself for being so healthy after four months in the tropics. 'I never was better in my life,' he assured Margaret. 'I have not swallowed five pills since I reached India. My appetite is good; my sleep is sound; I can do anything here that I could do in England, except taking strong exercise in the heat of the day . . . As yet the climate agrees perfectly with me. I do not think that I ever had better health in England than I have here.'[44] His health may have been perfect, but his emotional equilibrium was about to be shattered by two major blows in rapid succession.

5

Love, Death and Reform

Chowringhee Road was the most desirable address in nineteenth-century Calcutta, and it was here at Number 33 that the Macaulays set up home in a grand Palladian mansion in the Classical style so beloved of its proud, new occupant.* Even before he had moved in to the house, he was describing it as 'the best in Calcutta'.[1] Fully furnished 'very comfortably and handsomely', including even its own china and cutlery, it had dining and drawing rooms which were 'really magnificent' and could accommodate a party of forty 'with not the smallest crowding or inconvenience'. The drawing room was particularly spacious; fifty feet long with large windows at both ends, fine sofas, gilded pankhas and a floor which shone 'like the polished oak floors at the Temple', covered in the winter with a fine Oriental carpet.

The house had a very pretty garden, Macaulay wrote to his sister Margaret, 'not unlike our little grass-plot at Clapham',

---

* The house was taken over by the Bengal Club in 1845, partially demolished in 1908 and sadly replaced by an ugly tower block in 1970.

and since it remained shady till ten in the morning, he intended to walk in it for two hours every day before breakfast. Never one to be wholly satisfied, he complained that the other rooms were badly laid out, because one had to pass through one to get to another. 'I must either sleep in my library . . .,' he grumbled, 'or walk through the drawing room every time that I go from my bedroom to my dressing room.'

The domestic arrangements were completed by the hiring of a coachman 'of very high character', so presumably not given to drunk driving, and, most important of all, 'a cook renowned through all Calcutta for his skill'. The latter arrived with recommendations from 'a long succession of gourmands . . . who pronounced him decidedly the first artist in Bengal'.[2]

Surrounded by these creature comforts and, of course, his library of books, Macaulay soon settled into a daily routine. He rose at six in the morning, was shaved while he had his toast and coffee and then walked for a couple of hours while simultaneously devouring Greek and Latin texts. In one fortnight alone, his pre-breakfast reading had gobbled down three books of Herodotus and four plays by Aeschylus.[3] 'It is a dangerous thing for a man with a very strong memory to read very much,' Macaulay confided to a friend, because it could make him 'a mere pedant'. 'I feel a habit of quotation growing on me,' he confessed, 'but I resist that devil . . . It is all that I can do to keep Greek and Latin out of all my letters. Wise sayings of Euripides are even now at my fingers' ends.'[4]

After his morning reading, he would join his beloved Nancy at 9 o' clock for a large English breakfast, during which they talked, laughed and read the papers. Then he spent the rest of the morning receiving his visitors, often as many as forty a day; and on alternate mornings he went out for two or three hours to return these calls. He would be relieved on these occasions if he found those he visited out visiting others, so that he could just leave a card.

Cynical about organized religion and its practitioners, he made fun of 'the reverend gentlemen' on whom he was obliged to call, 'always within doors in the heat of the day, lying on their backs—regretting breakfast, longing for tiffin, and crying out "Punkah tund" and "Lemonade Serbet".' 'I have not been so lucky,' he joked, 'as to find one of them "not at home".'[5] Unlike these lazy clergymen, he prided himself on never having tiffin, eating nothing between breakfast and dinner and very seldom napping in the middle of the day. His afternoons were generally spent reading and writing till just after 5, when his carriage arrived for their afternoon 'airing'. 'This drive,' he noted, 'is never omitted by anybody at Calcutta who can afford to keep a carriage, except when the rain renders it impossible to stir out.'

He was pleased to find himself immune to the tropical illnesses to which his fellow expatriates were so prone, and he could afford to be amused by their obsession with their health. 'Everybody at Calcutta,' he wrote, 'leads the life of a valetudinarian, eats, drinks and sleeps by the rule, notes all the smallest variations in the state of his body, and would as soon cut his throat as expose himself to the heat of the sun at noon.'[6] 'The climate of Bengal,' he assured a former Whig colleague in London, 'is a far less noxious one than the climate of the House of Commons.'[7] Finding himself in the pink of health, he resented the compulsory health insurance the East India Company imposed on all its servants: they had to pay an annual fee of 1200 rupees (a substantial sum: approximately £120 at the time or £6,000 in today's money) to the physicians retained by the Company regardless of whether their services were required or not.[8]

~

The Calcutta society in which Macaulay found himself offered neither the intellectual stimulus of literary London circles, nor the fashionable glitter and political repartee of evenings at Holland House. But it had its round of official dinners and fancy dress parties and even the occasional English play or Italian opera. Macaulay was scathing about most of these events and grumbled that he kept being placed next to the highest-ranking lady present, 'or in other words next to the oldest, ugliest, proudest and dullest woman in the company'.[9] Not surprisingly, he preferred more intimate and intellectual evenings, with a few friends dining together and debating matters as abstract as Alexander Pope's theory of the ruling passions. Foremost within his small circle of friends was Charles Trevelyan, a young Deputy Secretary in the Calcutta government's Political Department. He was to become Macaulay's closest political ally, but also his rival for the affections of his sister Hannah. What followed was narrated by Macaulay himself in excruciating detail in one of his marathon letters to his other sister Margaret.

Trevelyan came from an old, wealthy and respected county family in Somerset and had been educated at Charterhouse and then Haileybury, the East India Company's training college for its Indian civil servants. His first posting had been under a very powerful and popular but extremely corrupt British Resident, Sir Edward Colebrook, at the Mughal court at Delhi. Though only twenty-one at the time, Trevelyan had had the courage to accuse Colebrook publicly 'of receiving bribes from the natives'.[10] This had caused 'a perfect storm' to be raised against the accuser, who had found himself abused 'and very generally cut' by the rest of the British community at Delhi. But Trevelyan, 'with a firmness and ability scarcely ever seen in any man so young', had stuck to his guns and argued his case with strong supporting evidence during an enquiry which lasted some weeks. In the end, the truth had prevailed and Colebrook was sent back to England in disgrace.

After this, Trevelyan had found his way open to the top jobs in the Company's service. He was a particular favourite of Governor-General Bentinck, who had appointed him to a senior post in Calcutta. Here he had produced a report on internal transit duties in India which Macaulay applauded as 'a perfect masterpiece of its kind'. 'That man is almost always on the right side in every question,' Bentinck declared to Macaulay, 'and it is well that he is so, for he gives a most confounded deal of trouble when he happens to take the wrong one.'

By the time of Macaulay's arrival, Trevelyan was the leading voice among those Company servants who were campaigning to promote Westernization among the native population. Macaulay dubbed him 'a most stirring reformer' and 'found him engaged in a furious contest against half a dozen of the oldest and most powerful men in India on the subject of native education'. He had already published a treatise on how to communicate European learning and civilization to Indians and had proposed applying the Roman alphabet to Oriental languages. 'I thought him a little rash in his expressions,' Macaulay noted, 'but in essentials, quite right. I joined him, threw all my influence into his scale, brought over Lord William, . . . or rather induced Lord William to declare himself.'

The key point at issue was whether the government's annual budget of £20,000 for native education should be transferred from Sanskrit and Arabic to the teaching of English. Bentinck, by all accounts, required little persuasion. His sympathies were unmistakably with the Westernizers against the Orientalists, and this became clear when he appointed Macaulay to the key post of President of the Education Committee (also known as the Committee of Public Instruction). But before their political partnership had matured, the relationship between Macaulay and Trevelyan was put to a severe personal test when Trevelyan fell in love with the pretty and flirtatious Hannah Macaulay.

She had, as we know, accompanied her brother to India with a heavy heart and much trepidation. 'I have taken leave for years of almost anything I care for on Earth and given up all chance of happiness,' she wrote to one of her sisters from *The Asia*, clearly in the depths of depression. '. . . I have sealed my destiny for the next six years and after that what will be left.'[11] But her spirits recovered soon, encouraged by the male attention she attracted as an unattached and very well connected young woman surrounded by lots of unmarried young men.

Soon after her arrival In India, she had received a curious letter from her married sister Margaret impressing on her 'the old-fashioned lesson "beware of men"'. 'You must remember,' Margaret lectured her elder sister, 'that to a man whose prospects are Indian you are as great a catch as you would [be] in England had you been an heiress . . . Above all do not become a flirt. I have no doubt that is your tendency and therefore I honestly warn you against it.'[12] Margaret's words proved prophetic, because, within weeks of her arrival in Calcutta, Hannah, though penniless, found herself being courted assiduously by its most eligible bachelor, the wealthy, daring and dynamic Charles Trevelyan, heir to an English baronetcy.

Macaulay's assessment of this new rival for Hannah's affections was studiously objective and dispassionate. On the debit side, he reported to Margaret that Trevelyan's reading had been 'very confined', that 'his manners are odd, . . . blunt almost to roughness at times, and at other times awkward even to sheepishness', and that he lacked tact and savoir faire. 'But these drawbacks,' he continued, 'were they ten times more serious, would be trifling when compared with the excellencies of his character. He is a man of genius, a man of honour, a man of rigid integrity, and of a very kind heart.' He was practical enough to add that Hannah's suitor had a personal fortune of £5,000 in England plus his annual Indian salary of £2,000 (£250,000 and £100,000 in today's money).

As to physical appearance, he remarked that 'nobody can think him handsome; and Nancy, I suppose in order to anticipate the verdict of others, pronounces him ugly'. As against this, Trevelyan had 'a very good figure', was very athletic, always looked like a gentleman on horseback and was 'renowned as a great master in the most exciting and perilous of field sports, the spearing of wild boars'.

Hannah was initially cool to his advances, probably because, as her brother pointed out, Trevelyan had no small talk and 'his topics, even in courtship are steam navigation, the education of the natives, the equalization of the sugar duties . . .' But faced with the prospect of eternal spinsterhood as her brother's housekeeper, she probably realized that marriage to Trevelyan was her best chance of an honourable escape. Practical as ever, she set herself to smoothening out the rough edges of his voice, gestures and appearance; and her brother acknowledged that 'under Nancy's tuition he is improving fast'.

Macaulay, too, had joined in the task of tutoring Trevelyan and was helping him to brush up his Greek. Watching Hannah falling in love with her rough diamond, Macaulay appears to have accepted the inevitable with as brave a face as possible, at least in public. He did nothing to come between the lovers, although he thought he could easily have ended the courtship with 'a little coldness' or 'the smallest rebuff'. 'Nature made the two sexes for each other,' he philosophized in a letter to Margaret. 'It is the fundamental law on which the whole universe rests that they shall mutually attract each other. The celibacy of women has always been to me an object of more pity than I can express. I never see an amiable girl passing the prime of life unmarried without concern. And as to my dear Nancy, I would as soon have locked her up in a nunnery as have put the smallest obstacle in the way of her having a good husband.'

On the subject of his own celibacy, he admitted candidly to Margaret that his intense attachment to her and Hannah had taken the place of 'any attachment which could possibly end in marriage'. But he had not foreseen 'that others might wish to marry girls whose society was so powerfully attaching as to keep me from marrying', and that there were 'ties between men and women dearer and closer than those of blood'.

Such common sense quickly gave way to a melodramatic torrent of self-pity at his own tragic situation: 'At thirty-four I am alone in the world,' he wrote to Margaret. 'I have lost everything —and I have only myself to blame . . . Since you left me she was everything to me. I loved her—I adored her. For her sake more than my own I valued wealth, station, political and literary fame. For her sake far more than for my own, I became an exile from my own country . . . She was everything to me: and I am henceforth nothing to her—the first place in her affections is gone.'

Emotionally abandoned, as he saw it, by both his beloved sisters, he turned to an old nursery rhyme to sum up his situation:

There were two birds that sat on a stone:
One flew away, and then there was but one.
The other flew away, and then there was none;
And the poor stone was left all alone.[13]

~

With a haste that remains unexplained, Hannah's wedding to Trevelyan took place within weeks of their first meeting, the day before Christmas Eve, 1834. Macaulay did his best to conceal his feelings from the young couple, though confessing to Margaret that 'sometimes within the last few days I have been unable, even at church or in the council-room to command my voice or to restrain my tears'.[14]

The wedding arrangements were taken in hand by the Bentincks themselves, with Lady Bentinck acting like a mother to Hannah, fixing the wedding date and furnishing the bride with a lace veil 'unique in India'.[15] The event took place in great style at the Calcutta Cathedral, with the Governor-General resplendent 'in his uniform and his star'. Hannah, dressed in white, 'looked very pretty and very much frightened', while Trevelyan had a swollen face, possibly due to toothache, which, Macaulay noted with impish glee, 'sufficed to keep him tolerably reasonable'.

As for Macaulay himself, he grandly compared his emotional loss to the grief of St Mark at the Passion of Christ and even hinted at the thought of suicide: 'My soul is exceedingly sorrowful even unto death . . . Everything is dark. The world is a desert before me. I have nothing to love—I have nothing to live for—I do not care how soon I am carried to the cathedral on a very different occasion . . .'[16]

The worst was yet to come. No sooner had the bridal couple left for their honeymoon—at the Governor-General's country lodge in nearby Barrackpore—than news reached Macaulay that Margaret had read none of the long, intimate letters he had been writing to her; she had died of scarlet fever in August 1834, leaving 'the poor stone' more alone than even he could ever have imagined. The Bentincks rushed over to comfort him and, according to Hannah, found him so distraught that they 'wrote to me begging us to return as soon as we could, as they were frightened about him'. 'I am sure his mind was disturbed,' she noted in her intimate memoir of her brother, 'for he wrote me the most fearful letter of misery and reproach, followed the next day by one begging me to forgive it.'[17]

The Trevelyans cut short their honeymoon and returned post haste. It had already been agreed that they would be living with Macaulay in a new ménage a trois, based on both practical and emotional considerations. 'Nothing can be kinder than Nancy's conduct has been,' Macaulay wrote. 'She proposes that we should form one family; and Trevelyan, (though, like most lovers, he would, I imagine, prefer having his goddess to himself), consented with strong expressions of pleasure.' Macaulay himself was less than enthusiastic about the proposed arrangement, fearing that to share Hannah on a daily basis with his emotional rival would be 'a slow torture instead of a quick decisive pang'.[18] 'Every day will remind me how little I am to her who was so much to me,' he complained in the language of a jilted lover.

As always, he found solace in books: 'My intellect remains and is likely . . . to absorb the whole man. I still retain, . . . strengthened by the very events which have deprived me of everything else, my thirst for knowledge, my passion for holding converse with the greatest minds of all ages and nations . . . books are becoming everything to me.'[19] Within days, he had also thrown himself back into the fray on behalf of Western education for Indians, assuring one of his former Whig patrons that 'no laws, however neatly framed . . . , can do much for them unless we can raise the standard of intelligence and morality among them'.[20]

Although Macaulay quickly recovered his external composure, there is no doubt that an important part of him had died during that terrible Christmas in Calcutta, when the news of Margaret's death arrived hours after Hannah's wedding. 'He never while we were in India at all recovered his spirits,' Hannah recorded in her memoir, 'nor do I think his former lighthearted vivacity ever returned, a certain amount of depression remained, and to his last day there are entries in his journals referring to this unhealed wound . . . '[21]

6

A Battle for Minds

The imperial capital, Calcutta, where Macaulay would spend the next four years was the centre of an indigenous cultural and intellectual ferment that finds little mention in his own writings. The Bengali renaissance, which reached its full fruition with Rabindranath Tagore in the late nineteenth century, had already begun in the 1820s with groups like the atheistic Young Bengal and the more spiritualistic Brahmo Samaj, who were trying to reconcile European Enlightenment thought with a return to the spirit of the Upanishads.* Led by pioneers like Raja Ram Mohan Roy and various members of the wealthy and aristocratic Tagore family, movements such as these were questioning Hindu orthodoxy, particularly with regard to the status of women, marriage, the dowry system and caste discrimination.

While the angry, free-thinking radicals of Young Bengal espoused militant rationalism, the more moderate, parallel Brahmo Samaj advocated a new version of Hinduism, purged of

---

* The ancient Hindu scriptures, handed down orally in Sanskrit, which collectively embrace the philosophy of Vedanta, with its emphasis on the illusory nature of material reality, and the doctrines of karma (divine fate) and reincarnation.

practices like sati and polygamy and synthesized with Christian monotheism. In practice, both groups were largely drawn from the same class of upper-caste, educated Hindus, and there was a good deal of crossover between the two. Movements like these were centred mainly on Calcutta's Hindu College, founded as far back as 1817 with the objective of providing tuition to the 'sons of respectable Hindus, in the English and Indian languages and in the literature and science of Europe and Asia'. The college had been expanding rapidly, and demand for its increasingly Western-oriented curriculum was soaring. By the mid-1830s, the moment was ripe for a reform-minded administration like Lord Bentinck's, inspired by British Utilitarianism, to reach out to these potential allies among India's own ruling elites.

Macaulay had begun his job as Law Member of the Governor-General's Council with some ambiguity about the precise limits of this newly created post. In theory, he was part of the Council in its legislative role, but not when it was making executive decisions. The constitutional distinction was a fine one and continued to be argued over at India House in London and even in the House of Commons. In practice, it was up to the Governor-General in Calcutta to decide on the extent of Macaulay's participation in Council business; and Bentinck welcomed him with open arms as his closest lieutenant in all matters—'*un miraculo*', as he described him to his wife.[1]

Macaulay was more measured in his own first appraisal of Bentinck. 'He cannot speak at all, and would make a bad canvasser or party leader in England,' he wrote home to a Whig politician. 'But he is really a personification of justice, wisdom and industry.'[2] He also, we are told, compared Bentinck to his historical hero William of Orange, who had led England's Glorious Revolution of 1689, but lacked personal charm and communication skills.[3] In the years that followed, Macaulay's own polemical talents and persuasive oratory would supply the political edge of what was to be the most radically reforming Governor-Generalship in the history of the British Raj.

Despite his very different background as an aristocrat and military leader, Bentinck shared Macaulay's faith in the enlightened values of the Whig tradition allied with Utilitarian philosophy. Like Macaulay, he had been strongly influenced by Evangelical Christianity, but unlike him Bentinck remained a fervent believer. By the time of Macaulay's arrival in 1834, Bentinck was already well established as an active reformer, with a track record of major interventions in traditional Indian law and customs. As far back as 1807, he had served as Governor of Madras and been recalled because he was blamed for provoking a mutiny among local sepoys by interfering with their dress and hygiene. He had returned in triumph as Governor-General in 1828 with the task of reforming the Company's sagging administration and finances. When Macaulay joined him six years later, Bentinck had already abolished the Hindu practice of sati, set up a new system of district commissioners and opened up judicial posts to Indians. Most important of all, he had encouraged freedom of assembly and of the press among Indians, established close ties with radical Indian reformers like Raja Ram Mohan Roy and launched a lively debate about the future education policies of the Raj.

Bentinck's Evangelical Westernizing approach was miles away from the Orientalism of his adventurous predecessor, the first Governor-General, Warren Hastings, of whom Macaulay later wrote:

> ... his enlarged and accomplished mind sought in Asiatic learning for new forms of intellectual enjoyment, and for new views of government and society. Perhaps, like most

persons who have paid much attention to departments of knowledge which lie out of the common track, he was inclined to overrate the value of his favourite studies. He conceived that the cultivation of Persian literature might with advantage be made a part of the liberal education of an English gentleman . . .[4]

But the intellectual pendulum was now swinging the other way, and Macaulay's arrival coincided with a key turning point in the debate between Westernizers and Orientalists. It was already clear from his own parliamentary speeches a year back that he was firmly and passionately on the side of what we today would call liberal interventionism, convinced that India, like medieval Europe, needed to undergo a cultural renaissance through an infusion of European values, literature, institutions and science.

The case for using the English language as the instrument for such a renaissance dated back half a century, when it was advocated by Evangelicals who saw Western learning as the means to promote Christianity. The cause was later taken up on secular grounds by Utilitarians like James Mill, who had argued that the task of colonial government must be to provide useful knowledge, instead of bolstering native traditions and superstitions.[5] Under pressure from such arguments, a General Committee of Public Instruction had been established in 1823, with the brief of educating those Indian intermediaries who would then go on to instruct others. A decade later, when Macaulay took over as president of this committee, its policy was still an uneasy compromise between promoting English education and subsidising the older Arabic, Persian and Sanskrit colleges.

The Utilitarian case for promoting English had gained

added urgency by the 1830s with the East India Company under pressure to retrench its finances and cut back on its administrative costs. An obvious means of making economies was to send out less British officers and rely on more Indians to fill judicial and administrative posts. But that meant educating more Indians in English to qualify them for those jobs. Cost considerations also meant that it was cheaper to supply English textbooks, rather than translate them on a large scale into Indian vernaculars. Driven by a convergence of economy, utility and ideology, the earlier notion of educating only a small class of Indian intermediaries was expanding into a belief in a far wider dissemination of Western knowledge.

This sense of an imperial mission to educate was converging with a significant popular groundswell in favour of the new learning among the rising, new middle class of Bengal. Based in Calcutta, they were predominantly Hindu, ranging from wealthy merchants and bankers to more lowly clerks and artisans, and they were eager to work for and with their British rulers and to copy their ways. Macaulay himself experienced their anglophile hospitality at first hand; and he was less scathing than he tended to be about his local British hosts when he was invited to the home of Dwarkanath Tagore, one of the leaders of the Bengali renaissance:

> I have been persuaded to go to a party at the villa of a very wealthy native who proposes to entertain us with a show of fire-works. As he is a liberal, intelligent man, a friend to education, and in opinions an Englishman, though in morals, I fear, a Hindoo, I have accepted his invitation. The party cannot possibly be so stupid as one of our great formal dinners, which unite all the stiffness of a levee to all the disorder and discomfort of a two-shilling ordinary.[6]

His reference to morals was to religious affiliation rather than probity of character. It was pro-British Bengali Hindus like Tagore who had clubbed together twenty years ago to establish the Hindu College, which despite its name taught a curriculum based on Western history, literature and science. Led by Raja Ram Mohan Roy, they had strongly protested against the establishment by government of a new Sanskrit College at Calcutta, which they argued vigorously would perpetuate ignorance rather than knowledge.[7]

Bentinck himself, on both Evangelical and Utilitarian grounds, was convinced that India's progress depended on a rapid assimilation of Western ideas and institutions via the English language. Thirty years ago, as Governor of Madras, he had endorsed the establishment there of free English schools; and as Governor-General he had already replaced Persian—the old Mughal court language—with English as the official language of government and the higher courts of justice. He had been egged on in his Anglicist policies by both the home government and the Company's Directors. In 1832, a parliamentary Select Committee, of which Macaulay significantly had been a member, had concluded that not enough was being done to meet native Indian demand for the English language and its literature.[8] Bentinck had responded by appointing more Anglicists to the Committee of Public Instruction, chief among them Macaulay's brother-in-law, Charles Trevelyan.

Trevelyan had already prepared the ground for a radical change in the Committee's general orientation and funding policies. In the months before Macaulay's arrival, he had been campaigning tirelessly, with a barrage of essays, letters and press briefings making the case for a grandiose scheme of comprehensive education, based on an alliance between English and the vernacular languages, which would eventually extend to every village in India and might even become a model for the rest of Asia. He had given his campaign a party political colour, attacking as 'ultra Toryism' the position of Orientalists who saw a continued role for classical Indian languages.[9] He had used the most intemperate language and extreme examples in his assault on Orientalism, accusing its academic defenders of printing erotic Sanskrit dramas encouraging lechery, instead of providing a useful popular education in either English or vernacular languages.[10] Condemning government subsidies to Calcutta's Sanskrit College and its Muslim Madrassa, he asserted that 'the youth of India are bribed, by the offer of excessive emoluments, to imbibe systems of error, which we all know to have been exploded, and their falsehood demonstrated years ago'.[11] Trevelyan used the Calcutta press to publicize his campaign and mobilize support from Bengali radicals; and he helped organize a petition from former students of the Sanskrit College, complaining that the Hindu law they studied there had left them unable to find employment.[12]

As the new President of the now evenly divided Committee of Public Instruction, Macaulay, despite his own clear sympathies with the Anglicists led by his brother-in-law, decided to adopt a neutral position until the matter reached the Supreme Council. But he made no secret of his pro-English views in private arguments and correspondence with the opposing faction. Addressing the Orientalist plea that people learned best in their mother tongue, he demanded of a retired British teacher with Orientalist sympathies: 'Does it matter in what grammar a man talks nonsense? With what purity of diction he tells us that the world is surrounded by a sea of butter? In what neat phrases he maintains that Mount Meru is the centre of the world?'[13]

Lampooning such unscientific Hindu creation myths, he asked whether the Orientalists would be willing to teach their own children astrology and accused them of double-standards. 'The native population if left to itself would prefer our mode of education to yours,' he admonished his opponents, citing the eagerness of Indian students to pay for Western learning at private institutions, while having to be subsidised by government to do Oriental Studies. The Western-oriented Hindu College, after all, had been founded without any government support or subsidy, was funded entirely by donations from wealthy Indians like the Maharaja of Burdwan and housed in privately rented accommodation.

~

In late January 1835, when the matter finally reached the Governor-General's Council, Macaulay unleashed his famous Education Minute, adopting the arguments of the Westernizers and putting them forward with a rhetorical force which even Trevelyan could not match.[14] The Minute was really a retrospective justification of a policy which had already been agreed in practice and successfully imposed by the Westernizers led by Trevelyan. A case in point was the establishment of an English-medium medical college in Calcutta only weeks earlier. But the Minute, nonetheless, deserves its fame because it articulated a cogent, authoritative and highly persuasive ideological basis for what was to become a distinctively British sense of imperial mission. Almost two centuries later, though never acknowledged, its underlying principles remain the Bible of Anglo-American nation-building in the world's trouble-spots.

The Minute began by brushing aside legalistic arguments that a change of policy would require fresh legislation and insisted that the Governor-General was just as free to reallocate educational grants as 'to direct that the reward for killing tigers in Mysore shall be diminished . . .' It then asserted that the Indian vernacular languages or mother tongues were at present demonstrably inadequate to the task of providing a modern higher education; hence the need for a foreign language, and which of these could be more suitable than English, 'pre-eminent even among the languages of the West', with a literature equal to that of classical Greece and offering unparalleled access to every branch of useful knowledge, past and present? If that were not enough, English was already the language of India's 'ruling class', 'spoken by the higher class of natives at the seats of government' and 'likely to become the language of commerce throughout the seas of the East'.

With his characteristic love of sweeping comparisons and rhetorical exaggeration, Macaulay presented a stark contrast between the educational alternatives now on offer. Even among the Orientalists themselves, he remarked in a much-quoted dictum, he had found none 'who could deny that a single shelf of a good European library was worth the whole literature of India and Arabia'.

Admitting his own ignorance of the languages he was dismissing, he maintained that he had read the most celebrated Arabic and Sanskrit works in translation and conversed 'with men distinguished by their proficiency in the Eastern tongues'. He had concluded that 'all the historical information which has been collected from all the books written in the Sanskrit language is less valuable than what may be found in the most paltry abridgements used at preparatory schools in England'; and the position was the same in every other branch of knowledge.

Now in full flow, he demanded 'whether, when we can patronize sound philosophy and true history, we shall countenance, at the public expense, medical doctrines which would disgrace an English farrier . . . astronomy which would move laughter in the girls at an English boarding-school . . . history abounding with kings thirty feet high and reigns thirty thousand years long . . . and geography made up of seas of treacle and seas of butter'.

The historian in Macaulay could not resist citing past precedents for how best to create a true Indian renaissance. The most obvious example, he claimed, was that of the revival of learning in Western Europe through the rediscovery of Greek and Latin literature in the fifteenth and sixteenth centuries. In a curious and logically flawed analogy, he equated the enlightening role of English in India with that of the classics in Europe, while lumping India's own classical heritage with the primitive, ancient dialects of pre-Roman Europe.

'Had our ancestors acted as the Committee of Public Instruction has hitherto acted,' he declared, '. . . would England have been what she is now? What the Greek and Latin were to the contemporaries of More and Ascham, our tongue is to the people of India.' In a display of his wide-ranging, if very selective, historical knowledge, he even cited Russia as a successful example of modernization through the teaching of Western European languages, 'which will do for the Hindoo what they have done for the Tartar'.

Returning to firmer ground, Macaulay invoked the economic laws of supply and demand, arguing that Indians themselves were voting with their feet: '. . . we are forced to pay our Arabic and Sankrit students, while those who learn English are willing to pay us.' 'The state of the market,' he maintained, 'is the decisive test.' Pointing to the recent petition from ex-students of the Sanskrit College, protesting that their Oriental Studies had left them unemployed, he declared: 'They have wasted the best years of life in learning what procures for them neither bread nor respect. Surely we might . . . have saved the cost of making these persons useless and miserable . . .' The Arabic and Sanskrit texts being printed in such large quantities by the Committee were languishing unread, with 23,000 surplus copies lying in 'the lumber-rooms of this body'. English school books, on the other hand, were selling in their thousands and raking in large profits.

While accepting that the British must be respectful of Indian religions, Macaulay maintained that it was not the job of the government to bribe students 'to waste their youth in learning how they are to purify themselves after touching an ass, or what text of the Vedas they are to repeat to expiate the crime of killing a goat'. He dismissed as patronizing Orientalist concerns that English might be too difficult for Indians to grasp in sufficient depth. 'There are in this very town,' he pointed out, 'natives who are quite competent to discuss political or scientific questions with fluency and precision in the English language.' He had himself heard 'native gentlemen' debating this very subject 'with a liberality and an intelligence which would do credit to any member of the Committee of Public Instruction'. Indeed, it would be difficult to find any European foreigner in the highest literary circles who could 'express himself in English with so much facility and correctness as we find in many Hindoos'. English was certainly a lot easier for Indians to learn than Greek for an English schoolboy: 'less than half the time which enables an English youth to read Herodotus and Sophocles ought to enable a Hindoo to read Hume and Milton.'

Looking ahead to what practical shape the new Anglicist policy should take, Macaulay accepted, on grounds of cost and practicality, that the Indian masses could not be taught Hume and Milton in the kind of comprehensive educational system that campaigners like Trevelyan had envisaged. Instead, in its most famous words, the Minute set the objective of creating 'a class who may be interpreters between us and the millions whom we govern; a class of persons, Indian in blood and colour, but English in taste, in opinions, in morals, and in intellect'. This class of enlightened intermediaries would, in turn, revive and modernize vernacular languages like Bengali, Hindi and Urdu 'to render them by degrees fit vehicles for conveying knowledge to the great mass of the population'.

Words such as these were to make Macaulay's Minute the template of liberal imperialism across the world and one of the most important and controversial political documents of the nineteenth century. It outlined an imperial mission more ambitious and global than any since ancient Rome. India was to become the crucible in which the British Empire would create a new, modern, rational and scientific society, Indian in ethnicity but British in education, values, thinking and—most important of all—language.

The Minute was a report to the Governor-General, with whom the final decision rested. Macaulay had concluded his perorations with a largely rhetorical request to retire from the Committee of Public Instruction if its policy remained unchanged. But the Anglicist view already had the full backing of Bentinck, and the new policy was formalized a month later by a Resolution of the Governor-General in Council, closely based on a draft prepared by Macaulay.[15] The resolution declared 'that the great object of the British Government ought to be the promotion of European literature and science among the natives of India; and that all the funds appropriated for the purpose of education would best be employed on English education alone.'[16] In future, no public money was to be spent on printing Oriental works, and the funds thus saved were to be 'henceforth employed in imparting to the native population a knowledge of English literature and science through the medium of the English language'.[17]

In some respects, the resolution was a good deal less radical than the rhetoric with which Macaulay had surrounded it. It stopped short of accepting his original recommendations that both the Calcutta Sanskrit College and Muslim Madrassa be shut down and that all state stipends to students of Oriental Studies be ended. This was largely due to a successful petition campaign in which thousands of Hindus and Muslims joined in protesting against such closures. In response to this public pressure, Bentinck adopted a more gradualist approach of natural wastage towards Oriental Studies. The existing colleges of Oriental learning would be allowed to continue, and all their existing teachers and students would continue to receive their stipends. But no new stipends would be awarded, and Oriental professorships that fell vacant would not be filled.

Despite such concessions to his opponents, Macaulay appears to have been content with the outcome. 'I am not fond of violent changes when it is possible to avoid them,' he wrote to James Mill, who had surprisingly mounted a campaign in London opposing the new policy. 'I like to see abuses die out quietly . . . I like to see good things come in . . . almost imperceptibly. Such revolutions produce no suffering to any human being. They excite no malignant passions: and though slow, they are sure.'[18] That, no doubt, was the Whig way, which Macaulay had celebrated in his speeches on the Great Reform Act. But it was hardly the tone of the violent polemics he had been addressing to his Orientalist opponents. Conveniently for him, two of them now resigned from the Committee of Public Instruction in protest against the new policy, opening the way for Bentinck to appoint five new pro-English members recommended by Macaulay, two of whom were to be Indians nominated by the management of the pro-Western Hindu College, with the door left open to similar Muslim representation in the future. It was a momentous, though much ignored, first step towards allowing Indians representation in the key government institutions that were deciding their future; and the credit for it must go largely to Macaulay himself.

'There are very few things in my life on which I look back with so much satisfaction as the part which I took in deciding this question,' Macaulay told James Mill a few months later. The language war he had waged and won had consumed most of his energies and emotions at a time when he was still reeling from the double blow of Margaret's death and Hannah's marriage. The campaign for English brought him closer to his newly acquired brother-in-law, and living together as they did would no doubt have helped them to coordinate their political struggle.

Macaulay's other great consolation, as always, had been his reading, which had concentrated increasingly on Greek and Latin classics. 'My admiration for the Greeks increases every day,' he enthused to a friend. 'It almost amounts to idolatry.'[19] A year after the emotional loss of his sisters, he confessed to his closest friend, Thomas Ellis: 'Even now I dare not, in the intervals of business, remain alone for a minute without a book in my hand.'[20] On his thirty-fifth birthday, in October 1835, he scribbled into a copy of the Greek tragedies the bleak words of Sophocles: 'The happiest destiny is never to have been born; and the next best, by far, is to return, as swiftly as may be, to the bourn whence we came.'[21] And yet, even as he wrote these words, his spirits were about to be revived by a new arrival to his family circle.

7

Educating India

Writing home to his family in September 1835, Macaulay painted a less than exciting portrait of the imperial capital:

> The monotony of our life is such as you can hardly conceive. One week is the express image of another. Breakfasts, councils, airings, dinners, sleeping, waking, follow each other in a rotation which is only now and then slightly interrupted by a great formal banquet which some great man gives to thirty or forty people. This monotony is not unpleasing to me. And I only wish that it were still more rarely disturbed by ceremonious festivities.[1]

Monotony for him meant the opportunity to retreat into his voluminous library, where he kept a regular 'reading account' of his rapid progress. His precious cargo of books, he informed his friend Ellis, had been unpacked in November 1834, and thirteen months later he had consumed a long list of Greek and Latin classics, including two readings each of the complete works of Aeschylus, Sophocles, Pindar, Plautus, Terence and Lucretius, one reading of the works of Euripides, Herodotus, Thucydides, Xenophon, Plato, Aristotle, Plutarch, Catullus, Caesar and Cicero, and sundry other less familiar authors; and he was now deep in the plays of Aristophanes.[2]

Such public entertainments as Calcutta could offer, Macaulay dismissed as 'vile acting, . . . viler opera-singing . . . and things which they call reunions'.[3] 'Nothing can be duller,' he grumbled about the formal dinners he had to attend. 'Nobody speaks except to the person next to him. The conversation is the most deplorable twaddle that can be conceived . . .' He much preferred small, male gatherings of lawyers and civil servants and would have invited them more often had it not been for some 'most particularly disagreeable wives, who must be asked with them'.

Fortunately, he was rescued from such misogynistic musings by the birth of a daughter to the Trevelyans, named Margaret after the beloved sister he and Hannah had recently lost. Nicknamed 'Baba' in the Macaulay–Trevelyan household, she soon became the centre of attention, and Macaulay became fonder of her 'than a wise man who has seen and suffered so much as I have done would be of anything but himself'.[4] Her arrival almost immediately lifted him out of his depression. 'The weather is delicious,' he wrote home on New Year's Day 1836, 'mornings colder than those of an English October, . . . a noon far hotter than the hottest noon of an English July . . . Our Christmas table is loaded with cauliflowers, green peas, and other vegetables which, at home, are the products of a warm summer.'[5]

A few months later, he was equally cheerful about the onset of another Calcutta summer, with a sun blazing so fiercely that British soldiers cooked their beef-steaks by laying them out on the cannons of Fort William. 'We all thrive and bloom under this raging heat,' he wrote, 'the baby and I in particular.'[6] Although he and his immediate family seemed so happily immune to the climate, he told his friend Thomas Ellis that, 'it destroys all the works of man with scarcely one exception. Steel rusts; . . . pins become quite useless; . . . razors lose their edge; thread decays; . . . clothes fall to pieces; . . . books moulder away and drop out of their bindings; . . . plaister cracks; . . . timber rots; . . . matting is in shreds'.[7] 'The storms of wind, rain and thunder which afford some relief from the intense heat are such as sometimes seem to threaten the dissolution of nature,' he wrote to his father, himself a veteran of tropical Africa. 'I never knew what thunder and lightning were till I came hither.'

One consequence of these harsh conditions was that their house, after only 18 months of occupation, was badly in need of being repaired 'from top to bottom'. The family had to move to temporary accommodation, which Macaulay, with characteristic exaggeration, described as 'a narrow hot dungeon, with no garden, surrounded by native huts, where we were deafened with the clang of native musical instruments and poisoned with the steams of native cookery'. What he would have made of today's British passion for Indian curry-houses is hard to imagine, let alone the arrival of Indian classical music in British concert halls.

Calcutta was still more or less a racially segregated city, although Black Town to the north of the city was rapidly spawning a dazzling array of palatial mansions for the new Bengali elite. A typical example, built in the year of Macaulay's arrival, was the famous Marble Palace of the Mullick Rajas, with its uninhibited Indo-Baroque fusion of the most ornate Eastern and Western styles. Macaulay would doubtless have disapproved of such vulgar ostentation. His own far more modest and restrained, neo-classical mansion, newly painted in elegant white and green, looked 'better than ever', and the 'tatties'* he had had hung up diffused 'a delicious fragrance through the rooms'. Thanks to them, he claimed . . . again no doubt with some exaggeration . . . 'sometimes when the sun is hot enough to melt metal on the outside of the window, we are as cool on the inside as if we were in an ice-house'.[8]

His daily routine was as regular as ever, rising at dawn to be shaved by a barber, followed soon after by a visit from the baby. Then there was his reading till it was time for his bath, 'luxuriating in an enormous tub'; then a hearty breakfast which included 'plenty of eggs, mango fish,** snipe-pies, and frequently a hot beef-steak, in addition to coffee and toast'. His hatred of tropical fruit like mangoes and bananas was unabated, though he could tolerate lychees which, to his rather peculiar palate, tasted 'very much like a grape'. Dinner was usually an eclectic mix of more mango fish, more snipes, a curry and asparagus, after which 'we fall on a very fine Stilton-cheese which my aunt has sent us'.[9]

His days were occupied by various committees. The Governor-General's Council sat twice weekly, as did the newly established Law Commission, of which he was Chairman; and then there was the Committee of Public Instruction, where he also presided, and another commission on prison reform. The Council meetings generally dragged on for six or seven hours, and Macaulay tended to regard them as an opportunity to catch up on his correspondence. 'Sir Charles is alternately yawning and punning,' he wrote to the Chancellor of the Exchequer in faraway Whitehall. 'The Commander-in-Chief has gone into the antechamber to take a cup of coffee. One of my colleagues is writing a note, and

---

* Rush matting designed to be kept damp with water.
** A river fish from the Ganges, so named because it coincided with the summer mango season.

another is drawing a man and horse on his blotting paper . . . I cannot employ the next hour better than in writing to you.'[10]

If his job involved such periods of tedium, he could not complain about its generous emoluments, from which he was saving £600 a month (the large sum of £30,000 today) while living very well. Within two years of his arrival, this had enabled him to invest £7,000 (£350,000 today) in government securities, at a return of 5 per cent, and another £2,000 (now £100,000) in movables, while remitting up to £3,000 (now £150,000) back home for the support of his father and siblings. Trevelyan, too, was prospering and had paid off all his debts, because he was saving £1,800 a year (now £90,000) by living with Macaulay.[11]

~

Within weeks of his historic resolution on the new education policy, Lord William Bentinck ended his term as Governor-General and returned to England in the spring of 1835. Appropriately, it was Macaulay who composed the inscription on the statue erected in his memory by the citizens of Calcutta. It eloquently thanked the departed 'head of a great empire':

> Who infused into Oriental despotism the spirit of
> British freedom;
> Who never forgot that the end of Government is
> The happiness of the Governed:
> Who abolished cruel rites:
> Who effaced humiliating distinctions:
> Who gave liberty to the expression of public opinion.

Although Macaulay had once called Bentinck the greatest man he had ever known,[12] in private his verdict was more critical. 'The art of conciliating was one of the few parts of an excellent ruler which were wanting to my friend Lord William,' he wrote in a letter to the Chancellor of the Exchequer a year after Bentinck's departure. 'Had he possessed that art, he would have been incomparably the best governor that England ever sent to India.'[13] It was a strange criticism from someone who had himself shown little talent for conciliating his opponents.

The Orientalist faction, whom Macaulay had so fiercely attacked and derided, now regrouped around Calcutta's long-established and much respected Royal Asiatic Society, which addressed a memorial to the Directors of the East India Company, appealing to them to override Bentinck's Resolution. The Directors took up cudgels against the new policy, which Bentinck had rushed through without consulting them, and they were egged on by the ideological backing of Macaulay's old opponent James Mill and his son, John Stuart, who had joined his father in the influential post of Assistant Examiner at India House.

As far back as the enquiry by the parliamentary Select Committee of 1832, James Mill, while approving the recruitment of more Indians into the British Indian administration, had been deeply sceptical, on Utilitarian grounds, about a policy of teaching them English, advocating instead a reliance on the vernaculars.[14] Macaulay had tried hard to convert him to the Anglicist policy. 'The stir in the native mind is certainly very great,' he wrote to Mill a few months after the Bentinck Resolution of 1835. 'We have just learned that the resort of pupils to our [English-medium] school at Dacca is such that the masters whom we have sent are not sufficient, and that it has been found necessary to repel many applicants.'[15] He went on to highlight the wastefulness of the previous system, under which the government had printed thousands of volumes of

Oriental literature which no one was willing to buy or read. Twenty-three thousand unsold books, he reiterated, had been lying in store. The government, having spent 60,000 rupees on printing costs in the last three years, had received a derisory sum of 900 rupees in sales. Referring to the stipends which had been offered for Oriental Studies, he stressed 'the absurdity of bribing people to learn Sanskrit and Arabic when they are willing to learn English gratis'.

But James Mill remained unconvinced, and the ideological battle was taken up by his son and successor, John Stuart. The younger Mill, with the full backing of the Company's Directors, now addressed a memorandum to the home government condemning the new policy because it was likely to provoke hostility from Indians who saw the promotion of English as a threat to their religions.[16] Even those Indians who embraced the new learning, he claimed, would acquire only a smattering of English, sufficient to get them government jobs. People learned best in their mother tongues, and the Indian vernaculars needed to expand their vocabulary by drawing on their classical roots in Sanskrit and Arabic. It was therefore the Orientalists, not the Anglicists, who would best diffuse knowledge down to the Indian masses; and public money should not be wasted teaching elementary English to Indians who could pay for it themselves.

The battle of the two manifestos, Macaulay's Minute and Mill's rebuttal of it, generated much heated debate between the Company's Court of Directors, who backed Mill, and the government's pro-English Board of Control, with whom the final decision rested. Thanks largely to Macaulay's old Whig colleague, John Hobhouse, who was President of the Board of Control, the Directors' protests were brushed aside and the new policy allowed to stand. Writing to Bentinck's successor as Governor-General, Lord Auckland, Hobhouse made it clear

111

that, although he had come down on Macaulay's side, he would have preferred him to take a less confrontational approach:

> He may rest assured I shall stand by him on this occasion, but I do wish he had delayed the change or brought it about more gradually. His paper on the subject bears the stamp of his genius, but he must excuse me for saying that it is not a state paper. It is a declamation, eloquent, vehement and argumentative but I repeat, too controversial, too much inviting and defying opposition. Give my kind regards to him . . . , and if he will bear criticism, tell him what I venture to think of this business.[17]

This correspondence confirmed that, although the ideological ground had been well prepared by Anglicists like Trevelyan, it was Macaulay and Bentinck who together forced the home government's hand in endorsing what was undoubtedly the first *imperial* education policy in British India. Macaulay had not been alone in adopting a more aggressive tone than necessary. John Stuart Mill, furious at the rejection of his memorandum, called Macaulay, once his respected mentor, 'a coxcombical dilettante litterateur who never did a thing for a practical object in his life'.[18] And yet, the difference between their two positions was not so wide. Both agreed that government should promote some English teaching; the question was how quickly and extensively. Mill wanted efforts to be concentrated on a small elite of Indians who were already scholars of Oriental Studies and through whom knowledge would trickle down to the vernacular-speaking masses. Macaulay, on the other hand, wanted to use English as the medium for giving as many Indians as possible a Western education, responding to the aspirations of a rapidly

Zachary Macaulay, a severe father and passionate anti-slavery campaigner.

Trinity College, Cambridge. Tom Macaulay lived on the ground floor between the entrance gate and the chapel.

The House of Commons at the time of the reform debates of the 1830s,
with Macaulay among those standing in the foreground.

Holland House, the stately hub of London Whig society, where young Macaulay
dined with the highest in the land.

The road to the Indian hill-station, Ooty, which inspired even Macaulay with its beauty: 'Imagine the vegetation of Windsor Forest or Blenheim spread over the mountains of Cumberland.'

The tomb of Tipu Sultan, whom Macaulay admired as a worthy opponent of the British. He thought the building very similar to 'the prettiest and most richly carved of our small Gothic chapels'.

Macaulay, on the eve of
his departure for India in 1834,
found portraits of himself
too flattering.

Hannah Macaulay, Lady Trevelyan,
the sister who accompanied Tom
to India and remained the greatest
love of his life.

Sir Charles Trevelyan, Macaulay's
brother-in-law and leader of the
westernizing lobby in Calcutta.

Macaulay's grand house in Chowringhee, which he considered 'the best in Calcutta'.

Calcutta view in the 1830s, 'not unlike that from the houses in Park Lane', wrote Macaulay.

Lord William Bentinck, the most reform-minded British Governor-General of India. Macaulay found his abilities 'not quite on a level with his moral qualities'.

Government House, Calcutta, facing the imposing statue of Bentinck, its inscription composed by Macaulay.

The Calcutta Esplanade, which Macaulay likened to London's Hyde Park,
as viewed from his home in Chowringhee.

Macaulay in the 1840s, back in London in the Whig Cabinet.

In his beloved library, where he died slumped over an open book.

Macaulay's funeral in Poets' Corner at Westminster Abbey, January 1859.

expanding middle class and eventually of the entire population. Though not explicitly stated in his Minute, his ultimate goal was of an Indian empire whose citizens, like those of Rome, would become equal partners of their British mentors, with English, like Latin, as their imperial lingua franca. Ironically, Macaulay, rooted in the cautious Whig tradition, had come up with a vision far more egalitarian and inclusive than the linguistic elitism of his radical critic, John Stuart Mill.

~

Macaulay's relations with the new Governor-General, Lord Auckland, were soon 'on a very friendly footing', in his own words, though never as intimate as they had been with Bentinck. 'He is in all essentials eminently fitted for his situation,' Macaulay wrote home to his father, who had himself once served as a colonial governor. He described Auckland as 'liberal yet cautious, industrious, judicious and truly desirous to do what is right', but could not resist adding: 'In the ornamental qualities of a Governor-General he is rather deficient. He is extremely shy, and his shyness sometimes has the air of pride. His utterance is not ready, and his figure is not very dignified.'[19]

Uninhibited by such shyness himself, and secure in the approval of the home government, Macaulay could now press ahead with his education policy. The means at his disposal were slender, without any professional staff, such as Schools Inspectors, or even training colleges for teachers. He had to rely largely on local, voluntary committees; and much of his time was spent mediating in their petty, internal quarrels and personal jealousies.[20] 'We were hardly prepared,' said a former critic, 'for the amount of conciliation which he evinces in dealing with irritable colleagues and subordinates, and for the strong, sterling, practical common sense with which he sweeps away rubbish, or cuts the knots of local and departmental problems.'

The ink was hardly dry on the government's new Education Resolution than five new schools had been opened in the principal towns of Bengal. Macaulay took a close personal interest in the staffing and running of the new schools. 'Our English schools are flourishing wonderfully,' he assured his father, a year and a half after the reforms began. 'We find it difficult, indeed at some places impossible, to provide instruction for all who want it. At the single town of Hoogly fourteen hundred boys are learning English.'

Perhaps because he wanted to flatter Zachary's Evangelical hopes, he told him that most Hindus who learned English quickly renounced their own religion for Christianity, unlike Westernized Muslims who held on to their own faith. The reason, he explained, was that Hinduism was 'so extravagantly absurd' that it was impossible to reconcile with a knowledge of astronomy, geography, or natural history. Islam, on the other hand, belonged to 'a better family', related as it was to Christianity, and even at its most extreme was rational compared with Hinduism. 'It is my firm belief,' he told Zachary, 'that, if our plans of education are followed up, there will not be a single idolater among the respectable classes in Bengal thirty years hence. And this will be effected without any efforts to proselytize, without the smallest interference with religious liberty, merely by the natural operation of knowledge and reflection. I heartily rejoice in this prospect.'[21]

His misplaced optimism about Hinduism being doomed was inspired more by a hatred of superstition and idolatry than by a love of Christianity. He certainly did nothing to encourage Christian proselytizing in the new schools; and his own educational interventions were practical, pragmatic and often humorous.

114

Within weeks of the opening of Hooghly College, he was advising against taking too pedagogic an approach to its curriculum and too much reliance on 'grammars of logic and grammars of rhetoric'. 'Give them Jack the Giant Killer and Tom Thumb,' he urged instead, 'and then let them have Robinson Crusoe and Gulliver.'[22] He had a keen sense of the absurd, especially when it was the result of a slavish imitation of Western practices. Dismissing a proposal to devise a coat of arms for Hooghly College, he wrote:

I do not see why the mummeries of European heraldry should be introduced into any part of our Indian system . . . Nothing can be more absurd and grotesque than armorial bearings, considered in themselves. Certain . . . associations make them interesting in many cases to an Englishman; but in those . . . associations the natives of India do not participate. A lion, rampant, with a folio in his paw, with a man standing on each side of him, with a telescope over his head, and with a Persian motto under his feet, must seem to them either very mysterious, or very absurd.[23]

His many minutes to the Committee of Public Instruction were full of detailed instructions, peppered with his characteristic satirical wit. He was particularly scathing about the prize-giving ceremonies at Calcutta's Hindu College. Not only were too many prizes being given—almost as many as there were students—but the recipients were required to subject the audience to histrionic performances which were excruciatingly painful and embarrassing. 'I can conceive nothing more grotesque,' he complained, 'than the scene from the Merchant of Venice, with Portia represented by a little black boy.'[24] He went on to make fun of other such performances which required Indian schoolboys to hiccup and stagger about in imitation of tipsy English sailors. His verdict was crushing: 'Really, if we can find nothing better worth reciting than this trash, we had better give up English instruction altogether.' As to the prizes themselves, he was firmly on the side of books that would both entertain and enlighten, as he reminded his subordinates:

> There is a marked distinction between a prize book and a school book. A prize book ought to be a book which a boy receives with pleasure, and turns over and over, not as a task, but spontaneously . . . I never was better pleased than when at fourteen I was master of Boswell's *Life of Johnson*, which I had long been wishing to read. If my master had given me, instead of Boswell, a Critical Pronouncing Dictionary, or a Geographical Class book, I should have been much less gratified by my success.[25]

Macaulay's educational minutes made it abundantly clear that he saw the teaching of English, far from replacing the vernaculars, as a channel for the transmission of European knowledge into the vernaculars and through them down to the wide mass of the Indian population. But the vernaculars must grow organically out of the new learning, rather than by government paying a few authors to produce books in those languages. 'Twenty years hence, there will be hundreds, nay thousands, of natives familiar with the best models of composition, and well acquainted with Western science,' he predicted. 'Among them some persons will be found who will have the inclination and the ability to exhibit European knowledge in the vernacular dialects.'[26]

His forecasts were largely justified. By 1838, when Macaulay sailed back to Britain, his Committee had established forty English-medium schools which were open to all regardless of caste, in itself a revolutionary step in a society where the lower castes had so far been strictly forbidden to study.[27] Forty years on, as his biographer nephew recorded, the new policy had produced 'hundreds of thousands of natives who can appreciate European knowledge when laid before them in the English language, and can reproduce it in their own'.[28] Indeed, as his father, Charles Trevelyan, had told a parliamentary Select Committee in 1853, some Indians now spoke purer English 'than we speak ourselves'.[29] The new schools had inevitably led on to the founding of new universities, endowed not merely by government but, as Macaulay had predicted, by the private philanthropy of wealthy Indians themselves.

~

Macaulay's chief diversion from the controversy and tedium of his official duties was the pleasure he now found in his infant niece. 'I am quite as fond of my little niece as her father,' he wrote to Ellis, and he spent at least an hour every day playing with her and teaching her to talk.[30] She alone was allowed to disturb his early morning reading with games such as feeding the crows in the garden with crumbs from his toast. It was 'a ceremony during which he had much ado to protect the child from the advances of a multitude of birds, each almost as big as herself, which hopped and fluttered round her as she stood on the steps of the veranda'.[31]

Baba, as little Margaret was called, was having the multicultural childhood typical of an Anglo-Indian home. 'Her English relations would laugh,' Macaulay wrote home to her grandfather, 'to see her playing with . . . a hideous earthen doll, while four or five Musselmans with long beards and white turbans, and as many Hindus wrapped up in shawls to guard them against the winter cold, are smiling at her and chattering Hindustanee and Bengalee to her.'[32] Her first birthday was to be a grand occasion, ' . . . celebrated with a sort of droll puppet-show, much in fashion among the natives; an exhibition much in the style of Punch in England, but more dramatic and more showy. All the little boys and girls from the houses of our friends are invited, and the party will, I have no doubt, be a great deal more amusing than the stupid dinners . . . with which the grown-up people here kill the time'.[33]

But even Baba's happy childhood was not free from concerns about language and learning. Anxious that she was slow to start speaking, Macaulay complained:

> This country is not favourable to the early development of the power of speech in children. They hear one language spoken half the day and another language during the other half. One person calls sugar *sugar*— another calls it *misri*. One gives them *tea*—another *cha*. One talks of *bread*—another of *roti*. The effect of this is that they cannot learn to talk so fast as children who always hear the same thing called by the same name.[34]

His concern about such linguistic confusion undoubtedly had some basis. But it made him no less dismissive of the Orientalist argument that children and adults learned best in their mother tongue, rather than a foreign language.

8

The Law-giver

Macaulay's view of Indians, or for that matter other subject nations of the British Empire, like the Irish, was unashamedly racist, judged by today's multicultural standards. But it's easy to forget that he belonged to an age when it was the norm for most cultures, including those of the East, to believe in their own innate superiority. What was unusual for this early phase of imperialism was Macaulay's passionate belief in the duty of imperial rulers to govern in the best interests of the ruled. It was a passion he shared with his illustrious predecessor, Edmund Burke, although he had no time for Burke's Romantic Orientalism. Macaulay wrote of early British rule in India:

> The superior intelligence and energy of the dominant class made their power irresistible. A war of Bengalees against Englishmen was like a war of sheep against wolves, of men against demons. The only protection which the conquered could find was in the moderation, the clemency, the enlarged policy of the conquerors.

That protection, at a later period, they found. But at first English power came among them unaccompanied by English morality. There was an interval between the time at which they became our subjects, and the time at which we began to reflect that we were bound to discharge towards them the duties of rulers. During that interval the business of a servant of the Company was simply to wring out of the natives a hundred or two hundred thousand pounds as speedily as possible, that he might return home before his constitution had suffered from the heat, to marry a peer's daughter, to buy rotten boroughs in Cornwall, and to give balls in St James's Square.[1]

The Raj had come a long way in the half century since the buccaneering times of Clive and Warren Hastings, and Macaulay saw it as his mission in India to establish an educated civil society based on the rule of law. Although Indian education took up much of Macaulay's energies, and remains his biggest claim to fame, it was secondary to his main role in the post of Law Member of the Governor-General's Council. The post had originated in Utilitarian concerns, articulated by James Mill, that good government in Britain's infant Indian empire needed a new legislative machinery for the creation of a uniform system of law for all its subjects. Mill had backed Macaulay's appointment to the post; and despite crossing swords over education, the two men seem to have remained friendly till the former's death in June 1836. At the time, Macaulay declared himself 'a sincere mourner' for Mill, with whom he had been 'on the best of terms', from whom he had received 'a most kind letter' only months ago, and whose services at India House were 'never so much needed as at this time'.[2]

The guiding principle of Macaulay's tenure as Law Member

was that, while India was manifestly not ready for 'free government', it could 'have the next best thing—a firm and impartial despotism'.[3] Towards this end, he set himself to a major reform of the entire legal and judicial system of British-ruled India, which comprised at this stage the province of Bengal and the two subordinate presidencies of Bombay and Madras. From the outset, he felt handicapped by what he considered the apathy and lethargy of Indians and 'their own passiveness under wrong'. 'What is the greatest difficulty which meets us whenever we meditate any extensive reform in India?' he asked in one of his minutes to Council. 'It is this: that there is no helping men who will not help themselves.'[4] Coming 'from a land in which the spirit of the meanest rises up against the insolence or injustice of the richest and the most powerful', he was frustrated to find himself 'in a land where the patience of the oppressed invites the oppressor to repeat his injuries'.

Despite lacking the kind of public support he could have mobilized in England, Macaulay used his talents of persuasion and confrontation to push through important legal changes, often in the face of stiff opposition from the far more conservative home authorities in London. His first target was the residual censorship powers of the government in Calcutta, which were hardly ever used in practice. When a group of European and Indian petitioners asked for the repeal of these powers in the interests of full press freedom, Macaulay responded with a Minute strongly endorsing their case. 'The question,' he wrote, 'is not whether the press shall be free, but whether, being free, it shall be called free.' The press-licensing powers, which the petitioners wished to abolish, were 'un-English' in character and virtually unused, and the government had vast emergency powers at its disposal to deal with any genuine crisis. 'It is surely mere madness in a government to make itself unpopular for nothing,' he advised the Council, 'to be indulgent and yet to disguise its indulgence under such outward forms as bring on it the reproach of tyranny.'[5]

Macaulay's persuasive arguments prevailed, and the Governor-General in Council passed a new Press Act removing the licensing controls. The result was an outcry from the Home Government, the Company's Directors in London and even the King, who were all furious about not being consulted and declared that the Act had the potential to undermine British rule in India. The Directors went so far as to demand that the measure be annulled by Parliament; but wiser counsels prevailed, and it was decided to leave the decision to the new Governor-General, Lord Auckland. Macaulay was seen as the main culprit; and his old Whig colleague, John Cam Hobhouse, now President of the Board of Control, wrote to Auckland in an official despatch that 'such wretched unsubstantial pretexts for a great change in a system of government never, I am sure, were before invented by the most inconsiderate reformer'.[6]

In a private letter to Auckland, Hobhouse was even more candid, stressing that it was the Prime Minister Lord Melbourne's desire that the 'inconsiderate reformer' be kept 'a little more quiet' and not allowed to rush the Home Government into reforms without previous consultation. 'Of his vigour and genius, I have no doubt,' Hobhouse wrote, 'though I say to you, confidentially, that I entertain some alarm. However, you are the master, and will repress his ardour.'[7] Macaulay was unrepentant and responded with a letter to Lord Lansdowne ridiculing the 'panic' into which his Press Act had thrown both the Court of Directors and the Board of Control as 'childish to the last degree'. The English language papers were no more or less scurrilous than before, he pointed out, while the handwritten native gazettes, on which there had never been any restrictions, were still 'extravagantly abusive'.[8]

Macaulay's opponents were less sanguine. Based on the anti-British sentiments of many handwritten news-sheets which were circulating underground, they feared that press freedom would open the door for the vernacular press to spread mass sedition and disaffection, raising even the prophetic spectre of a sepoy mutiny. The Act's main opponent in Council had warned: 'When you have a free press on board of a man-of-war, then you may think of giving one to India.'[9] But Auckland agreed with Macaulay that it had all been a storm in a teacup and allowed the new Act to stand unchanged.

~

It was ironic that Macaulay was defending the freedom of the Calcutta press at the very time that its journalists 'could find for him no milder appellations than those of cheat, swindler, and charlatan'.[10] The cause of this press campaign against him, which lasted through most of his stay in India, was the so-called Black Act of March 1836, which had ended the special privilege enjoyed by British settlers of bringing civil appeals to the Supreme Court at Calcutta. As with the Press Act, the battle was one of principle rather than practice, because such appeals were extremely rare; but as in the former case, Macaulay took his stand on what he considered a fundamental human right, that of equality before the law.

Under the existing system, British litigants could bypass the jurisdiction of the East India Company's high court, called the Sadar Dewani Adalat, and take their cases to the Crown-appointed Supreme Court at Calcutta. This right of appeal was not available to Indian litigants, who could thus find themselves dragged into prolonged and ruinously expensive litigation at Calcutta by a British opponent. For Macaulay, such racial discrimination was contrary both to the Utilitarian concept of uniform justice and to the Whig principle of equality before the law. And he believed that the Charter Act of 1833, which had created his post, had expressly charged him with the duty to end such anomalies. The Act, while allowing new British settlement in India, had stipulated that the native population must be protected from 'the wrongs which may be apprehended from such settlers'.[11] Macaulay himself had articulated this concern in his parliamentary speech on the Act, saying: 'God forbid that we should inflict on her [India] the curse of a new caste, that we should send her a new breed of Brahmins, authorized to treat all the native population as Parias!'[12]

In one of several minutes on this subject, Macaulay made it clear that the continuance of a discriminatory legal appeal system would inevitably produce in future a kind of judicial apartheid based on race. The existing distinction, he argued, implied 'that the natives of India may well put up with something less than justice, or that Englishmen in India have a title to something more than justice'.[13] Allowing British settlers access to a higher court was proclaiming to Indians 'that there are two sorts of justice—a coarse one, which we think good enough for them, and another of superior quality, which we keep for ourselves'. Those who wished to retain their existing privilege 'call on us to recognize them as a privileged order of free men in the midst of slaves'.

To the fury of Calcutta's close-knit legal profession, Macaulay was scathing about the Supreme Court and their role in it. As the law stood, he pointed out, 'an Englishman at Agra or Benares who owed a small debt to a native, who had beaten a native, who had come with a body of bludgeon-men and ploughed up a native's land, if sued by the injured party for damages, was able to drag that party before the Supreme Court'.[14] That court, with the exception of the judges themselves, was 'the worst court in India, the most dilatory, and the most ruinously expensive'.

The reputation of the Supreme Court was so dreadful, Macaulay argued, that the mere threat of appealing to it was being used by dishonest British debtors to intimidate Indian claimants. 'I am quite certain,' he maintained, 'from what I have myself seen of the dread with which natives regard the Supreme Court, and from what I myself know of the expenses of that Court, that the threat would in a great proportion of cases be successful.' The terror and 'frightful magnitude' of native apprehensions about the Court had recently led 'hundreds of respectable and wealthy natives' to petition the government 'in language indicating the greatest dismay' about an attempt to extend the Court's jurisdiction to the suburbs of Calcutta.

On the question of equal access to justice, Macaulay pointed out that, even in England, 'people sit down quietly under wrongs and submit to losses rather than go to law' because of the expenses of litigation. But the cost of litigation in the Calcutta Supreme Court, he estimated, was five times that at the King's Bench in Westminster, with the barristers and Court officers 'enabled to accumulate in a few years, out of the substance of ruined suitors, fortunes larger than the oldest and most distinguished servants of the Company can expect to carry home after thirty or forty years'. 'To give to every English defendant in every civil cause a right to bring the native plaintiff before the Supreme Court,' he concluded, 'is to give every dishonest Englishman an immunity against almost all civil prosecution.'

Macaulay's frontal assault on the vested interests who wanted to preserve the status quo produced an equally vociferous response. A large section of the English community in Calcutta used the press, whose freedom he had just enshrined, to orchestrate a noisy and abusive protest campaign against the new measure and its author. At times the press attacks on him were so violent that he resorted to hiding the newspapers from his sister Hannah. 'They have selected me as the object of their invectives,' he wrote to Ellis, 'and I am generally the theme of five or six columns of prose and verse daily.'[15] One rather uninspired example of this sort of verse ran:

> Soon we hope they will recall ye,
> Tom Macaulay, Tom Macaulay.

A speaker at one of the public meetings went further and threatened 'the tyrant' with lynching:

> There yawns the sack, and yonder rolls the sea.[16]

As for the content of the 'Black Act', it was attacked with wild exaggeration as a measure to place British citizens under the jurisdiction of Indian judges. The Sadar Dewani Adalat, whose jurisdiction the Act upheld, was, like the Supreme Court, composed entirely of British judges. But that did not prevent the most obscenely racist caricatures of the prospect of savage and barbaric Indian judges oppressing Europeans. As a British speaker ranted at one of the protest meetings:

> I have seen at a Hindoo festival a naked, dishevelled figure, his face painted with grotesque colours, and his long hair besmeared with dirt and ashes. His tongue was pierced by an iron bar, and his breast was scorched by the fire from the burning altar which rested on his stomach. This revolting figure, covered with ashes, dirt, and bleeding voluntary wounds, may the next moment ascend the Sudder bench, and in a suit between a Hindoo

and an Englishman think it an act of sanctity to decide
against law in favour of the true faith.[17]

Macaulay, predictably, was only strengthened in his resolve
by such rantings and ravings. 'To a person accustomed to the
hurricanes of English faction,' he wrote scornfully to Ellis, 'this
sort of tempest in a horsepond is merely ridiculous . . . The
English settlers are perfectly contented; but the lawyers of the
Supreme Court have set up a yelp which they think terrible, and
which has infinitely diverted me.'[18] These lawyers, he scoffed,
were 'a miserable set of fellows, . . . most of them sots and
debauchees, perpetually engaged in discreditable quarrels, and
hardly ever admitted into good society'.

Macaulay's political response to the campaign against the
Act was to cite the nature of the opposition as the best reason
for having passed it. Replying to petitions against the measure,
he warned his colleagues in the Council not to be taken in by the
libertarian rhetoric of 'a small and noisy section of the society of
Calcutta', 'five hundred persons who have no interest, feeling,
or taste in common with the fifty millions among whom they
live' and who would oppose 'every measure which can prevent
them from acting as they choose towards the fifty millions'.[19]
A few months later, in a Minute to the home authorities, he
described the petitioners as being motivated by a 'spirit of caste'
and 'love of oligarchical domination', based on the claim 'that
the English were the conquerors, the lords of the country, the
dominant race'. According to 'the idle outcry of two or three
hundred people', he said, 'we were enemies of freedom because
we would not suffer a small white aristocracy to domineer over
millions'.[20]

While his opponents even tried to lobby Westminster for a
parliamentary enquiry into the Act, Macaulay could count on the

Home Government's support, led by his old friend, Hobhouse, who had been so critical of the previous Press Act.[21] He was also helped by the fact that English settlers in the mofussil (rural districts) appeared to be on his side, presumably because they had neither the time nor the money for appeals to Calcutta. 'The truth is,' Macaulay assured Lord Lansdowne, 'that the lawyers of the Supreme Court . . . were terrified for their craft.'[22] For his part, he was not afraid to be 'the chief mark of their abuse'. 'Mere child's play,' he wrote, 'to a man who has stood a contested election for a town of 140,000 inhabitants.' And he reiterated that the old right of appeal had been used as a threat by English settlers to intimidate and evade their Indian creditors. 'There is scarcely any native,' he said, 'who would not waive the most righteous claim rather than be forced to engage in a ruinous litigation before the most expensive tribunal in the world.'

As with the Press Act, Macaulay's firmness prevailed, and the so-called Black Act remained on the statute book, underpinning the important principle that European settlers would be subject to the same jurisdiction as Indians in civil cases.* But Lord Auckland, who had loyally supported his Law Member, voiced reservations in private about Macaulay's talent for stirring up more controversy than necessary. In a letter home to John Hobhouse he complained:

> Certainly his conduct has not been prudent. He has weakened his own just influence . . . He was encouraged to act too much alone, by the implicit reliance which my two predecessors placed in him, and he loved always

---

* The Ilbert Act of 1884, which extended the same principle of racial equality to criminal law, would provoke an even more vociferous outcry from the European settler community, but this time it would be matched by equally active lobbying by Indians in support of the change.

rather to provoke than to conciliate the antagonists whom he has found in the Council, and to disregard the opposition which he might otherwise raise . . . His great defect has been, and he does himself great injustice by it, in the exaggeration with which, when provoked to controversy, he states his own views and opinions.[23]

Nevertheless, it was largely thanks to Macaulay's vigorous and even strident campaigning that the British Empire followed the example already set by the French (after their Revolution of 1789) in granting full equality before the law to all colonial subjects. Other European colonial powers, such as the Spanish, Portuguese and Dutch were far slower to follow.

~

A second major provision of the so-called Black Act had confirmed the civil jurisdiction of middle-level and lower-level Company courts, staffed by Indian judges, over Europeans as well as Indians. A year later, another of Macaulay's Acts took this process of equalization further by allowing these lower courts, previously unable to decide disputes of more than 5,000 rupees, to hear suits involving any financial amount.[24] Here again, the opposition was mobilized largely on racial grounds. The exclusively English judges of the Sadar Dewani Adalat or High Court petitioned the government against such a measure because 'the official integrity of the Indian judges was not very high'.[25]

Macaulay responded with his favourite tactic of taking his opponents at their word and then exposing the absurdity of their arguments. Even if the Sadar judges were right about their Indian subordinates, he argued, 'we must work with such machinery as we have'.[26] Everybody knew that a Hindu witness was less trustworthy than an Englishman, but courts still had to rely on the testimony of Hindus even in capital cases. The same pragmatic principle should apply to native judges. 'We may regret that they have not the honourable feelings of English gentlemen,' he admitted. 'But what can we do? We cannot change the heart and mind of a nation in a day.' There was no question of the government being able to financially afford to replace the Indian judiciary with Englishmen.

Macaulay was equally pragmatic about the possibility of Indians in due course rising to the higher ranks of the judiciary. Comparing the respective abilities of English and Indian judges, he considered that the former were superior 'in energy, in powers of general reasoning, in extent of general information, in integrity and humanity'.[27] Indians, on the other hand, were obviously better acquainted with 'the language, the manners, the modes of thinking and feeling' of their countrymen and therefore much more competent to judge the value of evidence and 'all the shifts to which dishonesty generally has recourse in this country'. Since native judges were also much cheaper than Europeans, the judicial system must continue to rely on them, though 'under European superintendence'.

As for the monetary ceiling on lower courts' jurisdiction, Macaulay ridiculed the idea that it was reducing corruption: 'The argument of the Sadar court . . . is this: The native judges are bad and corrupt. Therefore leave to them more than nine hundred and ninety-nine cases in a thousand. Leave to them all the cases of the poor and almost all the cases in which the middle classes are concerned.' The result of such a course would be to perpetuate a two-tier system and reserve true justice for a tiny fragment of the population, whose cases differed from the rest only in their monetary value. If the lower courts were corrupt, far better that the rich rather than the poor should suffer from it, because only then would strong enough voices of protest be raised to expose judicial abuses or corruption and reform the system. Macaulay concluded:

> The petitioners would have us send the zemindar [landlord], the banker, the indigo planter, in all cases of importance, before a judge of undisputed integrity, while we send the ryot [peasant farmer] or the small shopkeeper in a case where his all may be at stake before a judge known to be undeserving of confidence. I regret that there should be abuses in our courts of justice. But, while such abuses exist, I think it desirable that all classes should suffer from them alike. Then they will be exposed, and I trust speedily reformed.

Macaulay's thinking was remarkably free of the kind of condescending paternalism which led so many of his contemporaries and successors to treat the Indian masses like backward children who must be protected from their own folly. Dismissing the idea that ryots should, in their own interests, be barred from making contracts for terms longer than one year, he declared: 'Grown-up men, not idiots or insane, should be suffered to make such contracts as are not injurious to others and as appear to them to be beneficial to themselves. To say that the ryots of this country are mere children and ought to be specially protected is, I conceive, quite incorrect.'

Government, Macaulay maintained, was 'almost certain to be wrong if, abandoning its legitimate function, it tells private individuals that it knows their business better than they know it themselves'.[28] In a warning that later colonial and post-Independence governments of India would have done well to heed, he urged that all legislation be based on the principle that 'freedom is the rule and restraint the exception; that the burden of proof lies on him who proposes to prohibit anything'.[29]

~

If, as Macaulay so forcefully argued, it was essential for rich and poor, White and Indian, to have access to the same courts and to be treated equally by them, it was clearly necessary to have a uniform code of law which could be applied across British India. The existing situation was confusing, to say the least, with British law supplying the latest layer of legal complexity to a sub-continent full of rival religious, caste and ethnic jurisdictions. Despite his belief in the innate superiority of British common law as it had evolved through the centuries, Macaulay had no illusions about the folly of trying to apply it unmodified to a subcontinent as alien as India. He later wrote after his return home:

> English law, transplanted to that country [India], has all the vices from which we suffer here; it has them all in a far higher degree; and it has other vices, compared with which the worst vices from which we suffer are trifles. Dilatory here, it is far more dilatory in a land where the help of an interpreter is needed by every judge and by every advocate. Costly here, it is far more costly in a land into which the legal practitioners must be imported from an immense distance . . . No English barrister will work, fifteen thousand miles from all his friends, with the thermometer at ninety-six in the shade, for the emoluments which will content him in chambers that overlook the Thames. Accordingly, the fees at Calcutta

are about three times as great as the fees of Westminster Hall; and this, though the people of India are, beyond all comparison, poorer than the people of England.

Yet delay and expense, Macaulay observed, were as nothing compared with the offence that English legal practices such as arrest on charging, the taking of oaths and the invasion of zenanas could cause to very different Indian sensibilities.[30] In one of his historical essays about the early years of British rule, he was scathing about a 'reign of terror' that the Calcutta Supreme Court had attempted to impose on the native population way back in the 1780s:[31]

No man knew what was next to be expected from this strange tribunal. It came from beyond the black water, as the people of India, with mysterious horror, call the sea. It consisted of judges not one of whom was familiar with the usages of the millions over whom they claimed boundless authority. Its records were kept in unknown characters; its sentences were pronounced in unknown sounds. It had already collected round itself an army of the worst part the native population, informers, and false witnesses . . . Many natives, highly considered among their countrymen, were seized, hurried up to Calcutta, flung into the common gaol, not for any crime even imputed, not for any debt that had been proved, but merely as a precaution till their cause should come to trial . . . The harems of noble Mahommedans, sanctuaries respected in the East by governments which respected nothing else, were burst open by gangs of bailiffs . . . No Mahratta invasion had ever spread through the province such dismay as this inroad of English lawyers. All the injustice of former oppressors, Asiatic and European, appeared as a blessing when compared with the justice of the Supreme Court.

Mercifully, this period of British judicial terrorism had been firmly ended by the home authorities, and Macaulay's 'Black Act' had completed the process of restricting the Supreme Court's jurisdiction. The Charter Act of 1833, which had given British India its own legislature, the Governor-General-in-Council, had also provided for a new Law Commission in Calcutta to advise on reforming and codifying Indian law. The guiding principle, as articulated in Macaulay's own famous parliamentary speech was: 'Uniformity where you can have it; diversity where you must have it; but in all cases certainty.'[32] Macaulay, 'at his own instigation',[33] was appointed President of that Commission, which soon set itself the Herculean task of framing a comprehensive Criminal Code for the whole of British India. Its work, he proposed, would be based 'on two great principles—the principle of suppressing crime with the smallest possible amount of suffering, and the principle of ascertaining truth at the smallest possible cost of time and money'.

A compelling reason for adopting such a code as soon as possible was the concern expressed in the recent Charter Act for bringing European settlers under the effective criminal jurisdiction of the Indian courts, so as to protect the natives from oppression. But that could not be done while the East India Company's courts applied a somewhat bastardised system of Islamic penal law inherited from the previous Mughal administration, while Europeans were judged separately in the Crown courts using English criminal law.[34] As Macaulay pointed out, there were many variations in the law applied in different provinces and lots of amusing anomalies. In Bombay, for instance, the death penalty applied across a range of offences from murder and arson to something as trivial as breaking a china cup in someone else's home.[35] Nor did the law make any distinction between intentional and unintended actions.

Macaulay insisted that only a comprehensive new code, rather than piecemeal reform, could create order out of this legal chaos; but the resources at his disposal were very limited. Of the five other commissioners appointed to assist him, there was scarcely one on whom he could count for both time and support.[36] Foremost among them was Sir John Macleod, a veteran civil servant 'with a mind fertile in objections'. 'One such member of a Commission is enough,' Macaulay wryly observed, 'but there ought to be one such.' Despite or because of this argumentative nature, he thought Macleod 'the cleverest man that I have found in India by many degrees'.[37] Unfortunately, Macleod's health proved so poor during the following year that 'the smallest effort seriously disordered him',[38] and he spent an average of two days a week in bed.[39] Another commissioner, Sir George Anderson, whom Macaulay thought 'utterly incompetent',[40] was the only one who was always present. 'Between ourselves,' Macaulay confided to his friend Ellis, 'if he would keep his bed all the week round, it would be the greatest service which he could render to the Commission.'[41]

He also faced opposition from the legal establishment in Calcutta, who were up in arms against his Black Act. Although the Chief Justice of the Supreme Court unexpectedly offered his support, Macaulay expected the British lawyers of the Court to 'give us all the trouble that they can'.[42] He was also anxious about the hostility of another Supreme Court judge, Sir John Grant, who 'is still, I am sorry to say, a wild elephant; and, in spite of all the exertions of his tame brethren, will not long keep his trunk and his tusks from us'.[43]

Two years into its monumental task, the Law Commission

found itself under fire in the Calcutta press for not having produced any concrete results; and the Directors in London were also complaining. Macaulay was contemptuous about the bad press he was getting. Dismissing 'the scurrility' and 'the clamorous abuse of the scribblers', he thought that the Calcutta press had 'fallen into the hands of the lower legal practitioners, who detest all Law-reform'.[44] Replying to an official inquiry from the Governor-General, Lord Auckland, Macaulay pleaded the ill health and other commitments of his colleagues as the reason for slow progress. He declared that a Code of this nature could not be 'written like an article in a magazine' and that he would not be hurried 'to gratify the childish impatience of the ignorant'.[45] Reminding his critics that the work in progress would decide 'the welfare of millions', he declared defiantly that, if anything, 'we have been guilty rather of precipitation than of delay'.

Writing to friends back home, Macaulay complained that 'all the Law Commissioners have been so ill that none of them but myself has done a stroke of work for months . . . '; he expected to have to write the entire Code single-handed.[46] To his father, he was more optimistic, promising that the Code would get rid of the death penalty, except for 'aggravated treason and wilful murder'. Also, in a measure dear to Zachary's heart, it would 'get rid indirectly of everything that can properly be called slavery'. Existing Indian conditions, it was felt, made outright abolition of slavery impractical; instead, it would be superseded by the law of civil contracts. 'No person will be entitled,' Macaulay explained to his father, 'on the plea of being the master of another, to do anything to that other which it would be an offence to do to a freeman.'[47]

A draft of the Penal Code was finally ready to submit to the Governor-General by the summer of 1837, and a final, printed version was published in October. No more than 200 pages long, it was a remarkable document—simple, elegant and succinct, with the laws it outlined illustrated by practical examples drawn from history, literature and everyday life, in order to make their meaning and intention clear to the judges who applied them. For instance, the crime of fabricating evidence was illustrated by a case clearly recognizable as that of Lady Macbeth, while theft and trespass were demonstrated, appropriately for Macaulay the bibliophile, by the rights of book-owners as against those who stole, borrowed or defaced books.[48] Although in theory the Code was the work of the whole Commission, it was generally regarded as being predominantly Macaulay's. None other than the contrary John Macleod testified to this when he declared that 'Mr Macaulay is justly entitled to be called the author of the Indian Penal Code'.[49]

His authorship was amply demonstrated by the clear, lucid and elegant prose of what might otherwise have been a dry and technical work. Unlike his Education Minute, the Penal Code was warmly welcomed by John Stuart Mill, who praised 'the accomplished President of the Commission', whom he had so recently abused, for 'making the body of the laws a popular book, at once intelligible and interesting to the general reader'.[50] Macaulay's humanitarian thinking made the Code the most liberal and humane of its time, in some respects more so than English criminal law. Apart from restricting the death penalty and indirectly outlawing slavery, it dispensed with punishments like flogging and resisted demands by some Indians to make adultery by women a capital offence. Well in advance of Britain, the Code recognized women's rights to own property and to legal redress for rape and other acts of violence. No doubt with Indian dynastic sentiment in mind, it refused to exempt highly placed families from the law, on the grounds 'that it is an evil that any man should be above the law; that it is a still greater evil that the public should be taught to regard as a high and enviable distinction the privilege of being above the law . . . '[51]

But at the same time, Macaulay was pragmatic about respecting certain Indian customs which were regarded as fundamental. Commenting on the intensity of caste sentiment among Indians, he noted: 'We are legislating for them, and though we may wish that their opinions and feelings may undergo a considerable change, it is our duty, while their opinions and feelings remain unchanged, to pay as much respect to those opinions and feelings as if we partook of them.'[52]

In keeping with this sentiment, the Code included an imprisonable offence of directly or indirectly causing a person to lose caste. To the anger of Christian missionaries, it included penalties for insulting Indian religious sensibilities or interfering with local religious practices, however offensive they might be to Europeans. But it also showed sensitivity to European anxieties in proposing banishment rather than imprisonment for Europeans convicted of serious offences. To subject Englishmen to native prison conditions, it declared, would be 'cruel and impolitic' and would lower native estimation of 'our national character'.[53] Local conditions were also reflected in the decision to reserve punishment for bribery to the recipient rather than the donor, since there was a much more widespread assumption in India than in England that no one could expect to get justice without paying a bribe.[54]

When he embarked on the Code, Macaulay had seen it, alongside his education policy, as the second major pillar of the new imperial citizenship he aimed to build. It would bring the highest standards of Utilitarian philosophy to bear, not just on the laws of India but on those of the imperial power itself.

Writing to James Mill, he had promised: 'When once the English people see the whole criminal law of a vast empire ... contained in a volume smaller than one of the hundred volumes of statutes and reports which a Templar must turn over to know whether a particular act be larceny or forgery, they will, I think, turn their minds to the subject of law-reform with a full determination to be at least as well off as their Hindoo vassals.'[55]

His comments on the completion of the task two years later were less grandiloquent. The Code, he confessed to his friend Ellis, 'is full of defects which I see, and has no doubt many which I do not see'.[56] Future generations would be more generous. Commenting three decades later, Macaulay's historian nephew, George Trevelyan, declared that the final verdict on his uncle's magnum opus was the gratitude of Indian civil servants, 'the younger of whom carry it about in their saddle-bags, and the older in their heads'.[57] But it was not until 1860, twenty-two years after it was written, that the Code was actually enacted into law.

According to one of Macaulay's successors as Law Member, the draft Code which he had submitted in 1838 was 'far too daring and original to be accepted at once'.[58] Its fate was closely interwoven with the wider political fortunes of the British Raj. Macaulay's immediate successor as Law Member opposed its enactment on the grounds of the fierce opposition it had aroused among the missionaries and their sympathizers in the judiciary. It was then circulated to judges and other law experts for their reactions and comments, a consultation which went on for more than a decade and produced various learned reports with opposing views. In the meanwhile, those judges who liked its provisions—and there were many—used their own discretion to start applying them in their own courts.

Although the overwhelming legal consensus was that the Code should be adopted with only minor revisions, this was delayed for another decade by a series of British wars against the Afghans and the Sikhs, which distracted the Calcutta government from domestic concerns about law reform. Eventually, it was the Great Mutiny of 1857 that concentrated the minds of imperial policy-makers on the urgent need for a new criminal Code to which both Indians and Europeans would be subject. Macaulay's Code, with minor revisions, was at last formally adopted in 1860 and came into operation two years later. It is a testament to its overwhelmingly rational, humane, egalitarian and modern guiding philosophy that it remains the basis of Indian criminal law to this day, long after the radical transformation of an enlightened, paternal despotism into a democratic, multicultural federation.

'It is the genius of this man,' one of independent India's most eminent historians wrote of Macaulay, 'narrow in his Europeanism, self-satisfied in his sense of English greatness, that gives life to modern India as we know it. He was India's new Manu, the spirit of modern law incarnate.'[59] During recent celebrations of the Indian Penal Code's 150th anniversary, senior Indian judges and lawyers paid tribute to the flexibility and pragmatism of Macaulay's vision, which have enabled the Code to survive and adapt to radically changing circumstances. The secret of his success, jurists have concluded, is that his Code does no more or less than necessary, which is quite simply—in the immortal words of Gilbert and Sullivan's *Mikado*—'to make the punishment fit the crime'.

Macaulay did not live to see his Code enacted, let alone hear these accolades; but with his characteristic self-confidence—some would say arrogance—he never doubted that his wisdom would prevail. In 1854, when a parliamentary commission decided that his draft Code was better than any of the alternatives, he wrote to his beloved sister Hannah:

> I cannot but be pleased to find that, at last, the Code on which I bestowed the labour of two of the best years of my life has had justice done to it. Had this justice been done sixteen years ago, I should probably have given much more attention to legislation, and much less to literature than I have done. I do not know that I should have been either happier or more useful than I have been.[60]

9

Return of the Native

'I have no words to tell you how I pine for England, or how intensely bitter exile has been to me,' Macaulay wrote home from India, comparing his feelings to those of Ulysses who 'was willing to forego everything else to see once more the smoke going up from the cottages of his dear island'.[1] 'A complete revolution in all the habits of life,' was how he summed up his years in India, 'an estrangement from almost every old friend and acquaintance; fifteen thousand miles of ocean between the exile and everything that he cares for . . .'[2]

With his usual talent for exaggeration, he did not mention the consolations of having managed to keep his beloved Hannah and her growing family by his side. Baba had been joined by a new arrival, of whom Macaulay was soon 'almost as fond as I am of her sister'.[3] But the new baby had died only three months later, a reminder that life could be harsh in the tropics. Macaulay was by now on friendly and relaxed, if not overly affectionate, terms with Hannah's very accommodating husband, Charles Trevelyan, whom he grudgingly described as 'not a bad brother-in-law for a man to pick up in 22 degrees of North latitude and 100 degrees of East longitude'.[4] Despite a somewhat rudimentary education, Trevelyan had 'an insatiable thirst for knowledge of every sort' and soon came to regard Macaulay, his intellectual mentor, 'as little less than an oracle of wisdom'.

Macaulay and Trevelyan joined in making fun of the latter's younger brother when he came to visit. A captain in the Madras Army, he bored everyone, most of all his own brother. 'Hannah and Trevelyan accordingly took to match-making,' Tom mischievously reported, 'and got rid of the captain by marrying him to a bouncing Scotch girl at the next house . . . Since that time the bridegroom has been boring his wife's relations instead of his own.'[5]

After three years in Calcutta, Macaulay was far less cheerful about the climate than he had been at the outset. 'We are annually baked four months,' he complained, 'boiled four more, allowed for the remaining four to become cool if we can . . . Insects and undertakers are the only living creatures which seem to enjoy the climate.'[6] His last summer in India was marked by a particularly fierce heat wave, 'far beyond anything . . . in the recollection of the oldest English inhabitants of Calcutta'. 'The tanks are dry,' Macaulay wrote home, 'the earth is baked as if it had been in a furnace; the peasantry have begun to quit their villages and to assemble in crowds on the banks of the river.'[7] Many died of heat stroke; others of a cholera epidemic that was raging. 'Black fellow die much, master,' Macaulay's barber told him. Even the master, despite his previous nonchalance about the heat, was forced to take refuge in his library, with all the windows and blinds 'most carefully closed; for if the smallest cranny were left open, a blast like that from the mouth of hell rushed in'. There he would lie from nine in the morning till six in the evening, on a sofa under his pankha, reading Voltaire and Plutarch for comfort.

When the heat finally broke and gave way to the monsoon,

Macaulay went down with his first and last of Indian maladies, 'a smart touch of fever' which lasted only an hour or two and against which he 'took such vigorous measures that it never came again'.[8] The climate and its hazards, however, were the least of his complaints about life in India. His views on Indian music and Hindu sculpture, or the little of it he bothered to see, were at best dismissive, at worst derisive. And the same applied to Indians themselves, especially the Bengali gentry and middle classes whom he encountered in Calcutta.

'The Castilians have a proverb,' Macaulay wrote with brutal irony, 'that in Valencia the earth is water and the men women; and the description is at least equally applicable to the vast plain of the Lower Ganges . . . There never, perhaps, existed a people so thoroughly fitted by nature and by habit for a foreign yoke.'[9] In an article he wrote about Warren Hastings, Macaulay listed in vitriolic detail the faults of this cowardly race:

> The physical organization of the Bengalee is feeble even to effeminacy. He lives in a constant vapour bath. His pursuits are sedentary, his limbs delicate, his movements languid . . . Courage, independence, veracity, are qualities to which his constitution and his situation are equally unfavourable. His mind bears a singular analogy to his body. It is weak even to helplessness for purposes of manly resistance, but its suppleness and its tact move the children of sterner climates to admiration not unmingled with contempt . . . What the horns are to the buffalo, what the paw is to the tiger, what the sting is to the bee, what beauty . . . is to woman, deceit is to the Bengalee. Large promises, smooth excuses, elaborate tissues of circumstantial falsehood, chicanery, perjury, forgery, are the weapons, offensive and defensive, of the people of the Lower Ganges.[10]

This rhetorically splendid diatribe is notable not so much for its unashamed, ethnic stereotyping, which was commonplace for its time, but for the unmistakable personal hostility towards the Bengali population among whom he had spent four years. While acknowledging their superior talents 'as usurers, as money-changers, as sharp legal practitioners', Macaulay was scornful of their lack of military prowess, evidenced by the fact that 'all those millions do not furnish one sepoy to the armies of the Company'. By contrast, he was full of praise for 'that noble Afghan race' who had settled in the adjacent region of Rohilkhand: '. . . the best of all sepoys at the cold steel' and 'the only natives of India to whom the word "gentleman" can with perfect propriety be applied'.[11] What he would have made of the twenty-first-century Afghan propensity for jihadism is hard to imagine.

~

Macaulay acknowledged that most of his colleagues in the Company's administration shared neither his alienation from nor his contempt for Indian ways:

> It is natural that they should not have it, for they are sent out while still schoolboys, and when they know little of the world. The moment of emigration is to them also the moment of emancipation; and the pleasures of liberty and affluence to a great degree compensate them for the loss of their home. In a few years they become Orientalized, and, by the time that they are my age, they would generally prefer India, as a residence, to England . . . A lad who six months before . . . could indulge in few pleasures for want of money . . . finds himself able to feast on snipes and drink as much champagne as he likes, to

entertain guests, to buy horses, to keep a mistress or two, to maintain fifteen or twenty servants who bow to the ground every time they meet him, and suffer him to kick and abuse them to his heart's content.[12]

It was a very different matter, he pointed out, to be transplanted as he had been at the ripe age of thirty-three; and he prided himself on not succumbing to a life of colonial luxury. 'I never suffer anybody to assist me in dressing,' he boasted, 'or in any of the thousand little offices which every man ought to be in the habit of performing for himself.'[13] He had little sympathy for the typical Anglo-Indian nabob who had 'a certain peculiar narrowness and Orientalism' about him and eventually returned to England a stranger to his own family, 'an old, yellow-faced bore, fit for nothing but to drink Cheltenham water . . .'

Macaulay's own colonial venture had been strictly pecuniary in motivation, and his objective of securing his own and his family's financial future had been achieved after only two years in Calcutta. As his draft of the new Indian Penal Code neared completion, he let it be known that he considered his work in India nearly done. As early as January 1837, rumours circulated that he would soon be resigning and provoked an outcry in the local press. The hostile Anglo-Indians who had only recently been clamouring for his removal now accused him of deserting his post, instead of staying to see through the implementation of his legal reforms.[14]

Macaulay had no compunctions about an early return home, especially as it would coincide with the Trevelyans taking the long furlough break in England to which Charles was now entitled. On May 1, 1837, the day before he submitted the draft of his Penal Code to the Governor-General, Lord Auckland, Macaulay wrote him a formal Minute announcing his intention to return home during the next cold season.[15] A few months later, the entire

Macaulay–Trevelyan extended family had booked their passage back to London on the *Lord Hungerford*, 'a huge floating hotel', whose luxuries included 'filtering-machines in all the cabins' and even shower-baths in the best cabins like Macaulay's.[16] 'She is more renowned for the comfort and luxury of her internal arrangements than for her speed,' he warned his friend Ellis, so the journey home was likely to take almost six months.[17]

In preparation for his return to Europe and its intellectual delights, Macaulay had resolved to use this long voyage to improve his German, one of the few Western European languages he had not yet mastered. Despite hearing it was a hard language, he declared with his usual self-confidence: 'I cannot believe that there is a language which I cannot master in four months with working ten hours a day.'[18] He had already made an impressive beginning by reading half of Luther's New Testament and much of Schiller's *History of the Thirty Years' War*.

Finally, there was the business of transferring back to London the thriving financial investments he had been accumulating in Calcutta with the large savings from his salary. He converted his holdings into government bills of exchange to carry with him on the journey home, grumbled about the loss of some £3,000 (about £133,000 in today's money) due to an unfavourable exchange rate and took the precaution of sending duplicates to England by land, just in case he and the originals should be lost at sea.[19]

∿

In an essay on Macaulay, the constitutional historian, Walter Bagehot, later remarked on his 'inexperiencing nature', pointing out that his several years in India did nothing to change his views on the empire one iota from what they had been before he went, as expressed most notably in his famous parliamentary speech on the Charter Act of 1833. 'You could never tell from any difference in his style,' said Bagehot, 'what he had seen, or what he had not seen.'[20] He was right, but only partially, because Macaulay's Indian years did much to strengthen and define his faith in Britain and all things British as the acme of global perfection. In one of his most lyrical eulogies, he hailed the British race for having 'become the greatest and most highly civilized people that ever the world saw', with dominions in every quarter of the globe, a maritime super-power 'which would annihilate in a quarter of an hour' the navies of all its predecessors, with a literature not inferior to the noblest classics of ancient Greece, and leading the world in everything from medicine, science and technology to political philosophy and institutions.[21]

As anticipated, his passage home on the *Lord Hungerford* was slow and took almost six months, causing anxiety among some Whig politicians, who we are told kept visiting 'the city to inquire at Lloyd's about the safety of her precious freight'.[22] His two spinster sisters, Selena and Frances, had been eagerly awaiting his return. 'It is as if the sun had deserted the earth,' one of them had written about his long absence. 'He was so unlike any other being one ever sees, and his visits amongst us . . . served not a little to enliven and cheer our monotonous way of life . . .'[23] His father Zachary's health had been failing rapidly, and sadly he died just a month before Tom's return. Though he had achieved little recognition in life for his services to the Abolitionist cause, he had the honour of being buried in Westminster Abbey, where a bust in his memory bore an inscription crediting him with having helped to 'rescue Africa from the woes, and the British Empire from the guilt of slavery and the slave-trade'.

Tom Macaulay was now the head of the large family he had already been supporting financially for some years, including three younger brothers whose careers and income he promoted generously for the rest of his life. The most difficult decision he had to face on his return was whether to return to active politics. The main motive for his Indian exile had been to accumulate the treasured 'competence' which would make him financially independent of the Whig oligarchs who dominated British parliamentary life. But time and distance had led him to wonder whether he should abandon politics altogether for historical writing, declaring in a letter to Ellis: '. . . that a man before whom the two paths of literature and politics lie open, and who might hope for eminence in either, should chuse politics and quit literature seems to me madness.'[24]

His feelings three years later, after his return to London, were much the same. 'All my tastes and wishes lead me to prefer literature to politics,' he wrote to McAvey Napier, his editor at the *Edinburgh Review*. 'When I say this to my friends here, some of them seem to think that I am out of my wits, and others that I am coquetting to raise my price. I, on the other hand, believe that I am wise, and know that I am sincere.'[25]

The longed for return to his native island had not lived up to expectations. 'I am quite unsettled,' he complained to his ever-patient editor. 'Breakfasts every morning . . . dinners every evening and calls all day . . . My books are at the baggage warehouse. My book-cases are in the hands of the cabinet-maker. Whatever I write at present, I must, as Bacon somewhere says, spin like a spider out of my own entrails. And I have hardly a minute in the week for such spinning.'[26]

He found London 'in a strange state of excitement' and the West End 'in a constant ferment' with preparations for the coronation of young Queen Victoria. 'The influx of foreigners and rustics has been prodigious,' Macaulay grumbled, 'and the regular inhabitants are almost as idle and curious as the sojourners. Crowds assemble perpetually, nobody knows why, with a sort of vague expectation that there will be something to see; and, after staring at each other, disperse without seeing anything . . . I am sick to death of the turmoil, and almost wish myself at Calcutta again . . .'

A month later, he was no more enthusiastic about the imperial metropolis, which he had once loved so dearly. 'I used to think that I liked London,' he complained again to Napier, who was based in Edinburgh, 'but, in truth, I liked things which were in London, and which are gone.'[27] Foremost among those lost attractions was his old, close family circle, now scattered. Without parliamentary or government business to occupy him, he feared 'becoming a mere diner-out' if he stayed on in London. He thought the writing projects to which he should now be devoting himself were 'almost incompatible with the distractions of a town life'.

Much of his first summer back in England was taken up with a furious row with a minor historian, one Mr Wallace, who had edited a history of the 1688 revolution by the late Whig historian Sir James Mackintosh. Macaulay, who much admired Mackintosh, had written an excoriating review of Wallace's editorial efforts, condemning him in typically colourful language for 'deforming' the text by his 'blunders', adding to it 'a bad memoir' and 'a bad continuation' and 'debasing it into one of the worst that we ever saw'.[28] The target of this diatribe responded even more dramatically by challenging Macaulay to a duel; but the latter for once decided that discretion was the better part of valour and agreed to issue a qualified apology negotiated by the Whig grandee Lord Strafford. While Wallace declared that he had meant 'nothing disrespectful or unkind to Mackintosh', Macaulay expressed regret for having used 'any language that could be deemed personally offensive'.[29]

~

While he pondered his political future, Macaulay decided to embark on a grand tour of Italy. The high point of the trip was his stay in Rome, and especially his visits to St Peter's. Though disappointed by the colonnade in front of the Basilica and the outside of its dome—'decidedly inferior' to St Paul's back in London—he was 'fairly stunned by the magnificence and harmony of the interior' and waxed lyrical in the daily journal he had started keeping: 'I never in my life saw, and never, I suppose, shall again see, anything so astonishingly beautiful. I really could have cried with pleasure.'[30] Despite his usual preference for all things English, he was sufficiently impressed by the splendours of the Vatican to want 'to see the walls of St Paul's encrusted with porphyry and verde antique, and the ceiling and dome glittering with mosaics and gold'.[31] Back in London a few months later, he would be 'grievously disappointed' by St Paul's and by 'the coldness and meanness of that interior which, before I visited Italy, I thought so wonderfully fine'.[32]

Macaulay's three months in Italy were both an aesthetic revelation and a delight to his classical scholarship. 'I had no notion,' he wrote home, 'that an excitement so powerful and so agreeable, still untried by me, was to be found in the world.'[33] The politician in him was also both fascinated and appalled by 'the strange Brahminical government' of the Papal States. 'Corruption affects all the public offices,' he observed. 'Old women above, liars and cheats below—that is the Papal administration. The States of the Pope are, I suppose, the worst governed in the civilized world; and the imbecility of the police, the venality of the public servants, the desolation of the country, and the wretchedness of the people, force themselves on the observation of the most heedless traveller.'[34]

Even here, amid the ruins of classical antiquity and the splendours of Renaissance Italy, British politics was never far away. Soon after his arrival in Rome, Macaulay received a letter from the Prime Minister, Lord Melbourne, offering him the minor government post of Judge Advocate and a seat in Parliament. He wrote back politely declining the job offer, but expressing his willingness to return to Parliament as a backbencher. To Whig patrons like Lord Lansdowne, he pleaded 'the dislike which I feel for official life' and that his support for the government would carry more weight if he were not compromised by being a placeman.[35] In private, he confided to his sister Hannah that only a Cabinet post would be a sufficient inducement to sacrifice his freedom and literary work.[36] 'A man in office and out of the Cabinet is a mere slave,' he remarked in his diary. 'I have felt all the bitterness of that slavery once.'[37]

His first Christmas back in Europe was spent in Rome, where he pronounced the procession in St Peter's to be the finest he had ever seen. Despite his Protestant roots, he was 'deeply moved' by 'the immense antiquity of the Papal dignity, which can certainly boast of a far longer, clear, known, and uninterrupted succession than any dignity in the world; linking together, as it does, the two great ages of human civilization'.[38] Among the crowds of tourists, he spotted the English politician, William Ewart Gladstone, to whom he introduced himself and chatted, finding him 'both a clever and an amiable man with all his [religious] fanaticism'.[39] Despite their temperamental and political differences, it was the start of a friendship which would endure till the end of Macaulay's life.

Returning to England via France, he was unimpressed by the splendours of Versailles, describing the palace as 'a huge heap of littleness', with the contrast between the red brick of its old part and 'the classical magnificence' of the later stone part 'simply revolting' and with little merit to justify Louis XIV's huge expenditure on it. 'Why there are a dozen country houses of private individuals in England alone which have a greater air of majesty and splendour than this huge [stone] quarry,' he noted. 'Castle Howard—a building in something of the same style, and not a third part of the length, is immeasurably finer.'[40] Perhaps he was prejudiced by his idolization of William of Orange, Louis XIV's historical nemesis.

~

Macaulay had resumed his essays for the *Edinburgh Review*, which had tapered off during his years in India, and his subjects ranged far and wide, from a critique of Gladstone's militant Anglicanism to the treatment of women as sex objects in Restoration comedies. He was welcomed back into his favourite London salons, elected to the Reform Club and, to his even greater delight, to The Club, famous as the hallowed meeting-place for past luminaries like Samuel Johnson, Edmund Burke, Edward Gibbon, Oliver Goldsmith, David Garrick and Sir Joshua Reynolds.[41]

In February 1839, Macaulay had his first sight of the young Queen Victoria and was less than enthusiastic about the future Empress of India. 'The separation of her lips,' he noted in his private journal, 'is certainly almost disagreeable, particularly as seen from below—as to the rest, she is rather a nice girl.'[42] He forgave her the buck teeth when she showed her preference for the Whig Party led by her beloved Lord Melbourne. The so-called Bedchamber crisis* opened the door to Macaulay's own return to active politics. With the return of Melbourne as Prime

---

* Queen Victoria's refusal to replace the Whig ladies of her bedchamber with Tories prompted the resignation of Sir Robert Peel's Conservative Ministry and the return of the Liberals under Lord Melbourne.

Minister, he was adopted as the Liberal candidate for a vacant seat in Edinburgh, appropriately also the home of his beloved *Review*. It was an offer he could not refuse, and he wrote back accepting, on condition that he would not be required to spend more than £500 on his election campaign.[43]

Macaulay's election manifesto declared his opinions as being fundamentally what they were when he had helped pilot the Great Reform Act seven years ago. Like the Radicals, he was in favour of introducing voting by secret ballot to stop powerful landlords intimidating their tenants, a practice which, he claimed, had been gaining ground since the abolition of pocket boroughs. He also wanted to reduce the legal term of the House of Commons from seven to four years.[44]

'I entered public life a Whig,' he assured his electors, 'and a Whig I am determined to remain.' He went on to explain that he used the term Whig 'in no narrow sense'. Being a Whig, in his view, did not involve slavishly following any particular political text or statesman. It meant being heir to a long struggle for civil and religious freedoms dating as far back as the parliamentary opposition to Elizabeth I. He credited the Whigs with the very existence of the House of Commons, for rightly opposing Tory wars against the American and French republics, for extending religious tolerance and for abolishing slavery.

Macaulay was returned virtually unopposed, since the Tories, or so he claimed, had not dared put up a candidate against him; and his only opponent, a Chartist, mustered just twenty votes. He had firmly opposed the Chartist demand for universal suffrage and insisted on the need to retain the £10 franchise, restricting the vote to householders whose property had an annual rental value of at least £10.[45]

Macaulay's return to politics had coincided with a personal tragedy in the life of his best friend, Thomas Ellis, whose young wife had suddenly fallen ill and died. 'Comfort him I could not,' Macaulay wrote to Hannah, 'except by hearing him talk of her with tears in my eyes . . . I would with pleasure give one of my fingers to get him back his wife, which is more than most widowers would give to get back their own.'[46] Despite his own bachelorhood, Macaulay could empathize, having experienced the pain of his sister Margaret's untimely death; and he spent several days comforting his friend. Later that summer, he took Ellis on a trip to France to help him recover.

They returned from Paris after a stormy crossing to find a letter waiting from Lord Melbourne. It offered Macaulay the post of Secretary at War, along with the seat in Cabinet which had been his long-coveted goal. 'Office was never . . . so little attractive, and therefore, I fear, I cannot, as a man of spirit, flinch, if it is offered to me,' he had written three weeks earlier to McAvey Napier, who had been awaiting his promised article on Clive.[47] Now, without hesitation, he promptly penned a reply to the Prime Minister accepting his offer.[48]

10

Secretary at War

The early years of Queen Victoria's reign were a period of heady optimism, symbolized by the young and conscientious new monarch and her enlightened German consort, Prince Albert. The royal couple seemed to epitomize the break with the seedy past of the Regency years, presided over by the Queen's dissolute and ineffectual uncles. Victorian Britain imagined itself on the threshold of a new Elizabethan age, in which Britannia would rule not only the waves but the worlds of science, medicine and technology.

The imperial metropolis to which Macaulay had returned from his Indian exile was a gigantic construction site, as its landscape was being transformed by an explosion of new building and redevelopment. While Buckingham Palace was being rebuilt as a suitably impressive royal residence, just behind it the Grosvenor family was developing aristocratic Belgravia. The land just east of the palace had already been cleared of the royal stables to create Trafalgar Square and the new National Gallery.

As Macaulay discovered, the Parliament to which he had been re-elected was also in the throes of being rebuilt, following the terrible fire of 1834 in which both historic Houses of Westminster had burned down, along with the greater part of their libraries, works of art and valuable records. For three decades, peers and M.P.s alike would have to make do with temporary, makeshift chambers, surrounded by a dusty and noisy building site, as the neo-Gothic palace we know today slowly rose around them from the ashes.

In this golden age of steam, London was becoming the centre of a booming railway network, with new stations popping up at Euston, Paddington, Waterloo and King's Cross. It was a period of rapid urbanization and industrialization as England became the economic power-house of the world. The population of London surged throughout the nineteenth century, leaping from about one million in 1800 to over six million a century later. But this growth far exceeded the city's infrastructure; and a combination of coal-fired stoves and poor sanitation made the air heavy and foul-smelling, with its famous pea-soup fogs and the stench of huge amounts of raw sewage dumped straight into the River Thames. The slums of the East End remained overcrowded, unsanitary and disease-ridden. And there were new and growing problems of crime and social order, which the recently formed Metropolitan Police was designed to address, with its uniformed 'Bobbies', named after their founder, the Tory leader, Sir Robert Peel.

Internationally, this was the heyday of *Pax Britannica*, a period of relative peace in Europe and the world, during which the British Empire controlled most of the key maritime trade routes and enjoyed unchallenged global power. Since the end of the Napoleonic War in 1815, the United Kingdom had played the role of Europe's policeman, maintaining the balance of power between far weaker continental states. The statesman responsible more than any other for maintaining this global order was Lord Palmerston, who would dominate British foreign policy for two decades from 1830 to 1850. His abrasive style earned him the nickname 'Lord Pumice Stone', while his manner of dealing with any foreign governments who crossed him was the original 'gunboat diplomacy'. Not surprisingly, given their similarity of outlook and temperament, Palmerston, now Foreign Secretary, had a staunch admirer in Macaulay when the latter joined the government as Secretary at War, a post which Palmerston himself had previously occupied for two decades.

Macaulay's entry to the Whig Cabinet and his swearing in to the Queen's Privy Council was still in the 1840s a remarkable achievement for a man of middle-class origins, who had risen purely on his intellectual merits, without the advantages of either aristocratic birth or a large private fortune. Unfortunately, it made him the target of satire and worse in the Tory press, and most notably in *The Times*. Deriding him as 'Mr Babbletongue Macaulay', with his reputation for loquaciousness, the paper scoffed: 'These men Privy Councillors! These men petted at Windsor Castle! Faugh! Why they are hardly fit to fill up the vacancies that have occurred by the lamented death of Her Majesty's two favourite monkeys.'[1]

Macaulay was by now inured to press attacks; and he found it hard to conceal his satisfaction at being a self-made man who had arrived at the pinnacle of political success without having to curry favour with the aristocratic elite who still had a near monopoly of power. His own political sympathies were firmly with the new commercial and industrial elites represented by the reformed House of Commons, as against the landed aristocracy which, he believed, was rushing 'headlong to its inevitable doom'.[2] He had already annoyed some of his colleagues by arguing that the existing composition of the House of Lords, dominated as it was by big landowners, was irreconcilable with that of the reformed House of Commons. He had anticipated, with remarkable foresight, that there were bound to be constant conflicts between the two Houses and had advocated, a century before its time, the very modern solution of diluting the hereditaries with large numbers of life peers from the new middle-class professions.[3]

Even so, the Romantic in Macaulay confessed 'to a much greater liking for the hereditary branch of the legislature than I can reconcile to my reason', and he felt 'pain and anguish' about its doomed future.[4] His ambivalence was not unlike that of other, more recent, political interlopers who forced their way into the British establishment, such as Lloyd George or Margaret Thatcher.

Ever prudent about his finances, Macaulay was pleased to discover that his ministerial salary would be £2,500 a year (£111,000 in today's money), and that his young brother Charles, whom he had employed as his private secretary, would also 'put a few hundred into his pocket'.[5] Invited to dinner at Windsor Castle after his swearing in to the Privy Council, Macaulay proudly described to his sister Fanny how he 'was presented; knelt down; kissed Her Majesty's hand; had the honour of a conversation with her of about two minutes, and assured her that India was hot, and that I kept my health there'.[6] The Queen, apparently, was not impressed by this first encounter. She observed to Prime Minister Melbourne that she thought Macaulay odd-looking. 'Uncouth, and not a man of the world,' the very suave Melbourne is said to have agreed.[7]

Macaulay's plebeian origins combined with his garrulous ways and his unattractive appearance to make him the butt of many similar comments. The poet, Matthew Arnold, thought him a great Philistine, while his old intellectual opponent, John

Stuart Mill, accused him of falsifying the truth in his essays. 'He is what all cockneys are,' Mill wrote with unmistakable undertones of jealousy, 'an intellectual dwarf—rounded off and stunted, full grown broad and short, without a germ of principle of further growth in his whole being.'[8] Sydney Smith, like Macaulay a leading intellectual light of the Holland House circle, commented cynically about his appointment to the Cabinet that he was 'too professional a Speaker, ... brought in for the express purpose of Speechification, and an air of ridicule is thrown over the appointment'.[9]

Only weeks before Macaulay was invited to join the Cabinet, the Duke of Wellington, the grand old man of British politics, had joked that 'Lord Melbourne would prefer to sit in a Room with a Chime of Bells, ten Parrots, and one Lady Westmorland [renowned for being garrulous] to sitting in Cabinet with Mr Macaulay'.[10] After his first Cabinet meeting, a colleague noted that Macaulay 'spoke with his usual volubility and eagerness; but I thought he spoke too much'. Others expressed alarm that 'if he was always so powerful in talking, no business would be done'.[11] Because of his 'waterspouts of talk', another colleague told Melbourne that Macaulay resembled a book in breeches. The Prime Minister repeated the joke to the young Queen, with the result that 'whenever she sees her new Secretary at War, she goes into fits of laughter'.[12]

Macaulay's weekend at Windsor, and his unconcealed pleasure at having arrived there, backfired rather badly in the weeks and months to come. Following the parliamentary convention of the time, he had resigned his seat on accepting office and sought re-election from Edinburgh. Not unnaturally, he decided to send a manifesto to his electors at Edinburgh explaining his reasons for joining the government. But he made the mistake of dating and addressing the letter from Windsor

Castle, where he happened to be staying at the time.[13] 'That unlucky slip of the pen,' his nephew later wrote, 'afforded matter for comment and banter in Parliament, on the hustings, and through every corner of the daily and weekly press.'[14]

The Times, of course, led the way in ridiculing the pretentious pomposity of this political upstart; and Macaulay even found himself satirized in one of Thackeray's novels as the Right Honourable T.B. Maconkey. Twenty years later in his obituary of Macaulay, Thackeray, by then a good friend, atoned for joining in that 'wretched outcry'. 'Was this man not a fit guest for any palace in the world . . . ?' he asked rhetorically, and went on to declare that 'the place of such a natural chief was amongst the first of the land . . .'[15] Macaulay himself did his best to shrug off the whole episode. 'You think a great deal too much about the *Times*,' he admonished his Edinburgh editor, McAvey Napier. 'What does it signify if they abuse me or not?'[16]

∼

Macaulay's first months in office were disturbed far more by domestic worries than by press attacks. 'Throughout the autumn of 1839,' his sister Hannah wrote, 'his misery at the prospect of our return to India was the most painful and hourly trial . . .'[17] The Trevelyans were only in England on a one-year furlough; and Charles was eagerly looking forward to being back at work in India and taking his family with him. Macaulay realized that his only hope of averting this emotional disaster was to find Trevelyan an interesting assignment nearer home. And with his new connections in government, he managed to arrange the offer to him of a senior civil service post as Assistant Secretary at the Treasury.

Trevelyan took the job, much to the relief of his wife and her

161

brother. 'When the joy and relief came upon us,' she reported, 'it restored the spring and flow of his [Macaulay's] spirits. He took a house in Great George Street, and insisted on our all living together, and a most happy year 1840 was.'[18]

Now secure in his domestic life, Macaulay appears to have been equally content with his official duties, which were surprisingly light compared with the burdens of running the War Office a generation later. He showed an unexpected mastery of departmental finances and had little difficulty getting parliamentary approval for his generous spending plans, despite the government having only a narrow majority of five. 'I have got through my estimates with flying colours,' he boasted in a letter to Ellis in March 1840. 'Made a long speech of figures and details without hesitation or mistake of any sort . . . stood catechizing on all sorts of questions, and got six millions of public money in the course of an hour or two. I rather like the sort of work, and I have some aptitude for it.'[19]

His main regret was at having to shelve his projected *History*, and the fact that the only time he had for reading was while dressing and undressing. But he consoled himself with the thought that, just as exercise aids digestion, 'some months of hard official and parliamentary work may make my studies more nourishing'.

Macaulay's first major parliamentary intervention as a minister was a defence of the government against a Tory motion of no confidence in January 1840. It got off to a rocky start when he referred to himself as 'the first Cabinet Minister' to enter the debate, whereupon the Opposition 'burst forth into a storm of ironical cheering', chose 'wilfully to misconstrue those words, as if he were putting forward an absurd claim to the leading place in the Cabinet' and spiced their attacks with allusions to his pretentious Windsor Castle address.[20] It was a humiliating day which Macaulay never forgot. More than a decade later, he referred to that speech as 'one of the few unlucky things in a lucky life', though 'far superior to many of my speeches which have succeeded'.[21]

The speech itself was a wide-ranging defence of his political principles. He rejected Tory accusations that he was a Chartist sympathizer, but defended his belief in voting by secret ballot, contrary to the views of his Cabinet colleagues, and his desire to extend the £10 householder franchise from the towns to rural constituencies. He also reiterated his opposition to the Chartist demand for universal suffrage and defended the Liberal government from the charge of fomenting agitation. 'The truth is that agitation is inseparable from popular government,' he declared. 'If you wish to get rid of agitation, you must establish . . . a despotism like that of Russia . . . Would the slave trade ever have been abolished without agitation?'[22]

He also took a defiantly liberal stance on government policy towards Catholics and Ireland. He defended the appointment of three Roman Catholics as Privy Councillors, accused the Tories of plotting to repeal the Catholic Emancipation reforms of 1829 and credited the government with bringing peace and the beginnings of prosperity to Ireland by replacing British military occupation with a policy of conciliation.

A few months later, Macaulay was again leading the government response to a Tory motion of censure, this time blaming the Liberals for 'interruption in our commercial and friendly intercourse' with China and for failing 'to provide against the growing evils connected with the contraband trade in opium'.[23] Not for the last time, British Conservatives were opposed to military intervention in a faraway place, especially when it risked jeopardizing British commercial interests.

Macaulay's own position on Britain's opium disputes with

China was unashamedly jingoistic, inspired partly by his dislike of what he considered Chinese xenophobia and racial arrogance and partly by a pragmatic, free market approach to the opium trade. The subject had dominated his first Cabinet meeting in September 1839, when Macaulay, according to a colleague, 'was exceedingly eloquent against the Chinese, and was decidedly for hostile measures'.[24] The issue turned on whether the Chinese imperial authorities were justified in holding British merchants and consular representatives at Canton collectively responsible for the activities of British privateers who were smuggling in opium grown in India. By April 1840, the dispute had escalated into the First Opium War, in which Chinese punitive action against the British in Canton provoked severe reprisals by the British navy and the imposition of a humiliating peace treaty on Peking.

It was Macaulay's first practical test as Secretary at War, and he was as delighted with the naval outcome as he was by his own 'great success' in defeating the Tory opposition at home.[25] His self-satisfaction was endorsed by an impartial observer who noted: 'Macaulay is thought to have spoken excellently on the China Question, because on that occasion, he kept out of sight his all-knowingness, and addressed himself straight to the matter in the Debate—an achievement, which the Dunces flatter themselves, was beyond his power.'[26]

Foreshadowing future twenty-first-century concerns about China, the speech began by stressing how impenetrable China was to Western minds, 'a country separated from us physically by half the globe, separated from us still more effectually by the barriers which the most jealous of governments and the hardest of all languages oppose to the researches of strangers'.[27] Macaulay pointed out that until recently the Chinese authorities had themselves been in two minds about whether it would be better to continue with a ban on opium, which was impossible to enforce along such an extensive coast-line, or else to legalize the trade and seek to tax and regulate it instead. It was therefore premature and unreasonable of them to have expected the British Superintendent at Canton to launch a major crackdown on British opium traders, nor would he have had the necessary powers or resources to do so. One had only to look at the large quantities of illicit brandy and tobacco smuggled into Britain across the Channel to see how impossible it was to cut off external supplies in the face of strong domestic demand, all the more so with a product like opium for which buyers were driven by a craving 'little short of torture'.

The Chinese authorities in Canton, Macaulay argued, had arrested British merchants 'of spotless character' to deter 'the redheaded devils' and 'Outside Barbarians' they blamed for the contraband trade. But for the British to have banned the trade in Canton would have risked diffusing it along the Chinese coasts, turning 'honest merchant adventurers into buccaneers', escalating violent clashes with the local population, and provoking the Chinese authorities into even more drastic punitive action.

The somewhat specious and disingenuous logic of Macaulay's argument was that, although China had every right to crack down on opium smuggling, it had no right to expect Britain to follow suit, even though the trade was being carried on by British smugglers under British protection. He accused the Chinese, having failed so abysmally to stop the smugglers, of instead taking innocent Britons as hostages, confiscating their property, threatening to starve them to death and insulting 'our Sovereign in the person of her representative'. They had 'confounded the innocent with the guilty' and acted 'in a manner inconsistent with the law of nations'.

Macaulay was sarcastic about the 'very pitiable ignorance' which led 'the Celestial Empire' to see Westerners as 'savages destitute of every useful art'. He was adamant 'that all nations, civilized and uncivilized, should know that, wherever the Englishman may wander, he is followed by the eye and guarded by the power of England'. But he begged the question of why, while condemning opium smugglers and even likening them to illegal slave traders, he saw no necessity for British action against them. Instead, he concluded with a splendidly rhetorical fanfare proclaiming Britain's new status as the world's leading imperial superpower. By giving China a bloody nose, Macaulay proudly declared that Britain had reminded its Cantonese expatriates

> . . . that they belonged to a country unaccustomed to defeat, to submission, or to shame; . . . to a country which had made the Dey of Algiers humble himself to the dust before her insulted Consul; to a country which had avenged the victims of the Black Hole on the Field of Plassey; to a country which had not degenerated since the great Protector vowed that he would make the name of Englishman as much respected as ever had been the name of Roman citizen. They knew that, surrounded as they were by enemies, and separated by great oceans and continents from all help, not a hair of their heads would be harmed with impunity.[28]

~

The Opium War was the first of three military operations in which Macaulay at the War Office was happy to enforce the gunboat diplomacy and liberal interventionism of his colleague Lord Palmerston, the powerful Foreign Secretary who dominated successive Whig administrations. In a letter to his Edinburgh editor, Macaulay enunciated a concept of what he considered just

wars, anticipating much of the logic of future British wartime
leaders from Lloyd George and Churchill to Margaret Thatcher
and Tony Blair:

> It is foolish and wicked to bellow for war, merely for
> war's sake . . . I would never make offensive war. I would
> never offer to any other power a provocation which
> might be a fair ground for war. But I never would abstain
> from doing what I had a clear right to do, because a
> neighbour chooses to threaten me with an unjust war;
> first, because I believe that such a policy would, in the
> end, inevitably produce war; and secondly, because I
> think war, though a very great evil, by no means so great
> an evil as subjugation and national humiliation.[29]

The next test of British resolve was over the so-called 'Eastern
Question', the problem of how to manage the disintegration
of the once mighty Ottoman Empire which extended from
the Balkans to the Arabian peninsula. Matters came to a head
when Muhammad Ali, the Ottoman viceroy of Egypt, backed
by France and Spain, threatened to establish an independent
kingdom of his own. Despite French military threats, Britain
joined Austria and Russia in coming to the rescue of the
beleaguered Turkish Sultan. In August 1840, a British fleet
bombarded Beirut, landed ground troops in Lebanon and spent
the next two months driving a large, occupying Egyptian army
out of the rest of Syria and Palestine. In the peace treaty that
Britain then imposed on him, Muhammad Ali, though left in
control of Egypt, was forced to renounce all claims to Syria and
to accept the nominal suzerainty of the Ottoman Sultan.

Although Britain and Russia had been on the same side in
the Syrian War, they were rivals in the great game that was being

played out for control of Afghanistan. Early in 1839, a British Indian expeditionary force had marched on Kabul with the aim of replacing the reigning, pro-Russian Amir, Dost Muhammad, with his pro-British rival. A few months later, their mission had been accomplished. The British candidate had been enthroned in Kabul, backed up by a permanent British occupation force; and by late 1840 Dost Muhammad had surrendered and been exiled to India.

Only a year later, this initial success backfired when a successful tribal revolt against the British occupation renewed the conflict. Hostilities dragged on till the end of 1842, when the British were finally forced to withdraw, release Dost Muhammad and allow him to return to the Afghan throne. Britain's First Afghan War later came to be known as Auckland's Folly, after the Governor-General who began it. But in January 1841, Macaulay could be forgiven for celebrating what looked like a triple win for British arms and diplomacy, especially gratifying for a fragile Whig government with such a narrow majority. 'Now that we have placed England at the head of the world,' he declared, 'we may be easy about the rest. To dictate peace at once in the heart of Bactria, at the mouth of the Nile and in the Yellow Sea is something new.'[30] With such 'glorious news from all corners of the world', he was confident that 'if we go out now, we go out with all the honours of war—drums beating and colours flying'.[31]

A year earlier, in a long article about Robert Clive, the founder of British power in India, Macaulay had cited the Raj as illustrating the maxim that honesty was always the best policy, in international relations as in domestic life. 'The entire history of British India,' he wrote, 'is an illustration of the great truth that it is not prudent to oppose perfidy to perfidy, and that the most efficient weapon with which men can encounter falsehood is truth . . . The greatest advantage which a government can possess is to be the one trustworthy government in the midst of governments which nobody can trust. This advantage we enjoy in Asia.'[32]

Confident that he and his colleagues had dispelled any myths about perfidious Albion, Macaulay was ready for a return to private life and pining for the freedom to get on with his writing. By the spring of 1841, as the government faced renewed pressure to resign, he was even hopeful that defeat in a Commons censure vote would release him from office. The government finally resigned in June and lost the general election that followed. Macaulay, comfortably returned from his own seat in Edinburgh, declared himself thoroughly content with his lot as a backbencher and happy to be in opposition 'for a few years' while he wrote his history of England.[33]

11

Elder Statesman

At no point in Macaulay's life is there any indication of another person, living, historical or fictional, whom he regarded as a role model. Even at his lowest moments, he was remarkably free of envy, happy to be himself, comfortable in his own skin and satisfied with what he had achieved as a middle-class prodigy who had risen by his own efforts to a position unique in the highest circles of the land. The nearest he came to adulation for another public figure was with Warren Hastings, the controversial first Governor-General of British India. About to review a new biography of Hastings, Macaulay pronounced him 'one of the greatest men England ever produced', with 'pre-eminent talents for government, and great literary talents too; fine taste, a princely spirit, and heroic equanimity in the midst of adversity and danger'.[1] Although he never explicitly said so, Macaulay did his best to emulate Hastings's magisterial stoicism in his own later years when chronic illness increasingly blighted his public and literary ambitions.

For the present, he was delighted with the freedom and

comfort of his new life as a backbench M.P. of independent means, no longer 'a member of a government wretchedly weak, and struggling for existence'.[2] 'Now I am free,' he assured his editor at the *Edinburgh Review*, 'I am independent. I am in Parliament, as honourably seated as man can be. My family is comfortably off. I have leisure for literature; yet I am not reduced to the necessity of writing for money. If I had to choose a lot from all that there are in human life, I am not sure that I should prefer any to that which has fallen to me. I am sincerely and thoroughly contented.'

Now that Macaulay had successfully averted the dreaded prospect of the Trevelyans returning to India, it was agreed that they would move to a permanent house of their own in Clapham, the leafy suburb where the Macaulay family had once lived and Tom had grown up. Macaulay, meanwhile, decided to exchange his own town-house in a dreary and narrow Bloomsbury street for a far more fashionable and compact apartment in Piccadilly, on the second floor of the Albany, an Oxbridge-style retreat for successful academics and intellectuals, which survives relatively unchanged to this day. Macaulay's nephew George, who was a frequent visitor, described it as a 'luxurious cloister, whose inviolable tranquillity affords so agreeable a relief from the roar and flood of the Piccadilly traffic'.[3] Here, Macaulay told his friend Ellis, he intended to lead a 'college life at the West-end of London'.[4]

His Albany flat was very spacious by modern standards, with an entrance-hall, two sitting rooms, a bedroom, a kitchen, cellars and two rooms for servants. All this, he proudly announced, was his for only 90 guineas a year (a peppercorn rent of about £4,200 in today's money) and 'in a situation which no younger son of a Duke need be ashamed to put on his card'. The move itself caused him 'agonies' and 'a week of confusion' in which he had to transport and rearrange his vast library of four thousand books.[5] But once furnished, the flat, 'every corner of which was library', was very comfortable, though not overcrowded by ornaments. The walls were hung with half a dozen fine Italian engravings from his favourite Great Masters; a handsome French clock provided 'a singularly melodious set of chimes'; and there were bronze statuettes of Voltaire and Rousseau, old gifts from his former patroness Lady Holland.

On his return from India, Macaulay had inherited his father's faithful servants, a couple called William and Elizabeth Williams, who remained with him for nearly 20 years, till he pensioned them off in 1858, the year before his death. Attended by them at the Albany, and surrounded by good restaurants, Macaulay expected to have 'some very pleasant breakfasts there, to say nothing of dinners'.[6]

~

'A strong opposition is the very thing I had wanted,' Macaulay had confided in Ellis soon after the Whig's election defeat.[7] A few years out of the government, he calculated, would give him time to finish his monumental *History*. Meanwhile, he was happy to play the role of respected elder statesman in a party with a substantial bloc of 300 seats in Parliament. Ever economical about his finances, he boasted to Ellis about his re-election: 'I got through very triumphantly at Edinburgh, and very cheap. I believe I can say what no other man in the kingdom can say. I have been four times returned to Parliament by cities of more than a hundred and forty thousand inhabitants; and all those four elections together have not cost me five hundred pounds.'[8]

The loss of his ministerial salary had been substantially recompensed by the increased literary earnings that were flowing in from his essays and reviews, mainly for the *Edinburgh Review*. He told its editor, McAvey Napier, that he was 'more than satisfied' with his fees.[9] 'At present I consider myself as one of the richest men of my acquaintance,' he assured him, 'for I can well afford to spend a thousand a year [£45,000 today], and I can enjoy every comfort on eight hundred. I own, however, that your supply comes agreeably enough to assist me in furnishing my rooms, which I have made, unless I am mistaken, into a very pleasant student's cell.'

A month later, he was well into his 'historical labours', delighted to be filling what he considered an almost complete void in English history from 1688 onwards.[10] Parallel with his *History*, he was busily churning out learned essays on other subjects for the *Review*. Having finished with Warren Hastings, he had moved on to Frederic the Great of Prussia, an article which provoked an amicable intellectual duel with his editor over what Napier considered Macaulay's excessively colloquial style. 'The English language is not so poor but that I may very well find in it the means of contenting both you and myself,' Macaulay assured his editor, but not before setting out his own manifesto of journalistic style:

> The first rule of all writing . . . is that the words used by the writer shall be such as most fully and precisely convey his meaning to the great body of his readers. All considerations about the purity and dignity of style ought to bend to this consideration. To write what is not understood in its whole force, for fear of using some word which was unknown to Swift or Dryden, would be, I think, as absurd as to build an Observatory like that at Oxford, from which it is impossible to observe, only for the purpose of exactly preserving the proportions of the

Temple of the Winds at Athens. That a word which is appropriate to a particular idea, which everybody high and low uses to express that idea, and which expresses that idea with a completeness which is not equalled by any other single word . . . should be banished from writing, seems to me a mere throwing away of power.[11]

Macaulay could be a harsh judge of the journalism of other authors, however prominent and popular. He was particularly scathing about a new book by Charles Dickens on the Americans, which he refused to review because it was 'at once frivolous and dull' despite 'some gleams of genius'.[12] Instead, he set himself to polish and complete what was to be his own best-selling work, *The Lays of Ancient Rome*, which he had begun while in India. It consisted of four epic poems which aimed to reinvent the lost ballads and founding myths of the early Roman Republic. This foray into poetry was surprisingly well received by the critics; and by 1875 it was to sell more than a hundred thousand copies, with the poems themselves indelibly etched in the memory of successive generations of schoolchildren.[13]

Politics now came second to the demands of his writing. But it was said of him that 'no member ever produced so much effect upon the proceedings of Parliament who spent so many hours in the Library, and so few in the House'.[14] For a backbencher, he had an unusually major impact on the new legislation Parliament was debating to extend the period of copyright in the interests of authors. Macaulay's decisive intervention swung the House in favour of calculating the duration of copyright from the date of publication, rather than the death of the author, and his proposals were adopted with some slight modifications. The Tory Prime Minister himself, Sir Robert Peel, walked across the floor after Macaulay's speech to assure him that the last twenty minutes had radically altered his own views on the Bill.[15]

The other political issue which preoccupied Macaulay at this time was a tireless campaign he waged for the recall of Lord Ellenborough, the controversial Governor-General who claimed to have saved British India by winning the Afghan War of 1842. In February 1843, the Tory government moved a vote of thanks to Ellenborough, and the Whigs, for tactical reasons, decided to let it pass unanimously, even though most of them shared Macaulay's view of Ellenborough as 'vain, self-willed and insolent'.[16] Macaulay was furious about what he considered 'the stupid and disgraceful course which our leaders have resolved to take'. 'I did not think that any political matter would have excited me so much,' he confided to Ellis; but he decided to stay away from the House, rather than incite a backbench revolt.[17]

His forbearance paid off, and three weeks later the Whigs were united in support of a new Opposition motion censuring Ellenborough for his proposal to restore the gates of the historic temple of Somnath in Gujarat. The temple had been razed by Muslim invaders in medieval times and its massive gates incorporated into a mosque. Now that there were plans to rebuild the temple, Ellenborough had decided to curry favour with Hindus by magnanimously returning the gates to the site of the temple ruins. The motion of censure, with Macaulay as its most eloquent speaker, accused the Governor-General of directly disobeying the East India Company's declared policy of 'discontinuing any seeming sanction to idolatry in India'.[18]

Macaulay's Somnath speech was important for spelling out his vision of militant secularism for the British Empire, in stark contrast to the more emollient approach of the Orientalists whom he had already defeated over the education policy. Although this secular stance equally prohibited any official support for Christian proselytizing, its vitriolic condemnation of Hindu idolatry was unmistakably coloured by Macaulay's own Evangelical roots. Describing Hindu doctrines and rites as 'in the highest degree pernicious', he declared: 'In no part of the world has a religion ever existed more unfavourable to the moral and intellectual health of our race.' Despite his love of classical Greek mythology, he condemned its Hindu equivalent as 'so absurd that it necessarily debases every mind which receives it as truth' and blamed it for having produced 'an absurd system of physics, an absurd geography, and absurd astronomy'. He applied the same sweeping condemnation to Hindu art: 'Through the whole Hindoo Pantheon you will look in vain for anything resembling those beautiful and majestic forms which stood in the shrines of ancient Greece. All is hideous, and grotesque, and ignoble.'

Though far from puritanical by Victorian standards, Macaulay was particularly outraged by what he considered the sexual immorality of Hindu iconography. His revulsion may well have been exaggerated by his own long suppressed sexuality. 'Emblems of vice,' he railed, 'are objects of public worship. Acts of vice are acts of public worship. The courtesans are as much a part of the establishment of the temple, as much ministers of the god, as the priests.' His greatest rage was reserved for the worship of Shiva, whose temple at Somnath Ellenborough was proposing to honour. Referring to the phallic cult of shivalingams,* Macaulay declared: 'I am ashamed to name those things to which he [Ellenborough] is not ashamed to pay public reverence. This god of destruction, whose images and whose worship it would be a violation of decency to describe, is selected as the object of homage.'

Ellenborough, according to Macaulay, had fallen into the old

---

* Phallic pillars representing the Hindu god Shiva.

Orientalist habit of pandering to Hindu sentiment, which had meant in the past tolerating practices such as sati and female infanticide. Worse still, he would infuriate Muslims by removing the gates from the mosque which had been their new home for several centuries. If the Raj must take sides in India's religious conflicts, Islam as a sister religion to Christianity was 'entitled to the preference'. 'To affront a mosque of peculiar dignity,' he warned, 'not from zeal for Christianity, but for the sake of this loathsome god of destruction, is nothing short of madness.'

There is no record in Macaulay's Indian letters or journals of his visiting any major Hindu temple; so one can only conclude that this parliamentary diatribe was based on other people's descriptions and his own instinctive dislike of an alien culture and aesthetic so far removed from his Greco-Roman ideal. It was also indicative of how far Westernizers like Macaulay, Trevelyan and Bentinck had succeeded in constructing an aggressively British sense of imperial mission that Ellenborough's worst offence was to risk going native. Macaulay's speech mocked the florid language of the Governor-General's proclamation about Somnath and scorned 'all these tropes and hyperboles' as an imitation of Indian princes. One might as well ask, Macaulay added with a characteristic rhetorical jibe, 'why Lord Ellenborough should not sit cross-legged, why he should not let his beard grow to his waist, why he should not wear a turban, why he should not ride about Calcutta on a horse jingling with bells and glittering with false pearls. The native princes do these things, and why should not he?' The answer, quite obviously, was because he was an English Governor-General and because the native population respected 'the simplicity of our fashions'.

'Our plain clothing,' Macaulay elaborated, 'commands far more reverence than all the jewels which the most tawdry Zemindar wears; and our plain language carries with it far more weight than the florid diction of the most ingenious Persian scribe. The plain language and the plain clothing are inseparably associated in the minds of our subjects with superior knowledge, with superior energy, with superior veracity, and with all the high and commanding qualities which erected, and which still uphold, our empire.'

Despite all this imperialist eloquence, the motion of censure against Ellenborough was defeated. But Macaulay was determined not to give up. A year later he returned to the assault with a new motion of his own for Ellenborough's recall. Before it could be debated, the government and the Directors of the East India Company capitulated and announced the Governor-General's recall.[19] Macaulay's version of Britain's imperial mission had prevailed.

~

Macaulay's passionate dislike of Hinduism did not extend to all oriental cultures. His respect for Islam has already been noted. And despite his fierce prosecution of the recent war against China, he remained interested in and curious to learn more about Chinese culture. China was the subject of a major exhibition at Hyde Park Corner in September 1842, and Macaulay was enthusiastic about visiting it to see 'the wonders of the Celestial Empire', which included fifty life-size figures in different native costumes.[20] His only regret about being out of government, he confided to Ellis, was that he was no longer privy to the red boxes on the peace negotiations that were going on with the Chinese Emperor. 'We are good tutors, and the Chinese promising pupils,' he wrote optimistically. 'We taught them the meaning of a flag of truce first. Now we have initiated them into the mystery of ratifications.'[21]

Despite frequent trips to France to explore the Gothic and Renaissance architecture he loved, Macaulay was almost as scathing about the French as about Hindus. Writing home to Hannah from Paris in August 1843, he complained about everything—the French customs official who charged him the huge sum of 14 francs for bringing in an unused pair of cotton stockings; the inn which served him 'a cup of coffee worse than I thought any French cook could make for a wager'; the soap in his room which would have been 'an excellent substitute for Spanish flies in a blister'; and the disappointing cathedral of Chartres, which had the dubious distinction of appearing smaller than it was.[22]

His trip coincided with a state visit by Queen Victoria, designed to improve Anglo-French relations, which had been strained by Britain's military intervention against Egypt in the Levant while Macaulay had been Secretary at War. Now he thought the timing of her visit 'ill judged' and found the French in 'ill humour' about it because they thought their own king, Louis Philippe, had been too deferential to his British visitor. The French monarch, Macaulay reported, had acted merely with the 'chivalrous homage' due to a young woman, but there had been a press outcry about the welcome he gave her and about a French band playing 'God Save The Queen' when she landed on French soil. 'The French have taken it strongly into their heads,' he noted, 'that their government is acting a servile part towards England, and they are therefore disposed to consider every act of hospitality and gallantry on the part of the king as a national humiliation . . . They are wretched creatures . . . and will not be wiser till they have another lesson like that of 1815.'[23]

Back in London, he continued to plough his own furrow in Parliament, making major speeches on issues ranging from constitutional and social reform to Ireland. 'Macaulay's reputation and authority in Parliament,' his nephew conceded, 'owed nothing to the outward graces of the orator.'[24] On this, the Press Gallery was unanimous. *The Times* described him as 'rather ungainly', while the *Standard* found his delivery 'somewhat monotonous' and lacking in 'demonstrative or dramatic action', concluding: 'It was the matter and language, rather than the manner, that took the audience captive.'[25] The *Daily News* was more generous:

> Vehemence of thought, . . . language, . . . manner, were his chief characteristics. The listener might almost fancy he heard ideas and words gurgling in the speaker's throat for priority of utterance . . . He plunged at once into the heart of the matter, and continued his loud resounding pace from beginning to end, without halt or pause. This vehemence and volume made Macaulay the terror of the reporters; and when he engaged in a subject outside their ordinary experience, they were fairly nonplussed by the display of names, and dates, and titles.[26]

He was particularly famous for his unique method of preparing his speeches. Though he neither wrote down a word of them in advance nor spoke from prepared notes, his extraordinary powers of memory and instant recall enabled him to compose each speech word-perfect in his mind while he was on his long walks or pacing up and down in his study. As he confided to the Whig peer Lord Lytton, 'he himself never committed to writing words intended to be spoken, upon the principle that, in the process of writing, the turn of diction, and even the mode of argument, might lose the vivacity essential to effective oration . . .'[27]

Macaulay was just as meticulous when it came to editing

and correcting the published version of his collected speeches, to ensure that they read more like polished essays. Their message was rarely simple or merely partisan. Speaking in May 1842 on a motion favouring the Chartists, Macaulay endorsed their demands for a secret ballot and for removing the financial qualification for election to (but not voting for) Parliament, but he was adamant in rejecting their central aim of universal suffrage as being 'incompatible with property' and 'consequently incompatible with civilization'.[28] Foreshadowing the rhetoric of Thatcherism, he accused the Chartists of planning to nationalize land, factories and railways if they won power via adult suffrage, whereas progress and prosperity depended on the sanctity of private property and on 'the diligence, the energy, the thrift of individuals'. Rejecting the concept of class war implicit in the Charter, Macaulay proclaimed inequality as 'necessary to the wellbeing of all classes'. Universal suffrage would make the working class 'an irresistible majority', in which event 'capital will be placed at the feet of labour; knowledge will be borne down by ignorance', society would fall into anarchy, famine and chaos, out of which would emerge a new dictatorship. Universal suffrage, he concluded, must wait for universal education.

While this Hobbesian prophecy can be credited for anticipating the rise of Communist dictatorships, it can also be criticized for underestimating the instinctive conservatism of the British working class. Replying to a letter from one of his Edinburgh constituents, Macaulay maintained that 'a very large portion of them do not understand their own interest' and, if given the vote, would bring 'indescribable misery' on themselves by 'national bankruptcy' and 'the destruction of all property'. 'I refused them the franchise,' he declared with unabashed paternalism, 'not from disregard of their interests, but from the same feeling which would lead me to refuse a razor to a man who told me that he wanted it in order to cut his throat . . .'[29]

Despite his new conservatism on constitutional reform, Macaulay remained remarkably liberal in his attitude to Ireland, and in particular on the controversy about state funding for the Irish Catholic Church. Even though he recognized how unpopular this would be in his own staunchly Presbyterian constituency of Edinburgh, he was strongly in favour of transferring most of the revenues of the Anglican Church of Ireland, which served a tiny minority, to its Roman Catholic rival, which had the allegiance of the vast majority of the Irish.[30]

When Peel's Tory government introduced a Bill to give state funding to the Irish Catholic seminary at Maynooth College, Macaulay urged his Whig colleagues not to oppose it, arguing that it would 'promote the real Union of Great Britain and Ireland', and announced that he would vote for it 'regardless of the risk which I may run of losing my seat in Parliament'.[31] Citing the vast material and intellectual wealth that Britain had inherited from the Catholic Church, epitomized by the colleges of Oxford and Cambridge, he argued that it was time to repay a small part of that debt.

'A Church which is abhorred is useless or worse than useless,' he warned, referring to the established Protestant Church of Ireland, 'and to quarter a hostile church on a conquered people, as you would quarter a soldiery, is therefore the most absurd of mistakes.' The way forward, he urged, was to give the same status to Catholicism in Ireland as had already been allowed to the Presbyterian Kirk in Scotland.

As for the general state of Anglo-Irish relations, Macaulay was vocal in his attack on the Peel government's repressive policies against Irish nationalists. Ireland, he declared, was being governed like Britain's new conquests in Sind, 'not by means of the respect which people feel for the laws, but by means of bayonets, of artillery, of entrenched camps'.[32] 'Of all forms of tyranny,' he said, 'I believe that the worst is that of a nation over a nation', and England's repression of Ireland had been accentuated by the religious divide between the two nations after the Reformation.

~

Macaulay called these years on the backbenches the most contented period of his life, his views heard with respect in Parliament while he was free to immerse himself in his reading and writing. 'If anybody would make me the greatest king that ever lived,' he told his seven-year-old niece Baba, 'with palaces and gardens, and fine dinners and wine and coaches and hundreds of servants, on condition that I would not read books, I would not be a king. I would rather be a poor man in a garret with plenty of books than a king who did not love reading.'[33]

Despite his lack of interest in a return to government, Macaulay suddenly found himself at the centre of a Cabinet crisis in December 1845, when the Peel government came close to collapse because of its internal divisions over the repeal of the Corn Laws. These were the import tariffs which kept food prices artificially high in the interests of Britain's big landowners. Macaulay, like Peel himself, was a committed free trader. Speaking at a public meeting in Edinburgh, he made a strong case for lower food tariffs and prices benefiting both British labour and business. His argument was based on the inescapable fact of global interdependence through trade, with different products suited to different climates. 'Even if that dependence were less beneficial than it is,' he argued, 'we must submit to it; for it is inevitable. Make what laws we will, we must be dependent on other countries for a large part of our food.'[34]

With the Tories on the verge of resigning, the Whig leader, Lord John Russell, was trying to put together a minority government which, with support from Peel's Tory faction, would be able to push through the contentious Corn Law repeal. Macaulay, surprisingly for a backbencher, was one of the Whig inner circle of five that Russell convened to steer his negotiations with Peel and the Palace.[35] 'It is an odd thing to see a ministry making,' he confided to his sister Hannah. 'I never witnessed the process before.'[36] Lord John spent the day closeted in his inner library, while his ante-chamber was thronged 'with comers and goers, some talking in knots, some writing notes at tables'. Every few minutes some fortunate person would be summoned into the inner sanctum; and when he emerged was greeted with cries of 'What are you?' Macaulay was one of the first to be called in and was offered the very undemanding post of Paymaster-General because, as Russell explained, he 'wanted leisure and quiet more than salary and business'. 'I at once accepted it,' Macaulay told his sister. ' . . . I shall have two thousand a year [about £120,000 today] for the trouble of signing my name. I must indeed attend Parliament more closely than I have of late done; but my mornings will be as much my own as if I were out of office.'

His satisfaction was premature, because the leading Whig grandees, Lord Palmerston and Earl Grey, could not reconcile their mutual rivalry. Macaulay was mortified that his party had shown itself incapable of putting the public interest first 'because we are, as the French say, mauvais coucheurs, and cannot adjust ourselves to accommodate each other'.[37] Peel stayed on in office for another six months and managed to get his Corn Law Bill through Parliament, whereupon his government promptly imploded in a second and this time finally collapsed. Lord John Russell was again summoned to replace him, and Macaulay got the post he had originally been offered 'as the least likely to interfere with his historical labours'.[38]

According to the usual convention, on taking office, he had to resign his Edinburgh seat and seek re-election.* This time he faced stiff Tory opposition, which focused on his contentious support for funding of the Irish Catholic Church. The main election meeting brought a massive turnout of nearly three thousand electors, 'well-dressed people' who greeted Macaulay with 'immense cheering, mingled with a little hissing'.[39] He spoke for an hour; and when a show of hands was called for, he 'had a perfect forest, and the other side not fifty'. 'I am exceedingly well and in high spirits,' he assured Hannah. 'I had become somewhat effeminate in literary repose and leisure. You would not know me again now that my blood is up.'

~

During this second term in government, Macaulay spoke only five times in Parliament over a period of two years. But they were all star performances, carefully prepared and rehearsed, and 'advertised beforehand by the misgivings of the speakers who differed from him'.[40] According to an authoritative contemporary parliamentary historian, 'the popular voice' placed Macaulay 'in the very first rank of contemporary speakers', placing him fourth after Sir Robert Peel, Lord John Russell and the Duke of Wellington.[41]

---

* The practice of M.P.s who accepted government office having to get a new vote of confidence from their electors stemmed from the old battles between Crown and Parliament, when it was necessary to stop the King's ministers from packing the lower house.

His critics, nonetheless, complained that he was an intellectual exhibitionist whose torrents of talk were a symptom of vanity. Others were more generous and thought he could not help himself when 'he only pours out talk and listens to no other mortal man or woman'.[42] 'Did you ever see a beer barrel burst . . . ?' Sydney Smith asked a friend. 'Well Macaulay bursts like a beer barrel and it all comes over you but he can't help it. He really has no wish to shew off.'

His own favourite torrent and the speech he considered the best of his career was on the subject of child labour in the booming factories of Britain's industrial revolution. For all his passionate championship of property rights, the central tenet of nineteenth-century liberalism, Macaulay was not a believer in laissez faire capitalism. In May 1846, he spoke strongly in support of a Bill seeking to reduce the limit on factory working hours for children from 12 to 10 hours a day. Free markets, he argued, required regulation: even cab-drivers were not free to charge what they liked on a rainy day. 'Would you treat the free labourer of England like a mere wheel or pulley?' he demanded. 'Rely on it that intense labour, beginning too early in life, continued too long every day, stunting the growth of the body, stunting the growth of the mind, leaving no time for healthful exercise, leaving no time for intellectual culture, must impair all those high qualities which have made our country great.'[43]

Anticipating by a century and a half today's emphasis on the so-called knowledge economy, he proclaimed 'human intelligence' as Britain's greatest resource and declared: 'Man, man is the greatest instrument that produces wealth.' Leading inventors like Hargreaves and Crompton, he pointed out, came from working-class backgrounds but had had the education and time to design new textile-spinning machines. Mocking the notion that Britain could be undercut by cheaper labour working longer hours in other countries, he concluded: 'I laugh at the thought of such competition. If ever we are forced to yield the foremost place among commercial nations, we shall yield it, not to a race of degenerate dwarfs, but to some people pre-eminently vigorous in body and in mind.' He was referring, ironically, to German competition, but would presumably have felt much the same about cheap Chinese products today.

Macaulay returned to the same theme in a debate on public education in April 1847, in which he proclaimed it as 'the right and duty of the State to provide means of education for the common people'.[44] Even those who believed in extreme laissez faire, he argued, must agree that governments had a duty to protect the security and property of their citizens, and educating the masses was the best means of doing so. Adam Smith himself had warned that mass ignorance could cause major riots fuelled by religious fanaticism. Education was the rational and humane alternative to repression, a national good like defence, which could not be left to market forces and free competition. Scotland, he was proud to point out, was a prime example of success through education a century ago, thanks to the parish schools set up by the Scottish Parliament.

The Scots themselves were less than enthusiastic about their prodigal son. The Presbyterians disliked his sympathy for Catholic grievances; the Radicals were angered by his opposition to Chartism and universal suffrage; and the whisky trade attacked him for refusing to lobby on their behalf against excise duties. 'The truth is,' wrote a Scottish peer in July 1846, 'that Macaulay, with all his admitted knowledge, talent, eloquence, and worth, is not popular. He cares more for his *History* than for the jobs of his constituents, and answers letters irregularly, and with a brevity deemed contemptuous; and above all other defects, he suffers severely from the vice of over-talking, and consequently of under-listening.'

Another source of unpopularity as a constituency M.P. was his insistence on avoiding the slightest hint of corruption, which led him to refuse any financial contributions to entertainments like a race-cup or even donations to a charitable hospital or school. He had a strong sense of privacy and, on his visits to Edinburgh, lacked the common touch and shunned publicity. In the July 1846 by-election he had routed his Tory opponent by two to one; but only a year later the tide had turned strongly against him, and he faced an unholy alliance of 'Established Churchmen and wild Voluntaries, intense Tories and declamatory Radicals, who agreed on nothing except holding their peculiar religion as the scriptural, and therefore the only safe, criterion of fitness for public duty'.[45] Macaulay became the main target of their attacks, the charge being that he was too much of an essayist and too little of a politician. 'The burden of half the election-songs,' according to his nephew, 'was to the effect that he had written poetry, and that one who knew so much about Ancient Rome could not possibly be the man for Modern Athens.'[46] The hustings, we are told, had been packed by the advocates of cheap whisky, and Macaulay was heckled and jeered when he declared: 'I cannot ask pardon for my conduct. I cannot ask pardon for being in the right. I come here to state what I have done clearly, and to defend it.'[47] The voters of Edinburgh were not impressed; and Macaulay had the humiliation of coming third at the polls.[48]

He put a brave face on it. 'I have been completely beaten,' he wrote to Hannah, but maintained: 'I am not vexed, but as cheerful as ever I was in my life . . . I will make no hasty resolutions. But everything seems to indicate that I ought to take this opportunity of retiring from public life.'[49] His parting message to his former constituents was unrepentant: 'I shall always be proud to think that I once enjoyed your favour; but permit me to say that I shall remember not less proudly how I risked, and how I lost it.'[50]

In the weeks that followed, Macaulay was inundated with requests and offers to stand for various other vacant seats. 'I did not know how great a politician I was till my Edinburgh friends chose to dismiss me from politics,' was his acidic comment.[51] He firmly rejected the prime minister's offer of a seat for the pocket borough of Richmond, pointing out that it would compromise his role as an advocate of moderate electoral reform.[52]

His departure from government coincided with the revolutions that were convulsing most of Europe, in a tide of unrest not unlike today's Arab Spring. The French Revolution and the Napoleonic Wars had been followed by three decades of conservative reaction, during which democratic demands had been suppressed. But the political lid had been blown off by the rise of new and more militant middle- and working-class movements; and yet another Republican revolution in France had set off a chain reaction among its neighbours.

Despite its own more stable and liberal parliamentary system, Britain was not immune to the revolutionary tide, and London was the scene of a huge Chartist demonstration in April 1848. Two weeks later, Macaulay's letter of resignation from the government accepted that it was time to remove 'some evils and anomalies which the reform-bill [of 1832] spared'. 'Some concessions ought to be made with a good grace to the middle classes,' he advised Prime Minister Lord John Russell, 'and . . . at the same time, all innovations dangerous to order and property ought to be firmly resisted.'[53] It was a measure of how far the balance had changed in his own mind that he announced that he was now firmly opposed to the Chartist demand for the secret ballot, unlike most of his ministerial colleagues.

12

Indian Summer

For Macaulay, his second, enforced retirement from politics was a welcome opportunity to focus again on his *History*, 'rising at daybreak, and sometimes sitting at my desk twelve hours at a stretch'.[1] He seems to have been genuinely relieved at being out of the public eye and avoided it as far as possible. Despite the huge popularity of his books in the USA, he refused suggestions for a trans-Atlantic tour on the ground that his 'dislike of exhibition' had 'become almost morbid' since he had quit politics. He bluntly told an American admirer: 'What I hear of the form in which your countrymen show their kindness and esteem for men whose names are at all known deters me from visiting you.'[2] His worst fears of American sensationalism were confirmed four years later when the US press reported rumours that he had become an opium addict. This 'impudent lie', as he termed it, provoked an angry rejoinder that he had not swallowed more than 10 grains of opium in his entire life, had never taken laudanum except on medical advice and had last taken it during the cholera epidemic of 1849.[3]

Macaulay was more receptive to invitations from his Scottish ancestral homeland. He accepted the largely honorific post of Rector of Glasgow University, although he grumbled about the request to deliver a public speech at his inauguration and declared that he found such displays hateful. 'Nothing but a sense of duty surmounted my reluctance to harangue the House of Commons, or my own Constituents . . .,' he explained and wished he could 'escape without being exhibited like a Bengal tiger or an ourangoutan . . .'[4]

With two volumes of his *History* completed by the end of the year, he felt free to take a break from writing. His idea of a relaxing day off was to rise late at 9.30 in the morning, read Calderon in Spanish while dressing, then Pepys's *Diaries* at breakfast, followed by some Herodotus, and then a walk over to Clapham for lunch with the Trevelyans. After lunch, he walked back home again, read some more Herodotus, dined alone at a restaurant with a popular novel for company, walked the streets again for another hour while meditating on his *Lays of Ancient Rome*, and then went home to bed.[5]

Macaulay spent many of his evenings dining quietly at home with his old friend Thomas Ellis, refusing even an invitation to one of the Queen's balls because he 'preferred a quiet chat [with Ellis] over a glass of wine'.[6] A typical dinner for two at his Albany flat would be a lobster curry followed by woodcocks and macaroni.[7] Though still much in demand, he was becoming increasingly reluctant to do the London social rounds. 'He was peculiarly susceptible to the feeling of ennui when in company,' according to his sister Hannah, now Lady Trevelyan since Charles had inherited the family baronetcy. 'He really hated staying out even in the best and most agreeable houses. It was with an effort that he even dined out, and few of those who met him, and enjoyed his animated conversation, could guess how

191

much rather he would have remained at home, and how much difficulty I had to force him to accept invitations and prevent his growing a recluse.'[8]

Perhaps because of her encouragement, Macaulay remained a celebrity on the London social scene. On a visit to England in 1848, the American poet Emerson described him as 'the king of diners out' with 'the strength of ten men; immense memory, fun, fire, learning, politics, manners, and pride'.[9] 'I do not know when I have seen such vivacity,' Emerson wrote home to his wife. '. . . talks all the time in a steady torrent. You would say he was the best type of England.' But he added that unfortunately 'this most fashionable orator, scholar, poet, statesman, gentleman, is, in some companies of highest fashion, voted a bore'. Sydney Smith, known for his acerbic wit, was known to have delivered the crushing compliment that Macaulay 'had improved, he has flashes of silence'.

Macaulay, for his part, was less than complimentary about many of his hosts and fellow-guests. Despite his support for Jewish civil nights, in the privacy of his diary he felt free to joke about his 'Hebrew hosts of yesterday', the wealthy city financier and M.P. Lionel de Rothschild and his wife.[10] The 'Rothschildren', as he humorously called them, had a 'fine house, bad pictures and the most stupid of stupid parties', although the food and wine were good, 'as the dinners and wines of Israelites generally are . . .'

He was more generous about dinners at Buckingham Palace. 'The Queen was most gracious to me,' he noted after one such occasion, 'prettier than at a distance. She talked much about my book, and owned that she had nothing to say for her poor ancestor James the Second. "Not Your Majesty's ancestor," said I, "Your Majesty's predecessor."' Victoria, apparently, chose to take this rather pedantic genealogical correction as a compliment.[11] He remained on her guest-list, and some months later he was back to stay as a house-guest at Windsor Castle. He was graciously received by the royal couple and sat next to the Duchess of Norfolk at dinner, followed by a long chat with Her Majesty about German politics and a French history of the Reformation that she was reading.[12]

Although he usually accepted such royal invitations, Macaulay confided to his diary that he found them generally rather dull. The Queen, for her part, was less than complimentary about his company. 'I hear that Mr Macaulay is the most agreeable man in London,' she told another visitor, 'but I see very little of it.' When the remark was reported back to Macaulay, he noted in his journal: 'I do not know whether to be pleased or vexed.'[13]

Despite his professed reluctance to become 'a diner out', Macaulay himself hosted frequent and lavish breakfast parties at his Albany flat for his inner circle of friends and also for political bigwigs like Gladstone, Peel and various Whig grandees. 'If I had had a Duke, I should have had every gradation of rank,' he noted in his diary after one such 'very aristocratic' party.[14]

Although he could not conceal his satisfaction at being sought after by the rich and famous, Macaulay's happiest hours were spent with the Trevelyan children. His sister Hannah noted in her memoirs how he would arrive at her home after breakfast, dawdle away a whole morning playing with her children, and then spend the afternoon taking his favourite niece Baba for a long walk through the city of London.[15] To his delight, Baba shared his love of books.

Books apart, he was also happy to join in the rough and tumble of more childish games. 'He was beyond all comparison the best of playfellows,' his nephew George later wrote, 'unrivalled in the invention of games, and never wearied of repeating them. He had an inexhaustible repertory of small dramas . . . in which he sustained an endless variety of parts . . .'[16] One of the most popular was to play robbers and tigers from a den built up with newspapers behind the sofa, the girls shrieking with mock terror as their uncle roared menacingly at them. Despite his own dislike of dogs, he had bought Baba a pet spaniel and was amused when her younger sister Alice asked 'rather embarrassing' questions as to 'whether it was a boy dog or a girl dog'.[17]

As the children grew older, Macaulay spent many of his afternoons showing them the sights of London. This usually began with a sumptuous midday meal, at which their favourite food treats were accompanied by more rarefied gastronomic delicacies like oysters, caviar and olives, 'invariably provided,' wrote his nephew George, 'with the sole object of seeing us reject them with contemptuous disgust'.[18] Then it was off to places like the Regent's Park Zoo in summer or Madame Tussaud's in winter; or he would lead them 'through the lofty corridors of the British Museum, making the statues live and the busts speak by the spirit and colour of his innumerable anecdotes . . .'

Another Trevelyan family ritual was their Easter holiday, when Macaulay regularly took them on ecclesiastical history tours of the cathedral cities of England, Wales and, occasionally, the Loire Valley in France. He was a tireless guide, enlivening their long railway journeys with 'a running fire of jokes, rhymes, puns, never ceasing'.[19] His knowledge of British church history and architecture was encyclopedic, though his opinions were often original to the point of eccentricity. 'A striking specimen of rude barbarian power with little art or grace,' was his comment on Durham's magnificent Norman cathedral. 'There is something Egyptian about it.'[20]

The Trevelyan children also witnessed a surprisingly sentimental side of their uncle's nature. He was so easily moved to tears, especially by the suffering of children, that 'the sentiment of pity, whether in art or in nature, was nothing short of a positive inconvenience to him'.[21] One passage of Dickens's *Dombey and Son* about an orphaned little girl 'made me cry as if my heart would break', Macaulay confessed in his diary, noting on another day that a newspaper report of the suicide of a poor girl 'quite broke my heart. I cannot get it out of my thoughts, or help crying when I think of it'.[22] He avoided going to the theatre because he found 'the visible representation of distressing scenes' too upsetting; and his frequent re-readings of the *Iliad*, with its tragic portrayals of grief-stricken Achilles or Priam, often reduced him to floods of tears. 'I read the last five books at a stretch during my walk today,' he confided to Baba while holidaying at Malvern, 'and was at last forced to turn into a by-path, lest the parties of walkers should see me blubbering for imaginary beings . . .'[23]

This strongly Victorian streak of sentimentality did not affect Macaulay's excellent literary taste. He remained an ardent admirer of Jane Austen at a time when her novels had gone largely out of fashion and even out of print. 'There are in the world no compositions which approach nearer to perfection,' he noted, after re-reading all her novels.[24] 'How far inferior all our ranting artificial romancers are to that woman.' He rated *Northanger Abbey*, in particular, higher than all the works of Dickens and Pliny put together. 'Yet it was the work of a girl,' he exclaimed with wonder in his diary. 'She was certainly not more than twenty-six. Wonderful creature!'[25]

~

On his 49th birthday, Macaulay noted cheerfully in his journal: 'I have no cause of complaint . . . Tolerable health . . . competence

... liberty ... leisure ... very dear relations and friends, ... a great, I may say a very great literary reputation.'[26] He could afford to be immodest. By this time his fame and fortune had both been secured by the huge sales of his *History*, the first volume selling 35,000 copies in an expensive library format, when Volume II appeared to even greater acclaim and was sold out as soon as it was published. American sales were even more dramatic, reaching 100,000 within weeks of publication and putting Macaulay's *History* second only to the Bible in the list of US best-sellers. Later volumes of his essays and poetry also sold well, with lots of European translations and pirate editions.[27] His writing had made him a rich man, and he would never again have cause to worry about maintaining his independence in literary or political life.

Preparing to write the next section of his monumental *History*, which had now reached the crucial reign of its hero, William of Orange, Macaulay set himself a hugely ambitious five-year plan of research and writing. He would first spend eighteen months reading and travelling to steep himself in the period, visiting Holland, Belgium, Scotland, Ireland and France, ransacking local archives wherever he went. There were hundreds, even thousands, of pamphlets to be turned over, and the British Museum, the Bodleian and dozens of other libraries to be explored. Then, with the subject carefully mapped out in his mind, he would settle down to writing, aiming to produce a relatively modest average of two pages a day. The writing, he calculated, would take a further two years, followed by a year for 'polishing, retouching and printing'.[28]

His was a historical method which relied as much on live experience of historic locations as on written accounts of what had happened there. Researching the massacre at Glencoe in the Scottish Highlands, he insisted on visiting the site in both rain and sunshine. 'Yet even with sunshine what a place it is!' he exclaimed. 'The very valley of the shadow of death.'[29]

Despite his determination to concentrate on his writing, Macaulay found it hard to resist the continuing demands of public life. He was tempted by an unexpected offer from the Prince Consort himself. Prince Albert, as Chancellor of Cambridge University, was considering rival candidates for the post of Regius Professor of Modern History. Macaulay suddenly received a note from the Prince summoning him to the Palace the next afternoon and was 'greatly vexed' because it meant having to cancel a planned visit to Hannah at Clapham. 'I could almost have cried,' he noted in his journal. 'However, I answered like a courtier.'

Macaulay assumed that he was to be consulted about the relative merits of the two main candidates for the professorship; but Albert, to his 'extreme astonishment', offered Macaulay himself the Chair, pressing him 'very earnestly, and with many flattering expressions' to accept it. Macaulay politely but firmly declined, partly because he felt the demands of lecturing would conflict with his historical writing, but mainly because he could not, like the wolf in Aesop's fable, bear to sacrifice his independence. 'I cannot bear the collar,' he noted in his diary. 'I have got rid of much finer and richer collars than this. It would be strange if, having sacrificed for liberty a seat in the Cabinet and £2,500 a year, I should now sacrifice my liberty for a Chair at Cambridge and £400 a year [£3,500 today].'[30]

In the years to come, Macaulay jealously guarded his privacy and independence from continuing pressure to return to active politics. His own political sympathies remained firmly and consistently with the Whig right led by Lord Palmerston. Though fond of his old Tory adversary, Sir Robert Peel, Macaulay had nothing but contempt for the up and coming new Conservative leader, Benjamin Disraeli, 'that confounded Jew' whose 'gross folly and impertinence' had even led him to cast aspersions on the Queen's efforts to form a stable Whig government.[31] When Disraeli mocked Peel's government as 'organized hypocrisy', Macaulay found himself itching for 'a passage of arms' with this new Shylock in which he might riposte with Shakespeare's words: 'I thank thee, *Jew*, for teaching me that word.'[32] Perhaps it was a sign of the times that he saw no contradiction between his advocacy of Jewish rights and such personalized anti-Semitism.

The Whigs continued to regard Macaulay as one of their own, although his politics had been moving steadily to the right, especially after the failed European revolutions of 1848 convinced him of the dangers of radical republicanism and of the virtues of Britain's 'balanced' constitution. Based initially on alliances between middle- and working-class groups with moderate demands for national independence and democratic reform, most of these continental uprisings had rapidly descended into anarchy and violence, provoking a popular backlash and allowing the old monarchies to return more or less intact.

France was the only exception. Condemning the extremist policies of French Republicans, Macaulay had noted in his journal that 'they are refuting the doctrines of political economy in the way a man would refute the doctrine of gravitation by jumping off the monument'.[33] Visiting the newly born French Second Republic in 1849, Macaulay commented: 'No private person shows . . . the least love or respect for the present form of government. The word republic is hardly uttered without a sneer.'[34] Writing home from Paris, he declared: '. . . every human being that I saw, high and low, was cursing the revolution, and breathing vengeance on the Red Party.'

He was, of course, proved right when France returned

to monarchy only five years later with the Second Empire of Napoleon III. 'I do not like the Emperor or his system,' Macaulay cynically observed, 'but I cannot find that his enemies are able to hold out any reasonable hope that, if he is pulled down, a better government will be set up . . . The French have only themselves to thank; and . . . a people which violently pulls down a constitutional government, and lives quiet under despotism, must be, and ought to be, despotically governed.'[35]

Having turned down two parliamentary seats, Macaulay was eventually offered a Cabinet post in January 1852, with the tempting prospect of becoming President of the Board of Control for India. 'I might have had that place I believe,' he noted in his diary, 'the pleasantest in the Govt. and the best suited to me, but I judged far better for my reputation and peace of mind.'[36] Pleading 'health, temper, tasks, etc.', Macaulay refused to be persuaded by a somewhat half-hearted Prime Minister, Lord John Russell, who had himself been pressured by others to make the offer.[37]

A few months later, Macaulay received an offer he felt he could not refuse from the electors of Edinburgh, who had rejected him so decisively five years ago for his supposed Catholic sympathies. Plunged into a general election with the local Liberals badly divided, and facing the prospect of a Tory victory, a large public meeting in the Athens of the North voted 'by unanimous acclamation' for the return of its former tribune. 'No man has given stronger pledges than Mr Macaulay,' declared the city's leading Whig, 'that he will defend the rights of the people against the encroachments of despotism, and the licentiousness of democracy . . . If Mr Macaulay has a fault, it is that he is too straightforward; too open; that he uses no ambiguities to disarm opposition.'[38]

The Edinburgh Whigs now assured Macaulay that he

would win handsomely, without even visiting his constituency or canvassing in any way; all he had to do was agree to serve if elected. He graciously accepted, but firmly resisted pressure from the city's Presbyterians and his own party to withdraw his previous support for state funding of the Irish Catholic seminary at Maynooth. Edinburgh would have to accept him with no strings attached or not at all. Rather to his own surprise, he topped the poll: the voters of Edinburgh, it seemed, admired his courage and 'were rather proud, than not, of voting for a candidate who was probably the worst electioneer since Coriolanus'.[39]

~

Two days after his election triumph at Edinburgh, Macaulay found himself struck down by what appears to have been a serious heart attack. In his journal, he described himself as languid and oppressed; hardly able to walk or breathe. He was due to travel to Edinburgh to address a victory meeting, but dreaded the prospect of a public appearance in such a weakened state. His physician, Dr Bright, was summoned, examined him with 'a mysterious looking tube', pronounced that 'the action of the heart was deranged' and strictly forbade the journey to Edinburgh.[40] Instead, Hannah whisked him off to a quiet country retreat at Clifton near Bristol, where he would spend the rest of the summer convalescing.

His health had been troublesome for some years, with attacks of gout and arthritis which were so severe that he could barely walk for days on end.[41] There had been chronic tooth abscesses and a succession of bad colds and chesty coughs. He had also complained for more than two years of severe pains in the chest, back and left arm, which Dr Bright insisted on describing as 'latent gout' and rheumatism, although they were almost certainly attacks of angina.[42] 'I do not know that I ever felt so exhausted,' Macaulay noted during one such bout of illness. 'After climbing to my rooms, I could hardly take my great coat off. I fell into my chair panting for breath. I took a blue pill and some paregoric, put on a mustard poultice, drank a large bowl of tea and put my feet in hot water.'[43]

At Clifton, Macaulay put himself in the care of a local doctor whom he thought 'a very clever man, a little of a coxcomb, but, I dare say, not the worse physician for that'.[44] In the days before modern medication, diet was the chief remedy available to doctors, and their prescriptions tended to be more a matter of ingenuity than rationality. No doubt because he wanted to impress his patient, known to be a classical scholar, the Clifton doctor kept quoting passages from Horace and Virgil while he spent half an hour examining Macaulay with a stethoscope. He then prescribed a complicated new diet. While tea was forbidden, coffee was prescribed daily for breakfast along with eggs and a little boiled bacon. This was to be followed by a very small lunch and then a dinner of 'firm and brown meats'. While insisting that the patient give up green vegetables and fruit tarts, this cure was 'very liberal' as to wine, and indeed insisted that he could not do without it. Despite his customary scepticism, Macaulay resolved to give the eccentric new regime a fair trial.[45]

Whether or not diet had anything to do with it, his health slowly improved, though his physical stamina was still greatly reduced. By the autumn of 1852, he was well enough to deliver his postponed election victory speech at Edinburgh. It was a remarkably forward-looking and optimistic view of Britain's leading role in a world that was being rapidly transformed by industrialization and globalization. Macaulay began by declaring that he 'stood aghast' at the excesses of the European revolutions of 1848, which had threatened to plunge the entire continent 'in one generation from the civilization of the nineteenth century to the barbarism of the fifth'.[46] The new Huns and Vandals of European radicalism had been suppressed by a return to military despotism; but Britain alone had remained an oasis of tranquillity because of her noble and balanced constitution. Strongly defending free trade and the controversial repeal of the Corn Laws four years ago, Macaulay called for further parliamentary reform by a new Whig government to get rid of the remaining pocket boroughs and extend the franchise.

The most prophetic part of his speech looked forward to a world that was shrinking rapidly with better transport and communications. To illustrate the benefits of global trade and the mass prosperity it would bring, he cited the many thousands of Britons who had migrated abroad but continued to trade with their mother country:

> His candlesticks and his pots and his pans come from Birmingham; his knives from Sheffield; the light cotton jacket which he wears in summer from Manchester, the good cloth coat which he wears in winter from Leeds; and in return he sends us back, from what was lately a wilderness, the good flour out of which is made the large loaf which the British labourer divides among his children.

~

Because of his failing health, Macaulay served less than three years of this final term as an elected M.P. Since he was also struggling to complete his *History*, his parliamentary appearances tended to be few and far between. He attended the budget session of the new Parliament and made fun of the new Tory Prime Minister, Benjamin Disraeli, for making a five-hour speech to say what Macaulay himself might have said 'as clearly, or more clearly, in two hours'.[47]

When Disraeli lost the vote and his short-lived government fell, Macaulay was among the inner circle of Whig grandees who met to discuss a letter from the Queen, urging them to bury their differences and form a stable coalition government. 'I said that I could improve the Queen's letter neither in substance nor in language,' Macaulay noted approvingly and with rare modesty, 'and that she had expressed my sentiments to a tittle.'[48]

His first major parliamentary speech proved, as he admitted in his diary, 'a great trial to the nerves of a man returning after an absence of six years to an arena where he had once made a great figure'.[49] The subject was a Tory peer's Bill to exclude judges from membership of the House of Commons. Although expected to pass comfortably, the Bill suffered an unexpected defeat, with Macaulay claiming to have turned the tide. 'I spoke with great ease to myself; great applause; and better than applause, complete success,' he noted. '. . . I am glad . . . to find that, even for public conflict, my faculties are in full vigour and alertness.'

Judging by press reports, he was not exaggerating. His speech was a star attraction, with M.P.s dashing into the chamber from all directions when they heard that the once great orator was on his feet.[50] 'The old voice, the old manner, and the old style; . . . glorious speaking!' one paper enthused. 'Well prepared, carefully elaborated, confessedly essayish; but spoken with perfect art . . . A torrent of the richest words, carrying his hearers with him into enthusiasm, and yet not leaving them time to cheer.' At the end of this forty-minute tour de force, delivered 'with masterly vigour', Macaulay collapsed trembling and exhausted into his seat, too exhausted even to acknowledge the congratulations of ministers and other M.P.s.

Only three weeks later, he found himself under intense government pressure to make another major speech. This time the subject was India, about which he could claim more firsthand knowledge than any other M.P. The government's new India Bill of 1853 was meant to make good some of the promises of the previous Charter Act of twenty years ago, which Macaulay himself had shepherded through Parliament as a rising, young backbencher. Macaulay was now a member of the parliamentary Select Committee which had drafted the new Bill, and its most important provision was a project particularly close to his heart: the recruitment by open and competitive examination of Indian civil servants, a reform which the previous Act had approved, but which had remained a dead letter because of the reluctance of East India Company directors to give up their powers of patronage.

Careful arrangements were made by the government whips for Macaulay to speak during the crucial Second Reading of the Bill, which had run into unexpectedly strong parliamentary opposition. The problem was the timing of his speech, because his failing health meant that he could not speak for some hours after eating but also had a tendency to faint if he went late into the evening without food. To cap it all, he was suffering from persistent toothache, which must have made it difficult for him both to eat or speak.[51]

It was finally agreed that he should open the debate on an afternoon, but his place was usurped at the last minute by a rival, very long-winded speaker, and it was almost eight in the evening before Macaulay rose to speak. He spoke for an hour and a half and then came to an abrupt halt, too fatigued to cover the remaining points. 'I did not satisfy myself,' he confided to his diary, 'but, on the whole, I succeeded better than I expected. I was much exhausted, though I had by no means exhausted my subject.'[52] Another observer was more harshly critical, calling the speech a failure 'frigidly talked about and cruelly criticised' and describing the speaker himself as 'broken down in health, uncontrollably nervous, unable to sustain the pitch of his voice'; a far cry from his rousing performance in the House just three weeks earlier.[53]

The main thrust of the speech was that anything short of free, competitive exams would inevitably lead to nepotism and corruption by whoever controlled Indian appointments. He pointed to 'those shameful and lamentable years' which had followed the British conquest of Bengal, when even its rapacious Governor, Lord Clive, had been appalled by the virtual sale of Indian offices to people favoured by ministers and directors back in London.[54] Ridiculing some Tory claims that academic prowess was no guarantee of future success in one's career, he gave copious examples to demonstrate that 'the general rule is, beyond all doubt, that the men who were first in the competition of the schools have been first in the competition of the world'.

His speech was a powerful rejoinder to the traditional and typically English prejudice against intellectuals: 'As if a young fellow, who can get the heart out of a book, . . . must needs be less able to sit on a horse . . . or take charge of a famine-stricken district than the son of a person of fashion who has the ear of a minister, or the nephew of an influential constituent who owns twenty public-houses in a parliamentary borough.'

Macaulay also took the opportunity to reiterate his old arguments in favour of Western education for the natives of India. Dismissing the fears expressed by a Tory peer that education for Indians would hasten their rejection of British rule, he pointed to the inconsistency of those who argued that too much education was weakening for Europeans but empowering for Indians.

~

Despite his emphasis on India as the lynchpin of Britain's empire, Macaulay had no nostalgia for the years he spent there, and he positively avoided socialising with other India-returned Britons. On a trip to Holland, he had found himself trapped on board a ship with the same corrupt former British Resident at Delhi whom his brother-in-law, Trevelyan, had exposed and ousted a decade ago. The gentleman concerned and his wife, oblivious of Macaulay's knowledge of their past, had pestered him with their attentions and reminiscences of the East. They had waxed eloquent about India as 'the most delightful place in the world' and lamented the fate that had forced them to return to Britain. Macaulay's response had been scathing. India was well enough as 'a place of exile', he told them, and went on to assert 'that all the fruit of the tropics are not worth a pottle of Covent Garden strawberries, and that a lodging up three pairs of stairs in London is better than a palace in a compound at Chowringhee'.[55]

His contempt for things Indian extended, with the exception of his brother-in-law, to all Britons with Indian connections. In January 1853, he was delighted to see a reprinted copy of his own famous Indian Education Minute which, as he noted in his diary, had 'made a great revolution'. But, three days later, when he dined at the Trevelyans' with the future Chief Justice of Bombay and the future Governor of Bengal, his sole comment was to dismiss it as 'an Indian party and consequently stupid'.[56]

Whatever his views on Indians and their climate and culture, Macaulay remained ardently committed to the task of providing them with the best administration that Britain could offer; and his efforts resulted in an Indian Civil Service far superior in education, talent and integrity to Britain's own domestic service, for which it later became the model.

Despite his poor health, Macaulay agreed to take on the job of supervising the implementation of the new system of civil service exams for which the India Act of 1853 had provided. In March 1854, the government set up a special committee for this purpose, with Macaulay as its Chairman. A month later, the committee began work at his Albany flat, after one of his lavish breakfast parties. Macaulay thought one of his colleagues, a Whig peer, 'really a great bore and very unwise', but the others, who included the renowned classical scholar, Benjamin Jowett, were 'excellent men'.[57] Thanks, no doubt, to his efficient chairing, the task had been completed only three months later with a report written by Macaulay himself.

The guiding principle of his report was that depth of knowledge must count for more than mere breadth. A candidate must not be 'a mere smatterer' with superficial knowledge of lots of different subjects. Profound knowledge of a single language or subject must count for 'more than twenty superficial and incorrect answers'.[58] Candidates from the old English universities, with their emphasis on the Greek and Latin classics, must be allowed to compete on equal terms with those from newer academic institutions in other parts of Britain. The minimum entry age should be raised to 18 and the maximum to 23, to allow older university graduates to compete. The exam subjects should be those suited for 'English gentlemen who mean to remain at home', but the successful candidates must then go on to spend two years as probationers studying Indian languages, history, jurisprudence and economics.[59]

The government adopted Macaulay's report without any alterations, and the first advertisements for the revolutionary new exam appeared in the London *Times* in January 1854. Macaulay himself closely supervised all the details and suddenly found himself having to fight a last-minute battle over a change in the advertisement, reducing the maximum age of candidates from 23 to 22. This apparently innocuous alteration would have disadvantaged older Oxbridge graduates and favoured London and the Scottish and Irish universities.

As soon as he spotted the change, Macaulay wrote an indignant letter to the President of the Board of Control, complaining about not being consulted and protesting that he was 'a good deal vexed' by 'a change of great moment' which 'would exclude a very large number of the very best men'. He voiced his strong suspicion that it was a deliberate attempt at sabotage by the East India Company's Directors, whose 'object is that the whole plan may fail discreditably; and that the Indian Judgeships and Collectorships may again be apanages for the younger sons and nephews of the Chairman and Deputy Chairman'.[60] His fierce protests prevailed; and the government agreed to restore the age limit of 23 and to publish altered notices to this effect.[61]

~

Macaulay had hoped that his plan of recruitment by competitive examination would also be adopted at Whitehall, ending centuries of ministerial patronage and nepotism in British civil service appointments. But although such a reform had an ardent champion in Gladstone, opposition from vested interests proved too strong. 'The pear is not ripe . . . ,' Macaulay sadly admitted.

'The time will come, but it is not come yet.'[62] His reform of the Indian civil service proved to be his last major contribution to public life. From now on his main concern was to complete his *History* before his failing health forced him to a halt.

His 53rd birthday in October 1853 had found him surprisingly cheerful and optimistic, basking in the affection of his family and looking back on the year just passed as 'prosperous and, better than prosperous, happy'. 'My health improved—my fortune easy—my family everything that I could wish,' he noted gratefully, describing his frequent visits to and from the Trevelyans, with whom he dined several nights a week.[63] But a few months later came a grim reminder of mortality when his beloved Hannah came down with scarlet fever, the same illness that had carried away his other sister Margaret two decades ago. 'I was quite overset,' Macaulay noted in his diary, 'could eat nothing . . . could do nothing but weep for half-an-hour.'[64] Although the Trevelyans begged him not to visit Hannah and expose himself to infection, he could not bear to stay away and rushed over to their new Notting Hill home to find the crisis past and Hannah on the way to recovery.

Meanwhile, his own health was again proving troublesome. In April 1854, he complained of a toothache so severe that he could neither eat nor talk and was confined to a soft diet of turtle soup, eggs, sweetbreads, asparagus and jelly.[65] A few days later, he had dizzy spells, which his doctor attributed to his liver and treated with strong doses of calomel.[66] But the result was to make him feel even weaker, 'probably affected by the remedies rather than by the disease'.[67] Amid this succession of ailments, his thoughts grew increasingly morose: 'I am a little low—not from apprehension; for I look forward to the inevitable close with perfect serenity, but from regret for what I love. I sometimes hardly command my tears when I think how soon I may leave them. I feel that the fund of life is nearly spent.'

At other times, his moods could swing dramatically to optimism and even contentment, despite all his physical sufferings. 'It is odd,' he confided to his dear friend Ellis, 'that, though time is stealing from me perceptibly my vigour and my pleasures, I am growing happier and happier . . . It is shocking, it is scandalous, to enjoy life as I do.'[68] There were times when he even welcomed the excuse his ailments gave him to decline invitations and stay at home to concentrate on his *History*. 'On the whole I am working to good purpose,' he noted in his diary while he spent New Year's Eve, 1853, dining quietly at home with Ellis. 'So ends the year. Happily on the whole. My health is failing. My life will not, I think, be long. But I have clear faculties, warm affections, abundant sources of pleasure.'[69]

'I have nothing to complain of,' Macaulay wrote stoically to another friend five months later. 'My health is indeed not good. But I suffer no pain; and, though my pleasures are fewer than they were, I retain the great sources of happiness. My mind is as clear and my affections as warm as ever. Nothing can exceed the tenderness of those who are nearest and dearest to me. On the whole, I find life quite as pleasant, now that I am confined, during many months every year, to my room, as when I was in the vigour of youth.'[70]

Despite this brave front, Macaulay had been finding his parliamentary duties increasingly onerous as his health deteriorated. 'I never go down to the House except in a case of life and death,' he told a friend in May 1854. 'The late hours and the bad air would kill me in a week.'[71] A few months later he had reached the conclusion that he could no longer do justice to the needs or demands of his constituents. In January 1855, he wrote to his Edinburgh agent begging leave to resign as the city's 'titular member'. It was, he explained, the ninth day since he had been well enough to venture out; and he felt, especially at a time when Britain was at war in the Crimea, that it was his duty either to attend the House or resign.[72]

13

The Bitter Cup

Macaulay regarded his heart attack in the summer of 1852 as a major turning point in his life. 'I became twenty years older in a week,' he noted in his journal a year later. 'A mile is more to me now than ten miles a year ago.'[1] He was convinced that his time was running out, and his main concern was that his *History* would remain unfinished. The afterlife held little consolation for him. Although he had started attending church on Sunday mornings,[2] he had never been religious and was openly hostile to prevailing Victorian beliefs in a spirit world.

'Never was there such paltry quackery,' he sneered, after witnessing a performance by a renowned hypnotist and mind reader. 'The fraud was absolutely transparent. I cannot conceive how it should impose upon a child.'[3] He was equally incredulous during an attempted session of table-turning at one of his own breakfast parties. 'There certainly was a rotary motion,' he observed wryly, 'but probably impressed by the Bishop of Oxford [one of his guests], though he declared that he was not quite certain whether he had pushed or not. We tried again;

and then . . . he certainly pushed, and caused a rotary motion exactly similar to what we had seen before.'[4]

As life seemed to be moving to its inevitable conclusion, Macaulay's greatest consolation lay in the large and very popular corpus of published works he was leaving to posterity. By the late 1850s, sales of his books had reached hundreds of thousands, with a worldwide circulation, especially in America, France and Germany, 'unequalled by any of his contemporaries'.[5] His *History* was translated into almost every European language, with no less than six rival translators competing just to bring out a German edition. His international fame also brought a shower of awards and honours, including the highly prized Prussian Order of Merit, election to the Institute of France and an honorary doctorate at Oxford.

Macaulay's global popularity in his own lifetime, rivalled only by Charles Dickens, rested partly on the irresistible sweep of his very colourful prose, but also on his standing as the most authoritative interpreter of what was then the world's unchallenged superpower. Along with his meticulous and encyclopedic scholarship, his caustic wit and mastery of gripping narrative made his grand, Whig interpretation of British history at once convincing, compelling, highly accessible and entertaining. A contemporary British equivalent in our own time might be a combination of Simon Schama, Niall Ferguson, David Starkey and William Dalrymple all rolled into one.

For Macaulay himself, by far the most enjoyable of his various honorific duties was his role as a Trustee of the British Museum, whose Board meetings he attended assiduously. Its library remained his favourite workplace; he did much of his writing at one of the oak tables in the centre of the room, where the light was best; and he enjoyed his privilege as a trustee 'to search the shelves at pleasure without the intervention of a librarian'.[6] He also foresaw the museum's future as a global centre of accumulated wisdom and cultural wealth. When its new Reading Room was being built, Macaulay lobbied the Chancellor of the Exchequer for an extra £5,000 (£216,000 in today's money) to gild the dome. There could be no better way, he argued, to 'do the nation more honour in the eyes of foreigners', because the new library would be 'the daily resort of perhaps three hundred people of highly cultivated minds, . . . learned and accomplished men from every country in the world'.[7]

Macaulay's flourishing finances were also a source of some comfort and security to him during these final years. He had a princely annual income of more than £4,500 a year (£200,000 today) from his royalties, and his capital—wisely invested — amounted to almost £100,000 (about £4.5 million today) at his death. For someone who had begun life as a penniless young barrister, fame and fortune could never be taken for granted. He could not resist boasting to his friend Ellis that a particularly large advance from his London publisher, Longmans, was 'a transaction quite unparalleled in the history of the book trade'.[8] He was 'a very opulent man', he noted in his diary in March 1856, and therefore 'well able to help others'. Among those who benefited from his philanthropy were his two spinster sisters, Frances and Selena, whom he supported for the rest of his life and theirs.

Now that he no longer needed to be near Westminster, Macaulay had decided to move from the Albany, where the stairs to his second floor flat were becoming increasingly difficult to negotiate with his various ailments. After considering a suburban villa in Clapham or Weybridge, he finally decided to buy the lease on a large and very comfortable house and garden at Campden Hill, Kensington, within easy walking distance of the Trevelyans at Westbourne Terrace.

The move itself was emotional, because he had grown more attached than he realized to his cosy Albany lodgings, where he had spent fifteen years. Ellis, his oldest and still his closest friend, came to dinner to cheer him up—'the last of probably four hundred dinners or more that we have had in these chambers'.[9] 'I hate partings,' Macaulay wrote in his diary. 'Today, even as I climbed the endless steps, panting and weary, I thought that it was for the last time; and the tears would come into my eyes . . . Everything that I do is coloured by the thought that it is for the last time.'[10]

His new home in Kensington needed extensive redecoration, and his sister Hannah helped him to furnish it 'with great taste'.[11] It was a large villa which combined the best of town and country. It was set in a quiet and secluded corner, concealed by 'a mass of dense and varied foliage',[12] sandwiched between Kensington Gardens and Holland Park; and Macaulay's only neighbour was the Duke of Argyll, known for his love of peace and quiet. At the centre of the house was its airy, light and spacious library with a classical, pillared recess, which opened directly onto a delightful garden. There was a large, sloping lawn graced by a pair of rare, variegated elm trees, a 'noble' willow, a mulberry tree and in 'abundance all that hollies, and laurels, and hawthorns, and groves of standard roses, and bowers of lilacs and laburnums could give of shade, and scent, and colour'.

It was the first time Macaulay had had a garden of his own, and he took to tending it with all the fanaticism of a new convert. 'How I love my little paradise of shrubs and turf!' he exclaimed. Although his health did not permit him to be a 'working gardener', he personally supervised the clearing of weeds and debris and the planting of new shrubs. 'I have just been putting creepers round my windows, and forming beds of rhododendrons round my fountain,' he wrote during his first

Christmas in the new house. 'In three or four summers, if I live so long, I may expect to see the results of my care.'[13] When he spotted dandelions in his borders, he could not resist attacking them himself. 'How I grabbed them up!' he told his young niece Alice. 'How I enjoyed their destruction! Is it Christian like to hate a dandelion so savagely?'[14]

In response to reports of a spate of burglaries in neighbouring Notting Hill, Macaulay overcame his dislike of canines to keep a fierce guard-dog and also installed the Victorian equivalent of a high-tech security system. He had alarm bells on all his shutters, crowned by 'a powerful alarm bell' on the roof with bell-ropes to all the main bedrooms. If the house were attacked, he assured his anxious sister, the whole neighbourhood would be roused, and his noble neighbours, the Duke of Argyll and Lord Holland, would rush to his aid.[15]

The move to his new surroundings and his interest in decorating the house and improving the garden seem to have lifted his spirits and improved his general health. 'I am wonderfully well,' he wrote, in an unusually cheerful letter. 'My sleep is deeper and sweeter than it has been for years . . . What a blessing to regain, so late, the refreshing sleep of early years! I am altogether better than I have been since 1852.'[16] He entertained often and very generously. 'The hospitality of Holly Lodge,' his nephew remarked, 'had about it a flavour of pleasant peculiarity.'[17] The food was ample and the wine cellar excellent, and the menus were often geared to esoteric Church feasts and fasts, with veal for Sunday dinner and goose on Michaelmas Day.

Macaulay was often confined indoors by a succession of bad coughs; but when his health permitted he attended occasional breakfast and dinner parties at the grand houses of the aristocracy and remained high on the royal guest list at Buckingham Palace and Windsor Castle. According to his journal, he was more often than not a reluctant guest at these august gatherings. One such entry noted that he had gone 'much against my will' to dinner at the palace, chatted to the Queen about an ongoing Cabinet reshuffle and been bored by the flood of compliments he received from the visiting King of Portugal, who was personally translating his *History* into Portuguese.[18] On another such occasion, he found the party 'more pleasant than usual', with the Queen 'very gracious' and chatting to him about *Jane Eyre*, which the royal couple were reading together.[19] But a year later, the palace figures as 'the dullest house in London', even though he was seated opposite the Queen and had his usual chats with her about historical books she was reading, such as Carlisle's biography of Frederic the Great and Catherine the Great's memoirs.[20]

Macaulay remained till the end of his life an ardent admirer of Prince Albert, whose intellectual rigour and strong opinions struck a chord with him, even though they made the Prince increasingly unpopular in political circles. He had staunchly defended the Prince from criticism that he was meddling in foreign policy in the run up to the Crimean War; and he maintained that such attacks were motivated by no more than cheap xenophobia, because of Albert's German origins, and that the Prince should simply ignore his critics.[21]

Despite his respect for the royal couple and his belief in constitutional monarchy, Macaulay was no servile courtier. Introduced to the Prince of Wales on one of his visits to Windsor, he was not impressed by the dubious privilege of being taken up to the prince's room by his tutor. 'Wretched work!' he exclaimed, having 'to stand before a boy of fourteen, sirring him and bowing to him . . . How much happier he would be with a more manly education'.[22]

~

Despite his retirement from active politics, Macaulay in his final years continued to have strong opinions on the major political issues of the day, especially in the sphere of foreign and imperial policy. He saw British intervention in the Crimea as defensive and legitimate and strongly supported Palmerston's alliance with the French against the Russians.[23]

His imperial pride rejoiced in what some called the gunboat diplomacy and others the liberal interventionism of Lord Palmerston, the Tony Blair of Victorian Britain. Palmerston, Macaulay lectured his teenaged nephew, had seen to it that 'an Englishman shall be as much respected as a Roman citizen'.[24] In private, Macaulay was critical of Palmerston for unnecessarily jumping into a second China war by backing up a trigger-happy Governor of Hong Kong; but he was even more hostile to the 'highly discreditable' anti-war alliance of opposition parties who had joined forces to bring down the government.[25]

Returned to power as Prime Minister in a general election, Palmerston chose to reward Macaulay's loyalty and talents with an entirely unexpected honour. 'A great day in my life . . . .,' Macaulay noted on August 28, 1857. 'I went . . . to dinner, and had hardly begun to eat when a messenger came with a letter from Palmerston. An offer of a peerage; the Queen's pleasure already taken. I was very much surprised. Perhaps no such offer was ever made, without the slightest solicitation, direct or indirect, to a man of humble origin and moderate fortune, who had long quitted public life.'[26] The recipient had no hesitation in accepting right away and went back to his dinner 'little discomposed'.

The peerage arrived on the eve of Macaulay's departure for a holiday in France. On his return a fortnight later, he was delighted to read how favourably the British press had been commenting on his elevation. 'There is a general cry of pleasure . . .,' he boasted in the privacy of his diary. 'I am truly gratified by finding how well I stand with the public, and gratified by finding that Palmerston has made a hit for himself in bestowing this dignity on me.'[27] Three days later, he was still gloating about 'my late elevation, which has been received by the public with more applause than anything of the sort since Wellington was made a Duke . . .'[28]

In memory of the Leicestershire country house where he had been born, he took ermine as Baron Macaulay of Rothley. Although he was proud of his title and sporadically attended debates in the Lords, he never spoke on the floor of the House. His health would not have permitted the physical and nervous strain that public speaking always caused him. In the summer of 1858, addressing a small gathering in Cambridge to accept the honorific title of its High Steward, Macaulay sadly announced: 'It is now five years since I raised my voice in public; and it is not likely—unless there be some special call of duty—that I shall ever raise it in public again.'[29]

~

Palmerston's offer of the peerage had coincided with news of the Cawnpore massacre of June 1857,* the worst of many atrocities on both sides of what came to be known either as the Mutiny or as India's First War of Independence. 'Very sad about India,' was Macaulay's comment in his diary. 'Not that I have any doubt about the result; but the news is heart-breaking. I went very low to dinner . . . God knows that the poor women at Delhi and Cawnpore are more in my thoughts than my coronet.'[30]

During the next months, he followed events in India with a

---

* Hundreds of British women and children were shot and drowned on the banks of the Ganges by the rebel leader, Nana Sahib.

passion and intensity that were as much personal as political. His letters and diaries were full of allusions to developments such as the rebel takeover of Delhi, the massacre of its European population, and its subsequent, equally bloody and vengeful recovery by the British. 'I am half ashamed,' he confessed in his diary after the Cawnpore massacre, 'of the craving for vengeance which I feel. I could be very cruel just now if I had the power.'[31] He was delighted by the arrest of the deposed King of Oudh, Wajid Ali Shah, who had been 'frightened out of his little wits' and had 'howled like a jackal'.[32] He wished for the massacre of the 'whole [rebel] garrison of Delhi, all the Moulavies and Mussulman Doctors there and all the accursed rabble of the bazaar . . .'[33] He dismissed a demand from the eccentric former Governor-General Lord Ellenborough that 'all the mutineers whose lives are spared should be made eunuchs', but only because of 'the utter impossibility of proposing such a thing in any English assembly'.[34] And he was jubilant when the tide in India finally turned in November 1857, with the fall of Delhi and the end of the last vestiges of the Mughal Empire: 'Huzza Good news—Lucknow relieved—Delhi ours—The scoundrel princes shot—the old dotard a prisoner*—God be praised!'[35]

'The Indian troubles have affected my spirits more than any public events in the whole course of my life,' Macaulay observed, surprised to find himself swept along by the mass fury of the British public and its lust for revenge, reading with delight of reprisals such as the blowing of captured sepoys from the mouths of cannons.[36] 'It is painful to be so revengeful as I feel myself,' he confessed. 'I really could at this moment commit acts such as I have thought monstrous when I read them . . . I

---

* A reference to the last, titular Mughal Emperor, Bahadur Shah Zafar, who was finally deposed while his sons were brutally shot before his eyes.

who cannot bear to see a beast or bird in pain, could look on without winking while Nana Sahib underwent all the tortures of Ravaillac.'*[37]

During the months that followed, the public outcry for revenge on the mutineers was accompanied by occasional doubts about whether the revolt had been provoked by too much British intervention in Indian religious and social customs. In February 1858, no less a person than Lord Ellenborough, whom Macaulay had once pilloried for Orientalist tendencies, moved the House of Lords for a debate on the responsibility of Christian missionaries for provoking the Indian backlash. Macaulay arrived at the House determined to break his long parliamentary silence with a speech rebutting Ellenborough; but his former adversary, 'taken aback by seeing me ready to reply', chickened out of a direct confrontation. 'I can only say that I was quite as much afraid of him as he could be of me,' Macaulay confided with relief to his diary, since public speaking had now become a major struggle of endurance for him.[38]

Macaulay's writings on the Mutiny, and his honest analysis of his own feelings about it, demonstrate that he was only too aware of how irrational anger and hatred could undermine the most deeply held belief in justice and humanity. The historian in him could not resist speculating about how the public appetite for violent retribution stirred up by the Mutiny would affect Britain's national character. 'The effect,' he concluded, 'will be partly good and partly bad. The effeminate mawkish philanthropy . . . will lose all its influence; and that is a very good

---

* Ravaillac, the assassin who killed Henri IV of France in 1610, suffered a particularly gruesome death, being torn apart by four horses after being scalded with burning sulphur, molten lead and boiling oil and having his flesh torn by pincers.

thing. The nerves of our minds will be braced. But shall we not hold human life generally cheaper than we have done? Having brought ourselves to exult in the misery of the guilty, shall we not feel less sympathy for the sufferings of the innocents?'[39] It was a prophetic anticipation of the massive civilian casualties that would be inflicted by the wars of the next century.

~

An American diplomat saw Macaulay cutting an impressive if eccentric figure at a Buckingham Palace reception in the spring of 1859, the last year of his life. He described him as 'a short, thickset man, with a face . . . in which thought and penetration are strongly marked . . . His chest is broad, his legs not so well adapted to his chest as they ought to be, his hair mixed with grey, his voice clear, his manners bland, and his expression intellectual and captivating . . . He was dressed in a naval blue uniform'.[40]

One can only speculate about the nature of the uniform, which is not mentioned anywhere in Macaulay's own papers. But the rest of the picture communicates the strong impact of his presence, even after the ravages of time and illness had accentuated what had always been an odd appearance, his lower half too short and slight for his large head and heavy torso.

Although he continued to impress observers on his increasingly rare public appearances, Macaulay was by now frail and easily tired. His original aim had been to bring his *History* up to his own times; but as he embarked on its fifth volume, it looked unlikely that he would complete even the reign of William III. He found it increasingly difficult to settle down to writing, the chief reason being, as he noted, 'the great doubt which I feel whether I shall live long enough to finish another volume of my book'.[41]

Although his articles for the *Edinburgh Review* and other journals had tapered off, he continued to write the occasional piece for *Encyclopaedia Britannica*. He also set himself memory tests and brain-teasers to keep his faculties well exercised. Strolling in his portico, he would memorize in two hours the full 400 lines of Act IV of *The Merchant of Venice*. Another day he could repeat from memory the entire membership of the House of Lords, adding for good measure a few days later the second titles of all the peers.[42] He kept up his German and Italian and enjoyed burying himself in financial calculations about the stock market and government spending estimates. He might even spend an evening calculating and comparing the average duration of the lives of Archbishops, Prime Ministers and Lord Chancellors.[43]

Whatever the occasion, Macaulay was rarely without a book in his hand, and his reading remained eclectic, including a surprisingly large number of light, popular novels. 'Some books which I never should dream of opening at dinner please me at breakfast, and vice versa,' he cheerfully confessed.[44] But Jane Austen remained unrivalled in his literary affections. 'If I could get materials,' he wrote, 'I really would write a short life of that wonderful woman, and raise a little money to put up a monument to her in Winchester Cathedral.'[45]

Macaulay was well cared for in his final years by the couple who had been his butler and cook/house-keeper for two decades. He prided himself on being a generous and considerate master, dining out at his club in all weathers to give them their Sunday evening off, planning long holidays for them and allowing them to invite their own relations to stay.[46] Even so, he chided himself for being irritable with those around him, blaming chronic illness for his mood swings. 'I have thought several times of late,' he wrote in his diary, 'that the last scene of the play was approaching; and I have been beginning to study it—I should wish to act it simply, but with fortitude and gentleness united.'[47] The curtain was about to come down sooner and far more abruptly than he had ever imagined.

~

Ever since the death of his sister Margaret twenty-four years ago, Macaulay's emotional life had centred on his other favourite sister Hannah Trevelyan, and by extension on her children. He had always been closer to his nieces than to his nephew. As George grew from adolescence to adulthood, first at Harrow and then at Macaulay's own alma mater, Trinity College, Cambridge, he showed an aptitude for the classics and a passion for history which should have endeared him to his uncle. But Macaulay's relations with him remained didactic, schoolmasterly and lacking in the humour and intimacy he shared with his favourite Baba, now happily married to the son of an old friend and living nearby with her husband.

A typical example was a long letter offering detailed criticisms of one of George's Latin compositions. Having complimented George on a Latin prose style 'so good and pure, . . . so redolent of Cicero', Macaulay could not resist asking: 'Are you not a little too fond of the subjunctive mood?'[48] When George went up to Cambridge in 1858, his uncle took the opportunity to renew his own ties with the university and paid him frequent visits, usually with his beloved sister and nieces in tow. On occasions such as these, after 'a sumptuous college breakfast, sausages, kidneys, broiled fowls',[49] Macaulay enjoyed regaling the assembled undergraduates with 'his stores of information on the history, customs and traditions of the University'.[50]

Visits like these emphasized the contrast between his

undimmed intellect and memory and his all too obvious physical decline. 'It was already apparent,' his nephew sadly recorded, 'that a journey across Clare bridge, and along the edge of the great lawn at King's, performed at the rate of half a mile in the hour, was an exertion too severe for his feeble frame.'[51] And yet the blow that finished him would be emotional rather than physical.

Twenty years ago, faced with the terrible prospect of life without Hannah, Macaulay had succeeded in getting her husband, Charles Trevelyan, a plum civil service job in London to lure him away from a career in India. But Trevelyan, like the curry-loving Nabobs whom Macaulay loved to mock, had struck roots in India that threatened to draw him back. In the autumn of 1853, Macaulay first heard rumours that Trevelyan might be offered the post of Governor of Madras. 'It would be madness in him to go,' he noted in his journal, but doubted that the offer would materialize.[52] His wish was answered, and nothing came of the rumour. And then, suddenly, five years later, the offer returned as a firm invitation, and Trevelyan—without a second thought—promptly accepted.

Macaulay's journal is a poignant record of his own sense of tragedy and doom as his brother-in-law's plans unfolded. On January 6, 1859, Trevelyan arrived alone at Holly Lodge to tell Macaulay he had been offered the Madras Governorship, wanted to accept it, but was proposing to leave Hannah behind in London. For Macaulay, it was like hearing a death sentence and a reprieve all at once. 'If she were to go, I should die of a broken heart . . .' he wrote about the prospect of parting from Hannah. 'But, if she is to stay, the question is very different. For much as I value and love him [Trevelyan], his society is not necessary to me.' But when Hannah arrived a few hours later, distraught at the prospect of losing her husband, Macaulay felt less secure. 'Everything must be done to prevent him going,' he noted. 'With her, or without her, it is madness, destruction, misery.'[53]

Two days later, the decision had been made. 'All is over,' Macaulay lamented. 'Go he will—a madman—I can hardly command my indignation. Yet what good can I do by expressing it?'[54] Yet express it he did the next day when Trevelyan and young George came to call, but to no avail.[56] 'Between ambition and public spirit,' an exasperated Macaulay wrote of his stubborn brother-in-law, 'he is as much excited, and as unfit to be reasoned with, as if he had drunk three bottles of Champagne.'[56]

Only a month later, they were saying tearful farewells as Trevelyan prepared to take ship for India. 'You have always been a most kind brother to me,' he assured Macaulay, apparently oblivious to the anguish he was causing him. 'Shall we ever meet again?' was Macaulay's sad response in his diary. 'I do not expect it . . . Another sharp winter would probably finish me.'[57]

His bitterness was enhanced by the fact that everyone outside the family circle 'fancies that we must be in raptures, and pesters us with congratulations'.[58] His only consolation was the thought that Hannah would be staying behind. 'Trevelyan will not hear of Hannah's going,' he wrote with relief to his other sister Fanny, 'and there he is quite right. It would be monstrous to deprive the children . . . of both parents at the very moment when parental affection is most needed.' But Baba, now happily married, and George, up at Cambridge, were hardly in need of parental care; and that left only young Alice.

By the summer of 1859, Hannah, who had never before been parted from her husband, was beginning to have second thoughts about their enforced separation. She began to talk of joining him in India in the autumn of 1860, a prospect which filled her brother with the deepest gloom. 'Yet what weakness,' he chided himself, 'to be crying in May 1859 for what will not happen till November 1860. How many events may long before November 1860 confound all our calculations.'[59]

Determined to make the most of having them to himself, Macaulay spent the summer of 1859 travelling in the Lake District and the Scottish highlands with Hannah and Alice. Wherever he went, he was treated with awe, reverence and hospitality so generous that he found it embarrassing. One frequent form of honouring him, we are told, was for hotels to serve up special dinners to his party and refuse any payment.[60] 'He was quickly recognized on steamers and at railway stations,' Hannah recorded with satisfaction; and the Scots, who considered him one of their own, were particularly enthusiastic.[61] According to his nephew George, who joined them for part of the trip, Macaulay 'was still the same agreeable travelling companion that we had always known him; . . . with the same readiness to please and be pleased, and the same sweet and even temper', although 'there sometimes was a touch of melancholy about his conversation'.[62]

His melancholia deepened dramatically in October, when Hannah, pining more than ever for her husband, announced that she would be bringing forward her departure to February 1860. It is a measure of how devastating she knew her decision to be that she conveyed it to Macaulay in a letter and not in person. 'She gives good reasons . . . ,' he noted in his diary. 'But though I cannot deny that it is right, I feel the blow dreadfully. I walked mournfully in the verandah till past ten musing.'[63]

Ten days later, he began his fifty-ninth year with a bad toothache and even more painful emotions. 'I am entering on a dark sad year,' he wrote. 'My health indeed is improved— my fortunes are flourishing. I have rank, wealth, fame and what are they worth? I wish that I were dead . . . I have had many happy returns. Those which remain are likely to be few and evil.'[64] Though he struggled to appear cheerful, he found himself constantly on the verge of tears in Hannah's company and unable to enjoy the time he had left with her. 'I dread the next four months more than even the months which will follow the separation,' he confided to his friend Ellis. 'This prolonged parting—this slow sipping of the vinegar and the gall—is terrible.'[65] He took refuge in his library, with books as his main anodyne, and tried to distract himself by a renewed assault on the reign of William III in his now languishing and neglected *History*.

'I am sick of life,' Macaulay remarked on the 3rd of December. 'I could wish to lie down to sleep and never wake.'[66] During the next three weeks, as a frosty winter set in, it looked as though he was dying quite literally of a broken heart. His diary is full of entries about chest pains, rheumatism, loss of appetite, sleeplessness, weakness and breathlessness. 'I could hardly use my razor for the palpitation of the heart,' he wrote on the 19th of December. 'I feel as if I were twenty years older since last Thursday, as if I were dying of old age. I am perfectly ready, and shall never be readier. It is a great thing to be emancipated from the fear of death . . . As soon as life becomes utterly waste and dull and dreary, death ceases to be a bugbear.'[67]

Two days later, Hannah and her children all came to dinner at Holly Lodge, and Macaulay felt well enough to enjoy their company. The doctors, he said, had diagnosed heart failure, but happily he was 'sensible of no intellectual decay, not the smallest'.[69] The thought of senility was clearly far more frightening to him than any physical decline. His last diary entry, on the 23rd of December, cheerfully refers to a narrow escape from death that morning when the ceiling above his lavatory collapsed just after he had finished using it.[69] His last letter, written two days later to Thomas Ellis, describes a fainting fit two days earlier: 'I . . . lay quite insensible. I wish that I had continued to do so. For if death be no more—Up I got however . . .'[70]

Christmas Day, 1859, found Macaulay physically weak and emotionally very depressed. Hannah spent the day with him, and the rest of the family came for Christmas dinner. 'He talked very little, and was constantly dropping asleep . . . ,' Hannah later wrote. 'When we were alone together, he gave way to so much emotion that, while he was so weak, I rather avoided being with him.'[71] With Hannah's departure for India now less than two months away, the family put his symptoms down to mental rather than physical distress.

On the morning of the 28th of December, Macaulay signed his name for the last time—on a charitable donation of £25 to an indigent curate who had appealed for help. Later that afternoon, his nephew George arrived, intending to stay with him for dinner. He found his uncle in the library, 'sitting with his head bent forward on his chest, in a languid and drowsy reverie', with a short story by Thackeray lying open before him. George's attempts at conversation only succeeded in eliciting 'painful and pathetic reflections which altogether destroyed his self-command'.[72]

George hurried back home to tell his mother things were worse; and she decided to spend the night at Holly Lodge to be near her brother. As she made her preparations, a servant arrived with 'an urgent summons' to come at once. 'As we drove up to the porch of my uncle's house,' George later recorded, 'the maids ran crying out into the darkness to meet us, and we knew that all was over.' They found him seated in his beloved library in his easy chair, dressed as usual, with his book on the table beside him, still open at the same page. Moments before he died, he had told his butler that he was very tired and wished to go to bed early. He tried to get up, sat down again and ceased to breathe.

'He died as he had always wished to die,' George gratefully observed, 'without pain; without any formal farewell; preceding to the grave all whom he loved . . .'[73] But his mother was inconsolable. 'We have lost,' she wrote, 'the light of our home . . . What he was to me for fifty years how can I tell? What a world of love he poured out on me and mine! The blank, the void he has left, – filling, as he did, so entirely both heart and intellect, . . . no one can understand. For who ever knew such a life as mine, passed as the cherished companion of such a man?'[74]

It was the lament of a bereaved lover, rather than a sister; and she must have suffered all the more for the knowledge that the impending separation from her had undoubtedly hastened his end and darkened his final months. Her son chose to look on the bright side. 'Our great comfort,' he wrote to a relative, 'is in the knowledge that my dear uncle was taken at a time when his happiness was already overclouded by the shadow of a great sorrow: my mother's separation from him he always feared more than death. Never did I witness greater mental agony than he suffered since she declared her intention of joining my father.'[75]

~

Macaulay had achieved the distinction of becoming a legend in his lifetime; and his status as a national treasure had been enhanced in recent years by his frail health and rare public appearances. Above all else, he was recognized as a key architect of the empire that had now been officially proclaimed. As a result of his civil service reforms, the old East India Company training college at Haileybury had been wound up; and a new generation of imperial administrators was being recruited from Britain's leading universities. In India itself, the suppression of the Mutiny and the replacement of Company rule by the British Crown seemed like a vindication of Macaulay's Westernising policies and the launch of an era in which the English language and its literature spread like wildfire across hundreds of new Indian schools and universities.

Writing two decades later, George Trevelyan estimated that English-speaking Indians now numbered hundreds of thousands, with more than 6,000 students in higher education, 200,000 in secondary schooling and nearly 7,000 training as teachers. More than 4,000 works of Western literature and science were being published each year across the subcontinent; the Government of India's education budget had multiplied more than seventyfold since Macaulay's time in Calcutta; and it was being generously supplemented by the philanthropy of a new generation of wealthy Indians who were busily endowing new schools and colleges.[76]

Back at Westminster Abbey, on a cold January morning, a solemn procession carried Macaulay to his honoured last resting place in Poet's Corner. The pall was carried by an impressive array of dignitaries, including the Duke of Argyll, Prime Minister Lord John Russell, the Lord Chancellor and the Speaker of the House of Commons. 'A beautiful sunrise . . .,' wrote one aristocratic pall-bearer. 'The whole service and ceremony were in the highest degree solemn and impressive. All befitted the man and the occasion.'[77] There he remains, buried near the west wall of the South Transept, among many of the other authors and poets whom he had so avidly read and admired.

Epilogue

High up in a Delhi tower-block, in the living room of a leading Dalit intellectual, Macaulay's portrait hangs proudly beside that of Dr B.R. Ambedkar, the brilliant academic who led the 'Untouchable' political and social revival during the first half of the twentieth century. There is a strong facial resemblance between the two men, but the similarities do not end there. Ambedkar, like Macaulay whom he greatly admired, was a classical liberal who believed that India's future lay, not with nationalist revivals of the past, but with the wholehearted adoption of Western education and institutions.

Ambedkar's own personal trajectory embodies the benefits which Macaulay believed that enlightened British rule would bring to the subcontinent. Though he was born into a very poor Dalit family, his father was a soldier in the British Indian army and managed to get his son into the village school, despite strong upper-caste hostility. A decade later, Ambedkar was the first Dalit to enrol at Bombay University, joining Elphinstone College, which had been founded to promote the Western education that Macaulay had advocated for young Indians. From there, Ambedkar, supported by scholarships from the enlightened, Western-oriented Gaekwad of Baroda, went on to a distinguished postgraduate career at Columbia University in New York and later took his doctorate from the London School of Economics and also a Bar degree at Gray's Inn.

He never forgot his debt to the Western institutions and values which had offered him a ladder out of caste oppression. Unlike his upper caste Congress contemporaries, who symbolically abandoned their Savile Row suits for homespun Indian clothing, Ambedkar was always attired in a suit and tie and, like Macaulay, is pictured waving a book in his hand in the many public statues and portraits of him. While Congress nationalists led by Gandhi and Nehru boycotted the legislatures of the Raj and insisted on full independence, Ambedkar was happy to cooperate with the gradualist, democratic reforms of the colonial authorities and embrace the opportunities they offered for acquiring Western education, science and technology. And when Independence arrived in 1947, he played a prominent role in India's Constituent Assembly, especially in the drafting and adoption of a Chapter of Fundamental Rights, which enshrined key elements of the British Whig tradition, such as the rights to free speech, to ownership of property and to equality before the law.

Macaulay would have been proud to have Ambedkar as his political heir; and he would have been both pleased and amused by the way that Westminster and Whitehall rituals still survive in the far more rowdy and chaotic parliaments of the Indian Republic. More than anything else, he would have been delighted with the rapid growth of the huge, Western-educated middle class that has made India the world's second largest English-speaking country, close on the heels of the United States. And he would have seen that middle class as the best hope for India's future both as a political democracy and also as an economic superpower.

What might have surprised Macaulay is that the spread of English across the Indian subcontinent has happened in spite of the resistance, or at best indifference, of the Indian state and in the teeth of fierce opposition from cultural and regional chauvenists like India's new Prime Minister, Narendra Modi. Macaulay's own policy of government funding for English-medium education was reversed after Independence, with state funding directed instead to the regional vernacular languages and the official national language, Hindi, which only a minority of India's population actually spoke. As Macaulay would have anticipated, the attempt to replace English triggered decades of serious linguistic conflict in the subcontinent, with major political campaigns, often violent, to re-draw the boundaries of Indian states on linguistic lines. The regional vernaculars became the languages of state governments; but in practice this made little difference to the popularity of English, both as an indispensable link language and as a passport out of poverty. Especially in urban areas, the Indian masses have continued to vote with their feet, preferring to pay higher fees for English-medium, private schooling rather than go to state schools which teach in Indian languages.

Macaulay would probably have been appalled by the very poor standard of English taught in most Indian schools and colleges, and especially in the language academies which churn out the many thousands of new trainees required for the call centres and back offices outsourced by Western companies. But language for him was only a means to an end. He would have welcomed the fact that the vast majority of India's 125 million English-speakers, a number rapidly growing, know it as a second language which they can use to access global knowledge and ideas, even while they retain their vernacular mother tongues.

Macaulay would have seen a parallel here with the way that

the European educated classes once used Latin and Greek to access classical learning and enrich their own native languages and literature. Ramchandra Guha, one of India's leading contemporary historian, writes:

> Something like this has indeed happened. Far from being destroyed, the vernacular languages have flourished and developed, in colonial times through the advent of the printing press, and since Independence through the creation of linguistic States. But English remains indispensable for technical education and as a means of inter-State communication. The software revolution in India might never have happened had it not been for Macaulay's Minute. And India might not have still been united had it not been for that Minute either. For, it was the existence and availability of English that allowed the States of south India to successfully resist the imposition of Hindi upon them.[1]

He might have added that the survival of a pan-Indian judiciary and civil service would also have been impossible without Macaulay's legacies. Hindi, though officially the national language, remains at best the most widely spoken regional language, largely confined to the most populous and backward states of north-central India. After more than sixty years of Independence, English survives intact as the language of the higher civil service and law courts, of medicine, science and higher education. Not even the most vocal regional chauvinists seriously believe that English will ever be supplanted in those upper echelons; and most of them see no contradiction in sending their own children to English-medium schools while making largely symbolic, populist demands to replace English road and shop signs with local languages. In creative writing, too, English has now firmly settled in as an indigenous Indian language, in much the same way as Persian and Arabic were assimilated into Urdu during the Mughal period. Macaulay might have disapproved of hybrid 'Hinglish' as we know it, but probably no more than he would have disliked the Americanization of his imperial mother tongue.

For Macaulay, an English education for India's ruling elites had been only the first step in a far wider diffusion of modern learning to the largely illiterate mass of the subcontinent's population. He had correctly predicted that the English language would be the key to success in a globalized knowledge economy. And he would almost certainly have lamented the fact that, almost two centuries later, Indian English, like medieval Latin in Europe, remains the preserve of the wealthiest 12 per cent of the population who can afford to pay for it. He would probably have blamed the Indian state for its failure to provide free and equal access to English, in much the same way as he castigated the Orientalists of his own day for their backward-looking revivalism.

In the international sphere, Macaulay always regarded the Russians as semi-Asiatic barbarians who were badly in need of Europeanization, and Putin's Russia would have confirmed his worst prejudices. He would no doubt have been equally worried about the rise of China to superpower status. Even way back in the 1840s, he was wary of Chinese claims to cultural exclusiveness and what he perceived as their xenophobia and racial arrogance. Of course, he saw no contradiction in similar Anglo-Saxon claims to superiority, because the latter were grounded in the liberal values of the Whig Enlightenment.

It's no accident that the language of Western interventionism in our own time, whether from Margaret Thatcher, Tony Blair,

David Cameron or Barack Obama, often echoes the splendid, imperial rhetoric of Macaulay's speeches and minutes way back in the 1830s. What he would have made of today's Western powers is hard to imagine. The Americans he regarded as ungrateful offspring, the French as spoilt brats and the Germans as dull workaholics. It's unlikely that he would see them very differently today. He would no doubt lament Britain's decline to second-class status; but it's safe to assume that he would be firmly on the side of liberal interventions by the West wherever possible and an enthusiastic exporter of the 'soft power' through which Western values and institutions permeate the rest of the world via the English language and global media.

Notes

1. Clever Tom

1. *Times of India*, October 26, 2006.
2. Sir George Otto Trevelyan, *The Life & Letters of Lord Macaulay* (Longmans, Green and Co., London, 1900), p. 18.
3. Trevelyan, Ibid.
4. Margaret Knutsford, *Life and Letters of Zachary Macaulay* (London, 1900), p. 8.
5. Trevelyan, op. cit. p. 8.
6. Ibid., p. 10.
7. Ibid., p. 18.
8. Ibid., p. 19.
9. John Clive, *Thomas Babington Macaulay* (Secker & Warburg, London, 1973), p. 21.
10. Trevelyan, op. cit., p. 19.
11. Clive, op. cit., p. 23.
12. Trevelyan, op. cit., p. 20.
13. Ibid., pp. 21–22.
14. Ibid., p. 26.
15. Ibid., pp. 23–26.
16. Ibid., p. 21.
17. *The Early Mental Traits of Three Hundred Geniuses* (Stanford University Press, 1926), pp. 690 and 149.

18. Thomas Babington Macaulay, *Letters*, Volume I, Cambridge Univeristy Press, 1974–81, p. 35, to Selena Macaulay, September 9, 1813.

19. Trevelyan, op. cit., p. 40

20. Macaulay, op. cit., p. 21, to Selina Macaulay, March 8, 1813.

21. Ibid., p. 22, to Selina Macaulay, March 17, 1813.

22. Ibid., p. 23, to Zachary Macaulay, March 23, 1813.

23. Ibid., p. 26, to Selina Macaulay, April 19, 1813.

24. Ibid., p. 30, to Zachary Macaulay, May 8, 1813.

25. Ibid., p. 78, May 14, 1816.

26. Ibid., p. 94, November 28, 1817.

27. Margaret Macaulay, *Recollections*, p. 32, quoted in Clive, op. cit., p. 32.

28. Letter from Zachary Macaulay, February 22, 1815, Trinity College, Cambridge, Manuscripts.

29. Trevelyan, op. cit., p. 54.

30. Ibid., pp. 56–57.

31. Idem.

32. Clive, op. cit., p. 43.

33. Macaulay, op. cit., p. 133, to Zachary Macaulay, September 1819.

34. Ibid., pp. 140–1, January 5, 1820.

35. Trevelyan, op. cit., p. 169.

36. Zachary Macaulay to Hannah More, July 12, 1820, quoted in Clive, op. cit., p. 46.

37. John Moultrie, *Poems,* Volume I (London 1876), pp. 421–22, quoted in Clive, op. cit., p. 47.

38. Thomas Babington Macaulay, *Letters*, Volume II, Cambridge University Press, 1974–81, p. 81, to Hannah Macaulay, July 30, 1831.

39. Clive, op. cit., p. 56.

40. Macaulay, op. cit., Volume I, pp. 189–90, to Charles Knight, June 20, 1823.

41. Trevelyan, op. cit., p. 72.

42. Macaulay, op. cit., p. 175, to Zachary Macaulay, July 26, 1822.

43. Trevelyan, op. cit., p. 41.

2. The Making of a Whig

1. Trevelyan, op. cit., p. 56, note 1.
2. Lady Hannah Trevelyan, 'Reminiscences', Trinity College Manuscripts, quoted in Clive, op. cit., p. 62.
3. Thomas Babington Macaulay, *The Works of Lord Macaulay* (London, Longmans, Green & Co., 1898), Volume XI, pp. 371–73, 'Mitford's History of Greece'.
4. Trevelyan, op. cit., p. 80.
5. Ibid., pp. 80–82.
6. *Proceedings of the First Anniversary Meeting of the Anti-Slavery Society* (1824), pp. 71–76, quoted in Catherine Hall, 'Troubling Memories', *Transactions of the Royal Historical Society* (Cambridge, 2011), p. 163.
7. Trevelyan, op. cit. pp. 85–86.
8. Macaulay, op. cit., Volume VII, pp. 42–43.
9. Ibid, p. 449, 'Utilitarian Theory of Government', 1829.
10. Ibid., 'The London University', 1826.
11. Ibid., Volume VII, p. 367, 'Mill's Essay on Government', 1829.
12. Trevelyan, op. cit., p. 106.
13. Macaulay, op. cit., Volume VIII, p. 207, 'Burleigh and his Times', April 1832.
14. *Edinburgh Review*, Volume XLV, 1827, pp. 383–423 and 388–389.
15. Macaulay, op. cit., p. 1, 'Civil Disabilities of the Jews', 1831.
16. Macaulay, op. cit., Volume VII, pp. 221 and 528, Volume VIII, p. 56.
17. Speech to the House of Commons, February 6, 1833, on Irish Coercion Bill, Macaulay, op. cit., Volume XI, p. 526.
18. Lady Hannah Trevelyan, quoted in Trevelyan, op. cit., p. 101.
19. Hansard, Volume XXIII, pp. 1308–1314, April 5, 1830.
20. Margaret Macaulay, *Recollections*, p. 10.
21. Macaulay, *Letters*, Volume II, p. 41, to Hannah Macaulay, June 13 and 24, 1831.
22. Ibid., p. 9, to Thomas Flower Ellis, March 30, 1831.

23. Clive, op. cit., pp. 158–159.
24. Blackwood's, August 1831, quoted in Clive, op. cit., p. 163.
25. Margaret Macaulay, *Recollections*, pp. 44 and 90.
26. Trevelyan, op. cit., pp. 123–125.
27. Macaulay, op. cit., p. 65, to Hannah Macaulay, July 8, 1831.
28. Macaulay, *Works*, Volume XI, pp. 425–426.
29. Speech on September 6, 1832, quoted in Clive, op. cit., p. 221.
30. Trevelyan, op. cit., p. 204.
31. Lord Greville, quoted in Clive, op. cit., p. 238.
32. Ibid., p. 239.
33. Ibid., pp. 244–245.
34. Margaret Macaulay, op. cit., p. 52, quoted in Clive, op. cit., p. 252.
35. Macaulay, *Letters*, Volume II, p. 28, to Hannah Macaulay, June 1, 1831.
36. Ibid., p. 255, June 14, 1833.
37. Ibid., p. 276, July 22, 1833.

3. Brotherly Love

1. Lytton Strachey, *Portraits in Miniature and other Essays* (New York, 1931), p. 177, and J.H. Plumb, *Men and Centuries* (Boston, 1963), p. 255.
2. Trevelyan, op. cit., p. 128.
3. Margaret Macaulay, *Recollections*, p. 39, May 31, 1831, quoted in Trevelyan, op. cit., p. 133.
4. Ibid.
5. Ibid., quoted in Trevelyan, op. cit., pp. 130–132.
6. Ibid., p. 132, March 24, 1831.
7. Ibid., p. 39, May 21, 1831.
8. Macaulay, *Letters*, Volume II, pp. 133–134, to Hannah and Margaret Macaulay, June 18, 1832.
9. Ibid., p. 69, to Hannah Macaulay, July 13, 1831.
10. Ibid., p. 148, to Hannah and Margaret Macaulay, July 6, 1832.
11. Hannah to T.G. Babington, April 19, 1830, quoted in Clive, op. cit., p. 272.

12. Margaret to Hannah Macaulay, January 28, 1833, quoted in Clive, op. cit., p. 276.
13. Macaulay, op. cit., pp. 210–211, to Hannah Macaulay, December 12, 1832.
14. Trevelyan, op. cit., p. 207.
15. Macaulay, op. cit., pp. 203–204, to Margaret Macaulay, November 26, 1832.
16. Ibid., p. 122, to Hannah and Margaret Macaulay, June 7, 1832.
17. Ibid., p. 129, to Hannah and Margaret Macaulay, June 10, 1832.
18. Ibid.
19. Ibid., p. 242, to Hannah Macaulay, May 21, 1833.
20. Ibid., p. 133, to Hannah and Margaret Macaulay, June 18, 1832.
21. Ibid., p. 47, to Hannah Macaulay, June 20, 1831.
22. *Edinburgh Review*, March 1827.
23. Owen Dudley Edwards, *Macaulay* (Weidenfeld & Nicolson, London, 1988).
24. Macaulay, op. cit., p. 268, to Hannah Macaulay, 11 July 1833.
25. Macaulay, *Works*, Volume XI, pp. 567–586, speech to the House of Commons, July 10, 1833.
26. Macaulay, *Letters*, Volume II, pp. 272–274, to Margaret Macaulay (now Mrs Edward Cropper), July 17, 1833, and to Hannah Macaulay, July 22, 1833.
27. Ibid., p. 301, to Hannah Macaulay, August 17, 1833.
28. Ibid., pp. 353–354, to Lord Lansdowne, December 5, 1833.
29. Ibid., to Hannah Macaulay, December 23, 1833.
30. Ibid., p. 301, August 17, 1833.
31. Ibid.
32. Ibid.
33. Ibid., p. 304, August 21, 1833.
34. Ibid., p. 332, November 2, 1833.
35. Ibid., p. 322, October 21, 1833.
36. Ibid., p. 328, October 31 and November 1, 1833.
37. Ibid.
38. Ibid., pp. 338–340, November 22, 1833.
39. Ibid., pp. 339–340.

40. Rev. Frederick Arnold, *The Public Life of Lord Macaulay* (London, 1862), p. 184.

41. Macaulay, op. cit., p. 340, to Hannah, November 22, 1833.

42. Ibid., p. 363, December 18, 1833.

43. Ibid., p. 350, December 5, 1833.

44. Ibid., pp. 365–366, December 21, 1833.

45. Ibid., p. 6, January 2, 1834, to Hannah Macaulay.

46. Macaulay, op. cit., p. 355, December 6, 1833, to Hannah Macaulay.

47. Ibid, p. 362, December 18, 1833.

48. Ibid.

49. Macaulay, op. cit., Volume III, p. 9, to Hannah, January 4, 1833.

50. Ibid., p. 352, to McAvey Napier, December 5, 1833.

51. Ibid., p. 26, to Zachary Macaulay, February 16, 1834.

52. Ibid., p. 25, footnote quoting letter from Hannah to Margaret Macaulay, February 16, 1834.

53. Ibid., p. 8, to Margaret Macaulay Cropper, January 2, 1834.

54. Ibid., p. 17, February 3, 1834.

4. Mangoes and Maharajas

1. Clive, op. cit., p. 290.

2. Trevelyan, op. cit., p. 262.

3. Macaulay, op. cit., p. 62, to Thomas Flower Ellis, July 1, 1834.

4. Ibid., p. 32, to Margaret Macaulay Cropper, June 15, 1834.

5. Ibid.

6. Macaulay, 'Warren Hastings', *Edinburgh Review*, Volume LXXIV, October 1841, pp. 160–255.

7. Ibid., p. 39.

8. Macaulay, *Letters*, Volume III, p. 62, to Thomas Flower Ellis, July 1, 1834.

9. Macaulay, 'Warren Hastings', *Edinburgh Review*, Volume LXXIV, October 1841, pp. 160–255.

10. Macaulay, *Letters*, Volume III, p. 42, to Margaret Macaulay Cropper, June 27, 1834.

11. Ibid.

12. Ibid., p. 60, to Thomas Ellis, July 1, 1834.

13. Ibid., p. 57, to Margaret Macaulay Cropper, June 27, 1834.

14. Thomas Babington Macaulay, *Lord Clive* (Longmans, London, 1851).

15. Macaulay, *Letters,* Volume III, pp. 54–57, to Margaret Macaulay Cropper, June 27, 1834.

16. Macaulay, *Lord Clive.*

17. Macaulay, *Letters,* Volume III, p. 50, to Margaret Macaulay Cropper, June 27, 1834.

18. Ibid., pp. 51–52.

19. Ibid., p. 32, June 15, 1834.

20. Ibid., p. 44, June 27, 1834.

21. Ibid., p. 83, October 3, 1834.

22. Ibid., p. 58, June 27, 1834.

23. Ibid., p. 59.

24. Ibid., p. 62, to Thomas Ellis, July 1, 1834.

25. Idem.

26. Ibid., p. 68, to Margaret Macaulay Cropper, August 10, 1834.

27. Idem.

28. Idem.

29. Ibid., p. 64, July 6, 1834.

30. Ibid., p. 67, August 10, 1834.

31. Ibid., p. 64, July 6, 1834.

32. Trevelyan, op. cit., p. 273.

33. Macaulay, op. cit., p. 77, to Margaret Macaulay Cropper, October 3, 1834.

34. Ibid., p. 79.

35. Ibid., p. 82.

36. Ibid., p. 84.

37. Ibid., p. 86.

38. Ibid,. p. 87.

39. Ibid., p. 109, to McAvey Napier, December 10, 1834.

40. Ibid., pp. 90–91, to Margaret Macaulay Cropper, October 17, 1834.

41. Ibid., p. 39, June 15, 1834.
42. Ibid., pp. 90–96, October 17, 1834.
43. Ibid., p. 93.
44. Ibid., p. 88, October 3, 1834.

5. Love, Death and Reform

1. Macaulay, *Letters*, Volume III, p. 93, to Margaret Macaulay Cropper, October 17, 1834.
2. Ibid., p. 94.
3. Ibid., to Thomas Flower Ellis, December 15, 1834.
4. Trevelyan, op. cit., p. 314.
5. Macaulay, op. cit., p. 95, to Margaret Macaulay Cropper, October 17, 1834.
6. Ibid., p. 84, October 3, 1834.
7. Ibid., p. 118, to Lord Lansdowne, December 27, 1834.
8. Ibid., p. 98, to Selena and Frances Macaulay, October 19, 1834.
9. Ibid., January 1, 1836.
10. Ibid., p. 99, to Margaret Macaulay Cropper, December 7, 1834.
11. Letter from Hannah to Fanny Macaulay, February 1834, quoted in Clive, op. cit., p. 284.
12. Ibid., p. 282, Letter from Margaret to Hannah Macaulay, May 28, 1834.
13. Macaulay, op. cit., pp. 99–106, to Margaret Macaulay Cropper, December 7, 1834.
14. Idem.
15. Ibid., p. 117, to Selina and Frances Macaulay, December 26, 1834.
16. Ibid., p. 114, to Margaret Macaulay Cropper, December 24, 1834.
17. Hannah Macaulay Trevelyan, op. cit., pp. 62–63, quoted in Macaulay, *Letters*, Volume III, p. 116, notes.
18. Macaulay, op. cit., pp. 115–116, to Margaret Macaulay Cropper, December 24, 1834.
19. Idem.
20. Ibid., p. 119, to Lord Lansdowne, December 27, 1834.
21. Hannah Macaulay Trevelyan, op. cit.

6. A Battle for Minds

1. Trevelyan, op. cit., p. 270.
2. Macaulay, *Letters*, Volume III, p. 119, to Lord Lansdowne, December 27, 1834.
3. Lady Hannah Trevelyan, 'Reminiscences', p. 60, quoted in Clive, op. cit., p. 316.
4. Macaulay, 'Warren Hastings', *Edinburgh Review*, Volume LXXIV, October 1841, pp. 160–255.
5. Clive, op. cit., p. 347.
6. Macaulay, *Letters*, Volume III, p. 198, to Selena and Frances Macaulay, November 28, 1836.
7. Raja Ram Mohan Roy to Lord Amherst, November 12 and December 11, 1823, quoted in H. Sharp, *Selections from Educational Records* (Calcutta, 1920), pp. 99–100.
8. Bruce T. McCully, *English Education and the Origins of Indian Nationalism* (New York, 1940), p. 62.
9. Charles Trevelyan, *The Application of the Roman Alphabet to All the Oriental Languages* (Serampore, 1834), p. 13.
10. Ibid., p. 24.
11. Ibid., pp. 37–8, Letter dated January 4, 1834.
12. Clive, op. cit., p. 364, quoting Salahuddin Ahmed, *Bengal*, pp. 152–153.
13. Macaulay, op. cit., pp. 122–123, to John Tytler, January 28, 1835.
14. Macaulay, *Selected Writings* (Chicago, 1973), edited by John Clive and Thomas Pinney, pp. 237–250, Minute on Indian Education, February 2, 1835.
15. Macaulay, *Letters*, Volume III, pp. 138–139, to Lord William Bentinck, February 27, 1834.
16. Resolution of March 7, 1835, Sharp, *Educational Records*, p. 130.
17. Macaulay, *Selected Writings*, pp. 237–250, Minute on Indian Education.
18. Macaulay, *Letters*, Volume III, pp. 148–9, to James Mill, August 24, 1835.

19. Ibid., p. 136, to Richard Sharp, February 11, 1835.
20. Ibid., p. 158, to Thomas Ellis, December 30, 1835.
21. Clive, op. cit., p. 301.

7. Educating India

1. Macaulay, op. cit., p. 156, Letter to Selena and Frances Macaulay, September 15, 1835.
2. Ibid., p. 159, to Thomas Ellis, December 30, 1835.
3. Ibid., p. 162, to Selena and Frances Macaulay, January 1, 1836.
4. Ibid., p. 173, to Selena and Frances Macaulay, May 9, 1836.
5. Ibid., p. 161, January 1, 1836.
6. Ibid., p. 173, May 9, 1836.
7. Ibid., p. 175, to Thomas Ellis, May 30, 1836.
8. Ibid., p. 173, to Selena and Frances Macaulay, May 9, 1836.
9. Ibid.
10. Ibid., p. 166, to Thomas Spring-Rice, M.P., February 8, 1836.
11. Ibid., p. 175, to Thomas Ellis, May 30, 1836.
12. Lady Hannah Trevelyan, 'Reminiscences', p. 60, quoted in Clive, op. cit., p. 316.
13. Macaulay, op. cit., p. 170, to Thomas Spring-Rice, February 8, 1836.
14. Evidence of James Mill, February 21, 1832, *Parliamentary Papers*, IX, pp. 55–57, quoted in Clive, op. cit., pp. 352–353.
15. Macaulay, op. cit., pp. 148–149, to James Mill, August 24, 1835.
16. Previous Communication, 1836, India Public Department: 'Recent Changes in Native Education'. Revenue, Judicial and Legislative Committee, Miscellaneous Papers, IX, India Office Library, quoted in Clive, op. cit., pp. 384–386.
17. Sir John Cam Hobhouse to Lord Auckland, December 15, 1836, Home and Miscellaneous, Volume 837, India Office Library, quoted in Clive, op. cit., p. 392.
18. Letter to Henry Taylor, Mineka and Lindley, *Later Mill Letters*, XVII, 1969–70, quoted in Clive, op. cit., p. 389.
19. Macaulay, op. cit., p. 172, to Zachary Macaulay, May 2, 1836.

20. Trevelyan, op. cit., pp. 292–293.

21. Macaulay, op. cit., p. 193, to Zachary Macaulay, October 12, 1836.

22. Ibid., p. 145, to James Sutherland (Secretary to the Committee of Public Instruction), May 1835.

23. Trevelyan, op. cit., p. 295.

24. Ibid., p. 296.

25. Ibid., p. 297.

26. Ibid., p. 298.

27. Charles Trevelyan, op. cit., pp. 16 and 19.

28. George Otto Trevelyan, op. cit., p. 298.

29. *Parliamentary Papers*, XXXII (1852–1853), pp. 148–149, June 16, 1853, quoted in Clive, op. cit., p. 408.

30. Macaulay, op. cit., p. 179, to Thomas Ellis, May 30, 1836.

31. Trevelyan, op. cit., p. 304.

32. Macaulay, op. cit., p. 193, to Zachary Macaulay, November 30, 1836.

33. Ibid., p. 192, October 12, 1836.

34. Ibid., p. 191, to Selina and Frances Macaulay, October 5, 1836.

8. The Law-giver

1. Macaulay, 'Warren Hastings', *Edinburgh Review*, Volume LXXIV, October 1841, pp. 160–255

2. Macaulay, Letters, Volume III, p. 193, to Zachary Macaulay, October 12, 1836.

3. C.D. Dharker, *Lord Macaulay's Legislative Minutes* (Oxford University Press, 1946), p. 180.

4. Ibid., p. 190.

5. Ibid., p. 165, 'The Freedom of the Press', April 16, 1835.

6. Hobhouse to Auckland, January 30, 1836, Home and Miscellaneous, Volume 833, India Office Library, quoted in Clive, op. cit., p. 327.

7. Ibid., p. 328.

8. Macaulay, op. cit., pp. 184–185, to Lord Lansdowne, August 22, 1836.
9. H.T. Prinsep quoted in Dharker, op. cit., pp. 45–46, Parliamentary Papers (*c.* 2078), 1878, lvii, pp. 3–4.
10. Trevelyan, op. cit., p. 284.
11. Dharker, op. cit., p. 192, October 3, 1836.
12. Macaulay, *Works*, Volume XI, p. 575, July 10, 1833.
13. Ibid., pp. 177–178, March 28, 1836.
14. Ibid., pp. 192–4, October 3, 1836.
15. Macaulay, *Letters*, Volume III, pp. 176–177, to Thomas Ellis, May 30, 1836.
16. Trevelyan, op. cit., p. 288.
17. Ibid.
18. Macaulay, op. cit.
19. Dharker, op. cit., p. 179, March 28, 1836.
20. Ibid., p. 194, October 3, 1836.
21. Sir John Hobhouse to Macaulay, August 30, 1837, Home and Miscellaneous, Volume 838, India Office Library, quoted in Clive, op. cit., p. 338.
22. Macaulay, op. cit., p. 186, to Lord Lansdowne, August 22, 1836.
23. Auckland to Hobhouse, June 20, 1836, Home and Miscellaneous, Volume 837, India Office Records, quoted in Clive, op. cit., p. 340.
24. Dharker, op. cit., p. 109.
25. Ibid., p. 107.
26. Ibid., p. 230, Minute to Council, July 31, 1837.
27. Ibid., p. 207, June 25, 1835.
28. Ibid., pp. 275–276, Minute of November 13, 1835.
29. Ibid., p. 282, Minute of November 14, 1836.
30. Macaulay, 'Warren Hastings', *Edinburgh Review*, Volume LXXIV, October 1841, pp. 160–255.
31. Ibid.
32. Macaulay, *Works*, Volume XI, pp. 578–582, July 10, 1833.
33. Trevelyan, op. cit., p. 299.
34. Macaulay, op. cit., pp. 5–9, 'Introductory Report Upon the Indian Penal Code'.

35. Ibid., p. 9.
36. Macaulay, *Letters*, Volume III, p. 147, to James Mill, August 24, 1835.
37. Ibid., p. 210, to Thomas Ellis, March 8, 1837.
38. Dharker, op. cit., p. 252, 'The Law Commission and the Penal Code', January 2, 1837.
39. Macaulay, ibid.
40. Ibid.
41. Ibid., p. 210, March 8, 1837.
42. Ibid., December 30, 1835.
43. Ibid., p. 165, to Sir John Hobhouse, January 6, 1836.
44. Ibid., p. 252, to McAvey Napier, August 14, 1838.
45. Dharker, op. cit., p. 252.
46. Macaulay, op. cit., p. 195, to McAvey Napier, November 26, 1836, and p. 202, to Thomas Ellis, November 30, 1836.
47. Ibid., p. 193, to Zachary Macaulay, October 12, 1836.
48. Trevelyan, op. cit., pp. 300–301.
49. Sir John Macleod, *Notes on the Report of the Indian Law Commissioners on the Indian Penal Code* (London, 1848), p. iv, quoted in Clive, op. cit., p. 443.
50. John Stuart Mill, *Westminster Review* (1838), p. 402, quoted in Clive, op. cit., p. 445.
51. Macaulay, *Works*, Volume XI, p. 20, 'Introduction to the Indian Penal Code'.
52. Ibid., p. 123, 'Notes on the Indian Penal Code'.
53. Ibid., p. 27, 'Introduction to the Indian Penal Code'.
54. Ibid., p. 86.
55. Macaulay, *Letters*, Volume III, p. 147, to James Mill, August 24, 1835.
56. Ibid., p. 237, to Thomas Flower Ellis, December 18, 1837.
57. Trevelyan, op. cit., p. 301.
58. Ibid., p. 302.
59. K.M. Panikkar, *A Survey of Indian History* (Asia Publishing House, 1966), p. 210.
60. Trevelyan, op. cit., p. 337.

9. Return of the Native

1. Macaulay, op. cit., p. 203, to Charles Macaulay, December 5, 1836.
2. Trevelyan, op. cit., p. 307.
3. Macaulay, op. cit., p. 210, to Thomas Ellis, March 8, 1837.
4. Ibid.
5. Ibid., pp. 232–233, to Selina and Frances Macaulay, December 15, 1837.
6. Ibid., p. 225, to Mrs Thomas Drummond, September 20, 1837.
7. Ibid., p. 217, to William Empson, June 19, 1837.
8. Ibid., p. 222, to Selena and Frances Macaulay, September 11, 1837.
9. Macaulay, *Lord Clive*.
10. Macaulay, 'Warren Hastings', *Edinburgh Review*, Volume LXXIV, October 1841, pp. 160–255.
11. Ibid.
12. Macaulay, *Letters,* Volume III, p. 222, to Selena and Frances Macaulay, September 11, 1837; and p. 203, to Charles Macaulay, December 5, 1836.
13. Ibid.
14. Ibid., p. 213, note 2, quoting *Bengal Hurkaru*, January 13, 1837.
15. Ibid., p. 214, to the Governor-General in Council, May 1, 1837.
16. Ibid., pp. 229–230, to Selena and Frances Macaulay, November 4, 1837.
17. Ibid., p. 235, to Thomas Ellis, December 18, 1837.
18. Ibid., p. 211, March 8, 1837.
19. Ibid., pp. 232–233, to Selena and Frances Macaulay, December 15, 1837.
20. Walter Bagehot, *Complete Works*, Volume I, pp. 399–401.
21. Macaulay, *Works*, Volume VIII, 'Mackintosh', p. 443.
22. Trevelyan, op. cit., p. 338.
23. Ibid.
24. Macaulay, *Letters*, Volume III, pp. 158–159, to Thomas Ellis, December 30, 1835.

25. Ibid., p. 243, to McAvey Napier, June 14, 1838.

26. Ibid., p. 246, June 26, 1838.

27. Ibid., p. 253, July 20, 1838.

28. Trevelyan, op. cit., p. 340.

29. Macaulay, op. cit., pp. 253–254, to McAvey Napier, August 14, 1838.

30. Thomas Babington Macaulay, *The Journals*, edited by William Thomas (Pickering & Chatto, London, 2008), Volume I, p. 50, November 15, 1838.

31. Ibid., p. 361, November 26, 1838.

32. Ibid., p. 164, February 13, 1839.

33. Macaulay, *Letters*, Volume III, pp. 266–267, to Lord Lansdowne, December 19, 1838.

34. Ibid.

35. Ibid.

36. Ibid., pp. 264–265, to Hannah Trevelyan, November 14, 1838.

37. Macaulay, *Journals*, Volume I, p. 43, November 10, 1838.

38. Trevelyan, op. cit., p. 366.

39. Ibid., p. 367, and Macaulay, *Letters*, op. cit., p. 278, to McAvey Napier, February 26, 1839.

40. Macaulay, *Journals*, op. cit., p. 157, February 2, 1839.

41. Trevelyan, op. cit., p. 373.

42. Macaulay, op. cit., p. 162, February 10, 1839.

43. Macaulay, *Letters*, op. cit., pp. 287–288, to Adam Black (a prominent Edinburgh civic leader), May 15, 1839.

44. Macaulay, *Works*, Volume XI, p. 589, speech to electors of Edinburgh, May 29, 1839.

45. Macaulay, *Letters*, op. cit., p. 290, to Hannah Trevelyan, May 29, 1839.

46. Ibid., p. 280, March 20, 1839.

47. Ibid., p. 298, September 2, 1839.

48. Ibid., to Lord Melbourne, September 20, 1839.

10. Secretary at War

1. Trevelyan, op. cit., p. 387.
2. Macaulay, *Letters*, op. cit., p. 187, to Lord Lansdowne, August 22, 1838.
3. Ibid., pp. 167–169, to Thomas Spring-Rice (Chancellor of the Exchequer), February 8, 1836.
4. Ibid., p. 187, to Lord Lansdowne, August 22, 1836.
5. Ibid., p. 301, to Selina Macaulay, September 25, 1839.
6. Ibid., p. 304, to Frances Macaulay, October 1839.
7. Clive, op. cit., p. 491.
8. Matthew Arnold, *Essays in Criticism* (London, 1889), p. 304; and J.S. Mill, February 17, 1855, in F.A. Hayek, *John Stuart Mill and Harriet Taylor* (Chicago, 1951), p. 223.
9. *The Letters of Sidney Smith*, ed. N.C. Smith (Oxford, 1953), p. 693, to Lady Grey, October 1839.
10. Wellington to Lady Wilton, September 5, 1839, *Wellington and His Friends: Letters of the First Duke of Wellington* (London, 1965), p. 123.
11. Macaulay, op. cit., p. 302, note 4.
12. Clive, op. cit., p. 498, quoting *Reeve Memoirs*, Volume I, p. 104, November 30, 1839.
13. Macaulay, op. cit., p. 303, to the Electors of Edinburgh, October 1, 1839.
14. Trevelyan, op. cit., p. 387.
15. Ibid., p. 388.
16. Ibid., p. 388.
17. Ibid., p. 389.
18. Ibid.
19. Macaulay, op. cit., p. 321, to Thomas Ellis, March 14, 1840.
20. Trevelyan, op. cit., pp. 390–391.
21. Macaulay, *Journals*, Volume IV, p. 73, July 28, 1853.
22. Macaulay, *Works*, Volume XI, pp. 610–634.
23. Ibid., pp. 636–645, April 7, 1840.
24. Macaulay, *Letters*, Volume III, p. 302, note 4.

25. Ibid., p. 324, to McAvey Napier, April 8, 1840.
26. Ibid., note 3.
27. Macaulay, *Works*, Volume XI, p. 641.
28. Ibid., p. 656.
29. Macaulay, *Letters*, Volume III, pp. 353–354, to McAvey Napier, December 8, 1840.
30. Ibid., p. 362, to Lord Ebrington, January 12, 1841.
31. Ibid., pp. 360–361, January 6, 1841.
32. Macaulay, *Lord Clive*, p. 51.
33. Macaulay, *Letters*, Volume III, pp. 372, 382 and 385, to McAvey Napier, April 30, 1841 and July 27, 1841 and to Thomas Ellis, July 12, 1841.

11. Elder Statesman

1. Macaulay, *Letters*, Volume III, pp. 361–362, to McAvey Napier, January 11, 1841.
2. Ibid., July 27, 1841.
3. Trevelyan, op. cit., p. 408.
4. Macaulay, *Letters*, Volume III , to Thomas Ellis, July 12, 1841.
5. Macaulay, op. cit., Volume IV, p. 5, to McAvey Napier, September 3, 1841.
6. Ibid., Volume III, to Thomas Ellis, July 12, 1841.
7. Ibid.
8. Ibid.
9. Macaulay, op. cit., Volume IV, to McAvey Napier, October 30, 1841.
10. Ibid., November 5, 1841.
11. Ibid., April 18 and 25, 1842.
12. Ibid., October 19, 1842.
13. Trevelyan, op. cit., p. 426
14. Ibid., p. 433.
15. Ibid., p. 436.
16. Macaulay, *Letters*, Volume IV, p. 124, to James Stewart-Mackenzie, May 12, 1843.

17. Ibid., p. 99, to Thomas Ellis, February 20, 1843.
18. Macaulay, *Works*, Volume XII, pp. 18–39, 'The Gates of Somnauth', speech to House of Commons, March 9, 1843.
19. Trevelyan, op. cit., p. 438.
20. Macaulay, *Letters*, Volume IV, p. 52, to Thomas Ellis, September 1, 1842.
21. Ibid., p. 74, November 26, 1842.
22. Ibid., pp. 137–139, to Hannah Trevelyan, August 21 and 28, 1843.
23. Ibid., p. 151, September 7, 1843.
24. Trevelyan, op. cit., p. 438.
25. Ibid., p. 439.
26. Ibid., p. 440.
27. Ibid., p. 439.
28. Macaulay, *Works*, Volume XII, pp. 3–17, 'The People's Charter', speech to House of Commons, May 3, 1842.
29. Macaulay, *Letters*, Volume IV, p. 291, to David Greig, January 30, 1846.
30. Ibid., pp. 161–163, to McAvey Napier, November 25, 1843.
31. Macaulay, *Works*, Volume XII, p. 120, 'Maynooth', speech to House of Commons, April 14, 1845.
32. Ibid., pp. 40–73, 'The State of Ireland', speech in the House of Commons, February 19, 1844.
33. Macaulay, *Letters*, Volume IV, p. 56, to Margaret Trevelyan, September 15, 1842.
34. Macaulay, *Works*, Volume XII, pp. 193–194, 'Corn Laws', December 2, 1845.
35. Macaulay, *Letters*, op. cit., p. 272, to Hannah Trevelyan, December 13, 1845.
36. Ibid., p. 276, December 19, 1845.
37. Ibid., p. 278, December 20, 1845.
38. Trevelyan, op. cit., p. 464.
39. Macaulay, op. cit., p. 301, to Hannah Trevelyan, July 9, 1846.
40. Trevelyan, op. cit., p. 465.

41. G.H. Francis, *Orators of the Age* (London, 1847), pp. 78–79.

42. Clive, op. cit., p. 499, quoting Letter from Maria Edgeworth, December 3, 1843, *Edgeworth Letters*, pp. 600–601.

43. Macaulay, *Works*, Volume XII, p. 199, 'The Ten Hours Bill', speech to the House of Commons, May 22, 1846.

44. Ibid., p. 234, 'Education', House of Commons, April 19, 1847.

45. Lord Cockburn, quoted in Trevelyan, op. cit., p. 471.

46. Ibid., pp. 472–473.

47. Ibid., p. 476.

48. Ibid., p. 473.

49. Macaulay, *Letters*, op. cit., p. 341, to Hannah Trevelyan, July 30, 1847.

50. Trevelyan, op. cit., p. 476.

51. Macaulay, op. cit., to Frances Macaulay, August 6, 1847.

52. Ibid., pp. 362–4, to Lord John Russell, April 23, 1848.

53. Ibid.

12. Indian Summer

1. Macaulay, *Letters*, Volume IV, p. 382, to Charles Macaulay, November 27, 1848.

2. Ibid., Volume V, p. 39, to undisclosed recipient, March 25, 1849.

3. Ibid., p. 360, to undisclosed recipient, October 14, 1853.

4. Ibid., p. 389, to Andrew Rutherford, December 21, 1848.

5. Macaulay, *Journals*, Volume II, pp. 1–3, November 18 and 19, 1848.

6. Ibid., p. 94, June 13, 1849.

7. Ibid., pp. 1–3, November 18 and 19, 1848.

8. Trevelyan, op. cit., p. 485.

9. Ralph Waldo Emerson, *Letters* (New York, Columbia University Press), Volume IV, pp. 42–43, to Lilian Emerson, March 23, 1848.

10. Macaulay, op. cit., pp. 101–102, 28 June 23, 1849.

11. Ibid., p. 218, March 9, 1850.

12. Ibid., Volume III, p. 59, January 14, 1851.
13. Ibid., p. 258, June 25, 1852.
14. Ibid., p. 228, April 3, 1852.
15. Trevelyan, op. cit., p. 485.
16. Trevelyan, op. cit., p. 485.
17. Macaulay, *Journals*, Volume II, p. 223, March 18, 1850.
18. Trevelyan, op. cit., pp. 492–493.
19. Ibid., p. 493, quoting from Margaret Trevelyan's memoir.
20. Macaulay, op. cit., Volume IV, p. 149, April 15, 1854.
21. Trevelyan, op. cit., p. 491.
22. Ibid.
23. Macaulay, *Letters*, Volume V, p. 178, to Margaret Trevelyan, August 19, 1851.
24. Trevelyan, op. cit., p. 551.
25. Macaulay, *Journals*, Volume IV, p. 179, August 11, 1854 and August 12, 1854.
26. Ibid., pp. 160–161, October 25, 1849.
27. Macaulay, *Letters*, Volume V, p. vii.
28. Macaulay, *Journals*, Volume II, p. 38, February 8, 1849.
29. Trevelyan, op. cit., p. 497.
30. Macaulay, *Journals*, Volume II, pp. 104–105, June 30 and July 1, 1849.
31. Ibid., Volume III, p. 73, February 14, 1851, and p. 79, February 24, 1851.
32. Macaulay, *Letters*, p. 261, Letter to John Evelyn Denison, July 31, 1852.
33. Macaulay, *Journals*, Volume II, March 4, 1848.
34. Macaulay, *Letters*, Volume V, p. 72, to Fanny Macaulay, September 11, 1849, and p. 75, to Margaret Trevelyan, September 26, 1849.
35. Macaulay, *Journals*, May 15, 1858.
36. Ibid., Volume III, January 31, 1852.
37. Ibid., January 19, 1852.
38. Trevelyan, op. cit., p. 562.
39. Ibid., p. 566.

40. Macaulay, *Letters*, Volume V, p. 257, to Sir William Gibson Craig, July 24, 1852.

41. Ibid., Volume IV, p. 366, to Lord Mahon, May 26, 1848, and Macaulay, *Journals*, Volume II, p. 24, January 6, 1849.

42. Ibid., pp. 227, 230 and 232, March 26, 1850, April 4, 1850 and April 11, 1850.

43. Ibid., p. 227, March 26, 1850.

44. Macaulay, *Letters*, Volume V, p. 271, to Hannah Trevelyan, August 15, 1852.

45. Ibid.

46. Macaulay, *Works*, Volume XII, pp. 276 and 290, Speech to electors of Edinburgh, November 2, 1852.

47. Trevelyan, op. cit., p. 579.

48. Macaulay, *Journals*, Volume IV, p. 7, December 20, 1852.

49. Ibid., p. 52, June 1, 1853.

50. Trevelyan, op. cit., pp. 582–583, quoting *The Leader*.

51. Ibid., p. 586, and Macaulay, op. cit., pp. 54 and 61, June 4 and 21, 1853.

52. Macaulay, op. cit., p. 62, June 24, 1853.

53. Macaulay, *Letters*, Volume V, p. 336, to Frances Macaulay, June 30, 1853.

54. Trevelyan, op. cit., pp. 588–592.

55. Macaulay, *Letters*, Volume IV, p. 217, to Hannah Trevelyan, October 9, 1844.

56. Macaulay, *Journals*, Volume IV, pp. 17–18, January 23 and 26, 1853.

57. Ibid., p. 146, April 5, 1854.

58. Trevelyan, op. cit., pp. 609–612.

59. Macaulay, *Letters*, Volume V, p. 431, to Sir Charles Wood, November 27, 1854.

60. Ibid., pp. 438–439, January 19, 1855.

61. Ibid., p. 440, to Thomas Ellis, January 23, 1855.

62. Trevelyan, op. cit., p. 612.

63. Macaulay, *Journals*, Volume IV, p. 103, October 25, 1853.

64. Ibid., p. 126, January 29, 1854.

65. Ibid., p. 150, April 21, 1854.
66. Ibid., p. 154, May 2, 1854.
67. Ibid., p. 155, May 6, 1854.
68. Macaulay, *Letters*, Volume V, p. 306, to Thomas Ellis, December 30, 1852.
69. Macaulay, *Journals*, Volume IV, p. 119, December 31, 1853.
70. Macaulay, *Letters*, Volume V, p. 400, to Edward Everett, May 30, 1854.
71. Macaulay, op. cit., p. 400, to Edward Everett, May 30, 1854.
72 Ibid., p. 441, to Adam Black, January 25, 1855.

13. The Bitter Cup

1. Trevelyan, op. cit., p. 577.
2. Macaulay, *Letters*, Volume V, p. 97, to Lady Holland, June 15, 1857.
3. Macaulay, *Journals*, Volume III, p. 244, May 18, 1852.
4. Trevelyan, op. cit., p. 560.
5. Ibid., pp. 622–623.
6. Trevelyan, op. cit., p. 624.
7. Macaulay, *Letters*, Volume V, p. 42, to Sir George Cornewall Lewis, May 17, 1856.
8. Ibid., p. 25, to Thomas Ellis, March 11, 1856.
9. Macaulay, *Journals*, Volume IV, pp. 280 and 284, April 22, 1856 and May 1, 1856.
10. Ibid.
11. Macaulay, *Letters*, Volume V, p. 25, to Thomas Ellis, March 11, 1856.
12. Trevelyan, op. cit., p. 628.
13. Macaulay, *Letters*, Volume VI, p. 74, to Frances Macaulay, December 25, 1856.
14. Ibid., p. 272, to Alice Trevelyan, 1858.
15. Ibid., p. 74, to Frances Macaulay, December 25, 1856.
16. Ibid.
17. Trevelyan, op. cit., p. 630.

18. Macaulay, *Journals*, Volume IV, p. 162, June 9, 1854.
19. Ibid., Volume V, p. 145, March 20, 1858.
20. Ibid., p. 291, April 13, 1859.
21. Macaulay, *Letters*, Volume V, pp. 377–378, to Frances Macaulay, January 17, 1854.
22. Macaulay, *Journals*, Volume 4, p. 241, January 29, 1856.
23. Ibid., p. 456, to undisclosed recipient, May 24, 1855.
24. Ibid., p. 647.
25. Macaulay, *Letters*, Volume VI, p. 79, to Thomas Ellis, March 2, 1857.
26. Macaulay, *Journals*, Volume V, p. 69, August 28, 1857.
27. Ibid., p. 76, September 15, 1857.
28. Ibid., p. 77, September 18, 1857.
29. Trevelyan, op. cit., p. 652.
30. Macaulay, *Journals*, Volume V, p. 69, August 28, 1857.
31. Ibid., p. 67, August 22, 1857.
32. Ibid., p. 66, August 16, 1857.
33. Ibid., p. 90, October 25, 1857.
34. Ibid., p. 97, November 8, 1857.
35. Ibid., p. 98, November 11, 1857.
36. Ibid., p. 90, October 25, 1857.
37. Ibid., pp. 77–78, September 19, 1857.
38. Ibid., February 19, 1858.
39. Ibid., p. 78, September 19, 1857.
40. Benjamin Moran, *The Journal of Benjamin Moran* (Chicago, 1948), Volume I, p. 524.
41. Trevelyan, op. cit., p. 662.
42. Macaulay, op. cit., September 1857.
43. Trevelyan, op. cit., p. 666.
44. Ibid., p. 677.
45. Ibid., p. 678.
46. Ibid., p. 641.
47. Macaulay, op. cit., p. 183, March 20, 1858.
48. Macaulay, *Letters*, Volume VI, pp. 98–99, to George Trevelyan, July 4, 1857.

49. Ibid., p. 212, to Charles Trevelyan.
50. Trevelyan, op. cit., p. 650.
51. Ibid., p. 651.
52. Macaulay, *Journals*, Volume IV, p. 108, October 25, 1853.
53. Ibid., p. 250, January 6, 1859.
54. Ibid., p. 252, January 8, 1859.
55. Ibid., January 9, 1859.
56. Macaulay, *Letters*, Volume VI, p. 188, to Frances Macaulay, January 12, 1859.
57. Macaulay, *Journals*, Volume IV, p. 267, February 18, 1859.
58. Macaulay, *Letters*, Volume VI, p. 188, to Frances Macaulay, January 12, 1859.
59. Macaulay, *Journals*, Volume IV, p. 301, May 1, 1859.
60. Trevelyan, op. cit., p. 682.
61. Ibid.
62. Ibid.
63. Macaulay, op. cit., p. 371, October 15, 1859.
64. Ibid., p. 374, October 25, 1859.
65. Macaulay, *Letters*, Volume VI, p. 244, to Thomas Ellis, October 24, 1859.
66. Macaulay, *Journals*, Volume IV, p. 389, December 3, 1859.
67. Ibid., p. 394, December 19, 1859.
68. Ibid., p. 395, December 21, 1859.
69. Ibid., December 23, 1859.
70. Macaulay, *Letters*, Volume VI, p. 261, to Thomas Ellis, December 23, 1859.
71. Trevelyan, op. cit., p. 686.
72. Ibid., p. 687.
73. Ibid.
74. Ibid.
75. Macaulay, *Letters*, Volume VI, p. ix, undated letter to Sir Walter Trevelyan.
76. Trevelyan, op. cit., p. 298.
77. Ibid., p. 687.

Epilogue

1. Ramchandra Guha, 'Macaulay's Minute Revisited', *The Hindu*, February 4, 2007.

List of Illustrations

The British Library

The Calcutta Esplanade, photographed by Samuel Bourne © The British Library

Macaulay, 1840s, print by John Sartain after Eden Upton Eddis © The British Museum

Select Bibliography

Arnold, Matthew: *Essays in Criticism* (London, 1889)

Arnold, Reverend Frederick: *The Public Life of Lord Macaulay* (London, 1862)

Clive, John: *Thomas Babington Macaulay* (London, Secker & Warburg, 1973)

Dharker, C.D.: *Lord Macaulay's Legislative Minutes* (Oxford University Press, 1946)

Dudley Edwards, Owen: *Macaulay* (London, Weidenfeld & Nicolson, 1988)

Edinburgh Review, Volumes XLV and LXXIV

Emerson, Ralph Waldo: *Letters* (New York, Columbia University Press, 1939)

Francis, G.H.: *Orators of the Age* (London, 1847)

Ghosh, P.R.: 'Macaulay and the Heritage of the Enlightenment', *English Historical Review*, 1997

Hall, Catherine: 'Troubling Memories', *Transactions of the Royal Historical Society* (Cambridge, 2011)

Hayek, F.A. von: *John Stuart Mill and Harriet Taylor* (London, 1951)

Macaulay, Thomas Babington: *The Works of Lord Macaulay*, Volumes I to XII (London, Longmans, Green & Co., 1898)

—*The Letters of Thomas Babington Macaulay*, Volumes I to VI, (London, Cambridge University Press, 1974–81)

—*The Journals of Thomas Babington Macaulay,* Volumes I to V (London, Pickering & Chatto, 2008)

—*Lord Clive* (London, Longmans, 1851)

—*Selected Writings,* ed. John Clive and Thomas Pinney (Chicago, 1973)

McCully, Bruce T.: *English Education and the Origins of Indian Nationalism* (New York, 1940)

Moran, Benjamin: *The Journal of Benjamin Moran* (Chicago, 1948)

Panikkar, K.M.: *A Survey of Indian History* (Asia Publishing House, 1966)

Plumb, J.H.: *Men and Centuries* (Boston, 1963)

Sharp, H.: *Selections from Educational Records* (Calcutta, 1920)

Smith, N.C.: *The Letters of Sidney Smith,* ed. N.C. Smith (Oxford, 1953)

Strachey, Lytton: *Portraits in Miniature and Other Essays* (London, 1931)

Trevelyan, Charles: *The Application of the Roman Alphabet to All the Oriental Languages* (Serampore, 1834)

Trevelyan, George Otto: *The Life & Letters of Lord Macaulay* (London, Longmans, Green & Co., 1900)

Wellington, Duke of: *Wellington and His Friends: Letters of the 1st Duke of Wellington* (London, 1965)

Index